The history and results of the present capital punishments in England : to which are added, full tables of convictions, executions, &c..

Humphry W. Woolrych

The Making of Modern Law collection of legal archives constitutes a genuine revolution in historical legal research because it opens up a wealth of rare and previously inaccessible sources in legal, constitutional, administrative, political, cultural, intellectual, and social history. This unique collection consists of three extensive archives that provide insight into more than 300 years of American and British history. These collections include:

Legal Treatises, 1800-1926: over 20,000 legal treatises provide a comprehensive collection in legal history, business and economics, politics and government.

Trials, 1600-1926: nearly 10,000 titles reveal the drama of famous, infamous, and obscure courtroom cases in America and the British Empire across three centuries.

Primary Sources, 1620-1926: includes reports, statutes and regulations in American history, including early state codes, municipal ordinances, constitutional conventions and compilations, and law dictionaries.

These archives provide a unique research tool for tracking the development of our modern legal system and how it has affected our culture, government, business – nearly every aspect of our everyday life. For the first time, these high-quality digital scans of original works are available via print-on-demand, making them readily accessible to libraries, students, independent scholars, and readers of all ages.

The BiblioLife Network

This project was made possible in part by the BiblioLife Network (BLN), a project aimed at addressing some of the huge challenges facing book preservationists around the world. The BLN includes libraries, library networks, archives, subject matter experts, online communities and library service providers. We believe every book ever published should be available as a high-quality print reproduction; printed on-demand anywhere in the world. This insures the ongoing accessibility of the content and helps generate sustainable revenue for the libraries and organizations that work to preserve these important materials.

The following book is in the "public domain" and represents an authentic reproduction of the text as printed by the original publisher. While we have attempted to accurately maintain the integrity of the original work, there are sometimes problems with the original work or the micro-film from which the books were digitized. This can result in minor errors in reproduction. Possible imperfections include missing and blurred pages, poor pictures, markings and other reproduction issues beyond our control. Because this work is culturally important, we have made it available as part of our commitment to protecting, preserving, and promoting the world's literature.

GUIDE TO FOLD-OUTS MAPS and OVERSIZED IMAGES

The book you are reading was digitized from microfilm captured over the past thirty to forty years. Years after the creation of the original microfilm, the book was converted to digital files and made available in an online database.

In an online database, page images do not need to conform to the size restrictions found in a printed book. When converting these images back into a printed bound book, the page sizes are standardized in ways that maintain the detail of the original. For large images, such as fold-out maps, the original page image is split into two or more pages

Guidelines used to determine how to split the page image follows:

• Some images are split vertically; large images require vertical and horizontal splits.
• For horizontal splits, the content is split left to right.
• For vertical splits, the content is split from top to bottom.
• For both vertical and horizontal splits, the image is processed from top left to bottom right.

THE

HISTORY AND RESULTS

OF

THE PRESENT

CAPITAL PUNISHMENTS

IN

ENGLAND;

TO WHICH ARE ADDED,

FULL TABLES

OF

CONVICTIONS, EXECUTIONS, &c.

BY

HUMPHRY W. WOOLRYCH,

OF THE INNER TEMPLE, BARRISTER AT LAW

LONDON·

SAUNDERS AND BENNING, LAW BOOKSELLERS,

(SUCCESSORS TO J. BUTTERWORTH AND SON),

43, FLEET STREET

1832.

JAN 2 1924

LONDON
PRINTED BY STEWART AND CO
OLD BAILEY

PREFACE.

In presenting the history and results of our capital punishments to the public, the author is desirous of saying, that the main effort of his book has been to prove the inefficiency of severe penalties in restraining crime. If the infliction of death, then, have failed in its object,—the prevention of the evil,—the continuance of capital punishment cannot be defended upon any other principle than that of wreaking vengeance on the criminal; and at this our law shudders.

The great end to be attained at present seems to be the due and *certain* application of secondary corrections, and here, it will probably be soon admitted, that these last should be as few, as mild, but at the same time as sure as possible. For, in order to reach a high degree of civilization, great forbearance and calmness are very necessary. Too anxious pains cannot be taken to promote reform instead of dealing in penalties; to raise character instead of debasing it; to lift up the moral standard, instead of leaving the criminal without hope. Whatever changes may be effected by the increasing intelligence of the Legislature, it is to be hoped, that the mischiefs of gaols may be removed by *speedy trials*, and quick punishments, or rather, in many cases, by the immediate restoration of the offender to society—that the prac-

tice of public whipping may no longer exist, to brand a poor
wretch already sufficiently depressed—that men, instead of being
told that their characters are lost, should be carefully won to the
principle, that it is never too late to become valuable members of
the community, and, in a word, that attention should be chiefly
directed, not so much (as at present) to the nature of the offences,
as to the *best means of reforming the offender*

Should the first part of this work succeed in satisfying its readers,
it is the author's intention to include, within a second part, proofs
that the repeal of capital punishments has not been attended with
an increase of crime, thereby disproving Dr. Paley's arguments, that crime would, at at all events, *increase* in the *absence* of
the punishment of death, after which, he will attempt to trace
the endeavours of individuals to procure the mitigation of our
penal code, summing up the arguments on either side in each
case, and relating a number of anecdotes illustrative of the utter
inefficacy, as well as the injustice of capital inflictions. The
author bespeaks the indulgence of a kind and enlightened public
in respect of many errors which he may, doubtless, have fallen
into in the course of his enquiries.

2, Hare Court, Temple,
    October 27, 1832.

TABLE OF CONTENTS.

GENERAL INDEX.

PART I.

CHAPTER I.

OF CAPITAL PUNISHMENTS IN GENERAL

IT is a remarkable fact, that the first person who committed the offence of Murder was spared by ONE no less than GOD himself. And this is not merely worthy of notice, (now that we are about to enter upon the important subject of capital punishment,) because it illustrates the clemency of Jehovah, but chiefly because the most important doctrine of prevention was thus early manifested by Divine Wisdom. Cain, instead of expiating his crime by instant death, was condemned to be a fugitive and a vagabond upon the earth, and the fruits of his labours were denounced by a perpetual curse. "And Cain said unto the Lord, My punishment is greater than I can bear "(a) "And the Lord set a mark (b) upon Cain, lest any finding him should kill him "(c) So awful an example could not fail to have its effect upon the descendants of Adam, and thus the great end of prevention was preferred n the first instance by the wisest authority to the dread sacrifice of human life. And let it not be said, that this judgment upon Cain was inconsistent with the subsequent command to Noah,— "Whoso sheddeth man's blood, by man shall his blood be shed "(d) For independently of the arguments against capital punishment for murder under the sanction of that text,(e) it is quite clear, that the penalty of being " a fugitive and a vagabond," would not be so heavy when the inhabitants of the earth became

---

(a) Gen. iv. 13

(b) Or, as some say, "*gave him a sign*" י שם וקן אות
a mark to Cain he set and

They render these words in this manner, that is, that God worked some miracle to convince Cain of his safety, and do not treat the mark in question as one of obloquy according to many commentators, or as a mark generally, in conformity with the translation.

(c) Gen. iv. 15. (d) Gen. ix. 6. (e) See post, Chap II.

numerous, as in times when it was less thickly peopled. Again, there would be many other perpetrators of the same offence, and as it did not please God to set his sign of vengeance upon every murderer as upon Cain, the atrocious culprit would escape detection, and the grand object of prevention would not be so well answered.

In conducting the proposed inquiry, it is our chief object to adhere as closely as possible to the subject, which is *the execution of criminals by virtue of judicial authority.* The early hostility, therefore, which seems to have prevailed between people of different nations, the accustomed slaughters which took place when prisoners were taken in battle, (*f*) the universal spirit which prompted man in former ages to take the life of his foe, the disregard, indeed, of every punishment which (except among the Jews) did not involve life or member—all these, although they sadly manifest the cruelty of uncivilized spirits, and although they partake in some measure of the nature of penalties for supposed injuries, are yet inapplicable to our present purpose, which is one of practical utility, and not of curious speculation.

Probably, the earliest legislation which included capital punishments within its provisions, was that of the Jewish Theocracy We have there, at least, the most compendious of our early records upon this subject Many crimes denounced under that form of government are still regarded by Christians with equal horror, some have become extinct. others have yielded to the enlightened spirit of the times, whilst others, again, are now treated with less severity under the dispensation of our Saviour, than under an ancient system of rigour whose wisdom we are called upon to admit, not to question. But in order that the reader may the better apprehend the real object of this chapter, he will just observe here, that the chief purposes we aim at, are to show the antiquity of capital penalties, the history of their execution, and the results of severity. We deny, at the same time, that we are necessarily bound by the experience of former days to adopt the same practical conclusions, for the obvious reason, that the circumstances of the world are now entirely different, and also, because, although light is spread abroad, iniquity yet abounds

MURDER]—Murder, by which we understand the killing of a person premeditatedly with malice, was always spoken of by the Almighty with peculiar detestation (*h*) Neither the sanctuary, nor the city of refuge could save the wilful shedder of blood, nor could any pecuniary satisfaction be accepted for a crime so enormous. The murderer was to be taken, (as Joab was), (*i*)

(*f*) 2 Chron. xxv. 12. Mitford's Greece, i. 165-369.

(*h*) Gen. ix. 5, 6 , Ex. xx. 13 , xxi 12, 14 , Lev. xxiv. 17 , Numb. xxxv. 16-21 incl , 31, 33 , Deut xix. 11-13 incl., xxi. 1-9 incl.

(*i*) 1 Kings, ii. 28.

even though he grasped the altar,(k) he was to be fetched from the
city of refuge that the avenger might slay him, (l) he was to perish
notwithstanding the offer of recompense for his deed,(m) an offer,
which, on many occasions, might have been accepted with propriety as an atonement (n)   And manslaughter, the accidental
killing of any one, and homicide committed without enmity, are as
anxiously distinguished by the same Omnipotent law-giver as
murder is plainly denounced   So odious, indeed, was this crime
of wilful blood-shedding,(o) that the neighbourhood was held in
some measure responsible for a violent death   The elders and
judges were obliged, upon such an occasion, to make the solemn
sacrifice of a heifer, to wash their hands over the beheaded beast,
and to aver, that their hands had not shed the blood, and that
their eyes had not seen it (p)

The slayer, however, whether a murderer, or an accidental
offender, was not to die without a trial   If he fell into the hands
of the avenger of blood, his death was in all cases justifiable, but
if he reached the city of refuge, the congregation proceeded to try
him.   The elders and the judges met,(q) and heard witnesses,
two at the least, (r) and according to their view of the case, judgment was pronounced.   If they held the man guilty of murder, he
was delivered forth to the avenger of blood, as we have seen, if
not, they permitted him to remain in the city of refuge, from
whence he could only depart in safety upon the death of the high
priest. (s)

BLASPHEMY.]—Blasphemy, too, was an offence punishable with
death.   This crime seems to have been different from that of pro-
fane cursing and swearing which the lower orders of this country
still indulge in to an unwarrantable excess.   The capital misdeed
among the Jews was a denying of the supremacy of GOD their
great KING.   It was tantamount to our idea of high treason.   It
was a cursing of the GOD whose authority was absolute throughout the land, a renouncing of the Divine Head.(t)   Very nearly

---

(k) Ex. xxi 14.
(l) Deut xix. 12.   (m) Numb. xxxv. 31.
(n) See Ex. xxi. 19, 22, &c.
(o) See Ex. xxi. 13, Numb. xxxv. 22 — Manslaughter   Numb.
xxxv. 23, Deut xix. 4, 5; Joshua, xx 3 — Casual Homicide. The
killing of a thief found breaking at night was justifiable, but it was
murder to destroy him between sunrising and sunset. — See Ex. xxii.
2, 3, Calmet, tit. Thief.
(p) Deut. xxi. 7. — See the same chapter, verses 1-9 incl.
(q) See Numb. xxxv. 12, 24, Joshua, xx. 6.
(r) Numb. xxxv. 30.
(s) At the time of the judgment, it should seem. — See Joshua, xx 6.
(t) See Lev. xxiv. 10-16 incl , 1 Kings, xxi. 10, Matt. xxvi. 64,
65; Mark, xiv. 62-64, Luke, xxii. 69-71, John, xix. 7. Naylor s

allied to this was the offence of enticing the people under the pre-
tences of prophecies, dreams, or otherwise to serve other gods
than *Jehovah*   This, again, was a repudiating of the true and legitimate dominion, and death was, accordingly, prescribed as the
consequence (*u*)

CRIMES AGAINST RELIGION.]—Usurping the priest's office by
presuming to offer incense, or interfering in any way with the service of the tabernacle was capital (*x*)   So also was a neglect of the
day of atonement, (*y*) of the Sabbath, (*z*) of the Passover, (*a*) and
of the rite of circumcision (*b*)   So were the undue eating of sacrifices, (*c*) and the eating of blood, (*d*) the offering of children unto
Moloch, (*e*) and the much abhorred crime of witchcraft. (*f*)   Such
as were accessory to either of these two last offences were involved
in the same punishment.

The witchcraft of these days had no relation whatsoever to the
puny arts which have been attributed to criminals in this once
benighted country, nor did the punishment proceed upon the same
principles.   For the chief object of the old necromancers was to
gain an insight into futurity, not to injure property or life by spells
and charms; and the severe penalty was enacted against the
lovers of familiar spirits, because it was a desertion of GOD, the
only potentate, to seek information at the hands of inferior powers.
It was a subversion of the principle of theocracy, and was, therefore, a species of treason

OFFENCES AGAINST NATURE]—It is only necessary to say concerning abominable offences, that they were visited with death
under the system of government which we have been describing. (*g*)

OFFENCES AGAINST PUBLIC MORALS.]—The Jews were directed
to punish with no less severity the crimes of adultery, fornication,
(in some instances,) disrespect and disobedience to parents, and
perjury, (in some cases.)

Adultery, which was capital here even in the days of Cromwell,

---

offence, for which he so nearly suffered death in the times of the Protec-
torate, was that of assuming to himself the person of Christ · it was
called blasphemy.

(*u*) Deut. xiii. 10 ; xviii. 2-5 incl. xviii. 20.
(*x*) See Numb. i. 51 , iii. 10, 38 , xvi. 40 , xviii. 7.
(*y*) Lev. xxiii. 29, 30.   (*z*) Numb. xv. 35.
(*a*) Numb. ix. 13 , unless unclean, or on a journey.
(*b*) Gen. xvii. 14.   (*c*) Lev. xix. 8.
(*d*) Lev. xvii. 10   (*e*) Lev. xx. 2-5 incl.
   (*f*) Ex. xxii. 18; Lev. xix. 31 , xx. 27 , ver. 6 — Accessories. See
also Deut. xviii. 10, 11 , 1 Sam. xxviii. 7, 8 ; Josephus' Antiq. fol.
p 188 : and Sir Walter Scott's Letters on Demonology and *Witchcraft*.
   (*g*) See Ex. xxii. 19 , Lev. xviii. 22-25 incl. , xx. 13, 15, 16 , and
see Lev. xx. 18.

met not with the slightest mercy among the Hebrews; (*h*) nor did
fornication, where it was committed with kindred, or with be-
trothed women, or by a woman who afterwards married. (*i*)   But
fornication between persons who were not related, and where
there was no promise of marriage on the part of the woman was
not capitally punishable.   The man and woman in this case were
commanded to marry; (*k*) unless, indeed, her father were resolved
to refuse his consent, and then the price of a virgin's dowry was
to be paid (*l*)

To strike father or mother, was capital, (*m*) so it was to curse
them; (*n*)   and to be obstinate in refusing them obedience (*o*)
To bear false witness was also capital, if the accusation supported
by the perjury were capital.   The author of the false testimony
was delivered to the same punishment which the law awarded
against the crime which he appeared to prove (*p*)

To suppress the truth also, was an offence which the law denounced as deserving the last penalty (*q*)

OTHER OFFENCES.]—Man-stealing, which was perpetrated for
the purpose of selling the captive into slavery, is denounced as a
capital crime by the law of Moses (*r*)   Likewise the illegal possession of a man under such circumstances. (*s*)

However we may regret the existence of slavery at present, it
is yet observable, that no argument against it can be built upon
these pages, because the use of slaves was absolutely permitted
amongst the Jews, and the texts referred to are applicable to those
who might steal their brethren, and such too of their brethren as
were free

The last capital offence we shall mention, is the negligence of
the owner of a mischievous ox, with a guilty knowledge of the
animal's dangerous propensity.   In England, such conduct would
be manslaughter at least, should a death ensue; among the Jews,
it was regarded as very nearly approaching to murder.   We have
reserved this case to the last, because it seems to be the only instance in which a man was allowed to redeem his life by a pecuniary recompence.   The offence consisted in not keeping in the
ox, after a due warning given to the proprietor. (*t*)   But a sum of
money might be awarded by the judges as the price of life in this
instance, (*u*) which could not be allowed where the offender was

---

(*h*) Lev. xx. 10, 11, 12, 14, 20, 21, Deut. xxii. 22, 23.
(*i*) Lev. xx. 17, 19, Deut. xxii 13-21 incl
(*k*) Ex. xxii. 16, Deut. xxii. 28.   (*l*) Ex. xxii. 17.
(*m*) Ex. xxi 15.   (*n*) Ex. xxi. 17, Lev. xx. 9
(*o*) Deut. xxi. 18-21 incl.   (*p*) Deut. xix. 19.
(*q*) Lev. v. 1.   " He shall bear his iniquity."   " Which is usually
understood of capital punishment "— Calmet, tit Perjury.
(*r*) Ex. xxi. 16, Deut. xxiv. 7.   (*s*) Ex. xxi. 16.
(*t*) Ex. xxi. 29.   (*u*) Ex. xxi. 30.

actually a murderer (*x*) Upon this institution of Moses, the commutation of the more serious penalty for money in cases of death, so common in the East, was probably founded⁜ · But there is the most marked of distinctions between the custom adverted to, and the law of the Jewish legislator, for he was directed by God to refuse a satisfaction for murder, at all events,—under all circumstances. Whereas assassination, the basest of murders, might be compounded for amongst succeeding nations, in Turkey, for example, (*y*) in the times of the Saxons, and in other places and generations.

PUNISHMENTS]—It does not belong to this essay, to treat of the varieties of punishments which were inflicted by the Jews, or by other nations Among the Jews, these were chiefly stoning, burning, and crucifixion; but there were also several others, as hanging, beheading, &c. which are mentioned at length by antiquarians, whose writings the reader may consult if he think proper. (*z*) However, it may just be said, that for blasphemy,(*a*) idolatry,(*b*) witchcraft,(*c*) sabbath-breaking,(*d*) adultery and fornication, (*e*) stoning was the sentence ordained, and so again, for disobedience to parents. (*f*) But, for adultery with a mother-in-law, burning was the prescribed punishment,(*g*) and particular directions are given in Deuteronomy concerning the bodies of malefactors which have been hanged on a tree (*h*)

But, although we have but little to say, concerning the punishments themselves, yet, upon the infliction of these severities, and the consequent results, we will add a few words First, with respect to the inflexible execution of the sentence amongst the Jews, we are led to conclude, that upon most occasions life was certainly sacrificed upon a satisfactory conviction of the offender. But the most painful deliberation was exercised by the judges before they arrived at the fatal conclusion, and the criminal might be brought back from his journey to execution no less than five times, if any one would step forward to say any thing in favour of the condemned. Then should all justification prove unavailing, and the guilt of the transgressor be established beyond a doubt, the cry was, *such a one is abandoned*, and the capital penalty was carried

---

(*x*) Numb xxxv. 31.

(*y*) See Calmet, Fragments, No. xi. p. 24   "There was a time," says Beccaria, "when all punishments were pecuniary. The crimes of the subjects were the inheritance of the prince." — p. 69

(*z*) Calmet, tit. Punishments of the Hebrews. That drowning was not one of their punishments, (καταπουτισμου) see Elsner, Obs. Sacræ, tom. 1. p 85.

(*a*) Lev. xxiv. 14, 16 ; Deut. xiii. 10.   (*b*) Lev. xx. 2.
(*c*) Lev. xx. 27.   (*d*) Numb xv. 35.
(*e*) Deut xxii. 21, 24.   (*f*) Deut xxi. 21
(*g*) Lev. xx. 14   (*h*) Deut. xxi. 22.

into effect.(*i*)   It seems, that if there were any doubt, hope might be entertained, but where the conviction was clear, the rule prevailed,

"*Lex nulla capto parcit, aut pœnam impedit.*"—SENECA.

This unremitting obedience to justice, will, however, be deemed the less surprising, when it is considered, that the death of the offender was held, among the Jews, to confer a benefit upon his soul, especially if he made confession   The criminal, said the Jews, suffered to satisfy the justice of God, and to make atonement for his sins, by confessing his faults, he gained a share in the life to come (*k*)   A similar doctrine, accompanied by the like custom of exhorting to repentance, is found in the Roman church, and it may be observed too, though less tainted with superstition, in the occasional conduct of our own priesthood (*l*)   It does not seem necessary to multiply remarks upon this head, and we will, therefore, pass on to the next consideration; namely, the results of these punishments   And while we cannot but come to the conclusion, that the Jews could not be well restrained from crime, notwithstanding the certainty of their capital inflictions, (so stiff-necked a people were they), we must disdain in the strongest manner even the idea of arraigning the wisdom and justice of God. Let it be remembered, that if prevention did not follow the executions which thus inflexibly prevailed, if a system of terror were insufficient to deter the Jewish citizens from fresh acts of insubordination, they suffered the sentences of the law under the *legal dispensation*, which was ordained as the guide for man's conduct in those ages   Reasons which we dare not venture to interpret, no doubt actuated the divine mind in those days, in permitting the life of man to fall more frequently than at present a sacrifice to justice.   But now that the *Christian dispensation* has been bestowed upon us, while we submit in silence to the sovereignty of Jehovah concerning that which is past, we cannot be surprised at the anxiety which is universally manifested in favour of life, nor at the increasing dislike to capital punishment.   If the dread of certain death did not arrest crime among the Hebrews, it is not for us to judge of the fitness of continuing the severest punishments.   The mercy of God is so conspicuous throughout the Old Testament,(*m*) that we may almost safely refer every instance or ordinance of severity to the theocratical government which he had established.   But under the *new dispensation*, if even the

---

(*i*) See Calmet, tit. Punishments, ut supra.   (*k*) See Calmet, ut supra.
(*l*) This observation is not intended to discourage the efforts of clergymen who strive to awaken convicted men to a sense of their crimes, although, perhaps, it may, indeed, have a tendency to check the sanguine hopes of late repentances.
(*m*) See 2 Sam. xii. 13 , 1 Kings, xxi. 29 , 2 Chron. xxxiii. 13.

great end of prevention were effected by the stroke of death, it might be questionable how far upon many occasions, we should be justified in maintaining such severity in the land,—much less, when we are compelled to acknowledge, that evil abounds in the very sight of the gallows

Hence, although we shall proceed to enumerate a few instances of the continuance of crime, notwithstanding the inexorability of the judges of Israel, it will be the less necessary to enter fully upon this subject, by reason of the greater light which now surrounds us,—the more improved days in which we are permitted to live. First, with respect to blasphemy, and the serving of strange gods. It is notorious, that in defiance of the strictest commandments, the Hebrews were scarcely ever steady in their allegiance to Jehovah; and that, although they were constantly punished both by the immediate visitations of their great King, as well as by the sword of the temporal judge, they were so prone to revolt and disobedience, as at length to become entirely incorrigible (n) They were, consequently, dispersed, and sold into slavery.(o)

Witchcraft was also an unpardonable sin, and yet, such were the iniquities of the times, or the temptations of gain, or the flattering homage paid to divinations, that it lifted its head in spite of the awful threatening, " Thou shalt not suffer a witch to live " (p)

Adultery was a crime which Moses ordained to inflexible punishment, a penalty which there is reason to believe was inflicted without remission But we cannot help collecting from the writings of the prophets,(q) and other sources, that this offence was very prevalent amongst the Jewish nation, although the sentence of the law continued to be enforced with rigour (s)

(n) See Ex. xxxii, Lev. x. 1-7 incl., Numb. xi. 1 . xvi. 1, &c., xxv. 2, Israel worship the gods of Moab, xxvii. 14, Moses and Aaron, Judges, ii. 1-3 incl., Baal, iii. 1-14 incl., Baal, iv. 1-3 incl., Canaanites, vi. 1-6 incl, Midianites, viii 27, Gideon's ephod of gold, x. 6, &c, Baal — the Ammonites, xiii 1, Philistines, xviii. 30, the graven image, 1 Kings, xi. 5, Solomon — the Goddess of the Zidonians, xii. 28, Jeroboam — the calves of gold, xviii. passim, 2 Kings, xxi. 3 — Manasseh, 2 Chron. xii. 1, Rehoboam, xxiv. 18 — groves and idols, xxv. 14, Amaziah and the gods of Edom; xxviii. 2, Ahaz and the molten images of Baal, xxxiii 3, Manasseh. xxxvi. 14. — See also 2 Sam. xii 14, Ps. lxxiv. 18, Is. lii. 5, lxv. 7.

(o) 2 Kings, xviii. 11, xxiv. 14.

(p) Ex. xxii. 18 See, upon this point, 1 Sam. xxviii. 3, 7, 8, 9, Saul and the witch of Endor, 2 Kings, xxi. 6, xxiii. 24.

(q) See Jer. vii. 9, xxiii. 10. "The land is full of adulterers," Hos. iv. 11, Mal. iii. 5.

(s) John, viii. 5

These may be sufficient for historical examples of the proposition which has been offered, although others may be found without difficulty, and are no doubt familiar to the diligent readers of the Scriptures. (*t*)

We have been more diffuse in our brief history of the capital punishments of the Jews, than we shall be concerning those of other countries, both because of the very early government under which that nation was established, as well as by reason of the full and distinct information of the sacred records (*u*) We proceed to say a few words on the punishments of other ancient nations.

Egypt]—We learn from ancient writers, that the Egyptians were extremely careful in the selection of their judges, and in eliciting the truth of each individual complaint. (*x*) They seem to have adopted, in regulating their scale of punishments, a system of retaliation proportioned to the nature of the offence As for example, they punished rape by excision, treachery by cutting out the tongue, and so on

Murder was capital amongst them So also was a neglect to aid a person attacked on the highway, when assistance could have been rendered Parricide was treated with the most dreadful severity, the criminal being put to death with a variety of torments

Perjury was also capital, and false accusers were ordained to undergo the same penalty with the innocent accused, had the latter been convicted (*y*)

And a breach of the law of Amasis, which obliged every Egyptian once in the year, to show the magistrate of his district his manner of life, was punishable capitally, and if the party could not prove himself to be in an honest employment, the consequences were the same (*z*)

We should not have mentioned the punishment for adultery amongst this people, but for the fruitless results which seem to have attended an infliction scarcely short of death Adultery was visited with a thousand lashes as the man's penalty, and in the woman with the loss of her nose (*a*) This was not, by any means, a mild sentence, yet, we are told, that " adulteries were not infrequent amongst the Egyptians "(*b*)

(*t*) Note, that neither theft nor arson were punished with death amongst the Jews

(*u*) See also Pastoret, Histoire de la Legislation, vols. iii. and iv.

(*x*) See Diodorus Siculus, Univ. History, 1747, vol. i, p. 463

(*y*) See Univ. Hist. ut sup, pp 464, 465.

(*z*) Herodotus, Euterpe, prope finem, Beloe, ii 125

(*a*) Univ. Hist ut supra, p. 465.

(*b*) Chambers' Cyclopædia, 1786, tit. Adultery, and in Ceylon, the punishment of the same crime with death has been said to fail in lessen-

Sabacus, the So of the Scriptures, during his reign of fifty years over Egypt, *abrogated the punishment of death altogether*, substituting the hard labour of raising the ground, near the place to which each criminal respective y belonged (c)

PERSIA]—In point of antiquity the Egyptians must probably yield to the Celtes and other northern nations, in like manner as the origin of the ancient Egyptian institutions is said to have preceded the ordinances of Moses. But the accuracy of the records, and fidelity of the details of legislation, must be allowed to remain with the people of Israel and Egypt, since we are unable even to trace an outline of the jurisprudence and punishments of many considerable governments. It seems, however, that the Druids and Bards, the judges of the Celtes or Celts, contrived to promote a system of religious disability amongst their people, which was more terrible than death itself. We have here an instance, therefore, even in these early days, of prevention through a medium which fell short of death Whoever refused to abide by the sentence of the Curetes, or interpreters of the law, " was by them excluded from assisting at their sacred rites, after which no man dared converse with him." (d) But notwithstanding this, our information is very scanty concerning the Assyrians, the Phrygians, the Scythians, the Medes, the Lydians, and many such celebrated people, so that we hasten forwards in search of some, although it still be slight intelligence We advance to Persia. And here it is pleasing to remark, that Herodotus not only relates the absence of capital punishment for the most part in ancient Persia, but declares his commendation of the custom which forbade the sovereign from putting to death for a single offence. (e)

There were, however, some qualifications of this merciful rule. One was, the case of poisoners, who were pressed to death between two stones, (f) another, that of high treason, which was visited by the loss of the offender's head and right hand; and it appears further, that, although death could not in general be inflicted for a single crime, the judges were invested with a power of balancing the faults and virtues of a delinquent. If the former predominated, he might have been adjudged to death, because more

---

ing the number of adulteries. Chambers, ut supra, citing Bibl. Univ. —Even among the Jews, the miraculous ceremony of the bitter water was disused, because adulteries had become so frequent as to render the ordeal of secrecy inoperative. It was unnecessary to institute a trial concerning clandestine acts of unfaithfulness, when so many of such acts were committed in the face of the public.—See Univ. Hist 1747, vol. iii p. 139 (note E).

(c) Herodotus, Euterpe, Beloe, vol. ii. p. 66.
(d) Univ. Hist., vol. vi p. 25.
(e) Herodotus, Clio, Beloe, i. p. 201.
(f) Univ. Hist., v. p. 129, citing Plutarch in vitâ Artaxerxis

than a single fault was found in him: if the good deeds prevailed, he was either pardoned, or punished less severely. (g) Some monarchs, however, occasionally departed from the custom of the realm, and ordained not only death, but the most painful cruelties in executing that sentence (h)   Indeed, the exceptions of poisoners and traitors seem rather to be departures from the ancient law than qualifications of it

GREECE |—From such a dearth of information concerning the laws and governments of very old times as we have above complained of, it is not disagreeable to escape, and to seek channels which are fed from more fruitful sources.   GREECE—enriched by the names of Draco, Solon, Lycurgus, Pericles, offers to us a more ample catalogue of laws, and (which is more valuable,) of the reasons which led to their enactment.   Draco (i) the first considerable lawgiver of the Athenians, came to his dominion, as Archon, in times of violence and over a turbulent populace.   He was well read in the ancient laws, and in those also which prevailed in the countries around him   Many of these were sanguinary in the extreme, but as we have already seen, they did not answer their intended purpose.   Draco mistook the result in a philosophical sense, he was a friend to prevention, but he falsely judged, that because the laws had failed to repress crime, life should, therefore, be universally sacrificed

The principle of Draco was good, but he began his career by violating the laws of nature   The theory of prevention has been immortalized, but the practice of many of its votaries has been unphilosophical and full of error.   Draco ought not to have hoped for success, when in his first endeavour to crush offences, he made an attack upon the very foundations of human feeling. He besieged nature in her citadel: no wonder then that his ordinances soon tottered beneath their own weight

Whether he borrowed his idea from the Phœnicians or otherwise, it is not within our province to determine, (k) it is however clear, that the smallest faults punishable by the laws were capital, and it is satisfactorily certain, that the severity of such legislation was productive of the most unfortunate results.

Yet, whatever might have been Draco's anxiety to enforce the most rigid institutions, he was, undoubtedly, more than ever inflexible in the case of murder.   Indeed, it is said that his laws against murder were the most ancient of the Athenian records (l)

(g) Herodotus, Clio, Beloe, i. p 201 , Un Hist. v. 129.

(h) Un. Hist v. 128.

(i) Ante Chr. 623 — about the days of Cyrus and Daniel

(k) See, on this subject, Joseph. cont. Ap. fol 1540. p. 784 · Univ. Hist. vol vi. p. 293.

(l) Joseph. contra Apion. ed. by Whiston, London, 1737, p. 977

He punished theft also, even the taking of an apple, with equal inflexibility, and, we are told, that idleness constituted a crime,—a crime, of course, capital. (*m*)

Plutarch and Aristotle unite in condemning this code of blood; and we learn from them, that so far from becoming a body of pure and free citizens according to the wish of Draco, the Athenians, were, if possible, still more addicted to transgress the laws (*n*) In fact, "*all offences not highly atrocious went wholly unpunished* (*o*) That this observation may apply to England, in a great measure, who can help admitting, after a careful consideration of our rules concerning crime and punishment?(*p*)

SOLON.]—Draco being compelled to quit Athens, by reason of the severity of his principles, room was made for Solon, a man of honourable family, who having before his eyes the fatal results of extreme justice, found it more easy to establish a character for humanity, by softening the despotism of his predecessor Being made the supreme legislator of Athens, he cancelled the laws of Draco, excepting only those relating to murder, (*q*) and he added very few other capital offences to his new system He restored the Court of Areopagus, which had lost much of its power through the preference which Draco had given to the Epheta (*r*) Capital offences were for the most part cognizable by this Court only (*s*) It possessed the most extensive jurisdiction, but Solon reduced the sanguinary punishments over which it had controul to a very small number

If an Archon (*t*) were detected in drunkenness, he was deemed worthy of death (*u*) If a husband surprised his wife in adultery, he was allowed to put her to death, (*x*) but this last sanction of severity, (together with a similar one on the subject of theft, to

---

(*m*) Univ Hist. vi. 293, citing Plutarch in vitâ Solon.—See Mitford and Gillies, ubi infra.   Pet. Leges Atticæ, Pref. in init

(*n*) See Aristot. Politic. l 2 c 12, Plutarch in vitâ Solon, Gillies's Greece, ii. 240.

o) Mitford's Greece, i 357.

(*p*) It is, however, worthy of observation, (as far as the individual concerned,) that Draco was appointed to his office of legislator at the instance of the nobility.   He was neither an usurper nor a conqueror, and his integrity has never been questioned, although it is impossible to applaud his judgment   Sir John Popham, Chief Justice of the King's Bench in the reign of Queen Elizabeth, entertained a similar opinion. He was heard to say, that inflexible executions were merciful, because they tended to prevent crime.   That this is not so, we shall see hereafter.

(*q*) Univ. Hist. vi. 308, φονικοὶ νόμοι —Potter, i. 139.

(*r*) Univ. Hist. vi. 309   (*s*) Mitford's Greece, i. 381.

(*t*) Those who executed the office of archon with credit were made Areopagites.—Mitford, ut supra, 380

(*u*) Univ. Hist, vi. 314   (*x*) Id. 312.

which we shall advert presently,) may, perhaps, be considered rather as a concession to revenge, than a capital infliction (*y*)

But *murder*, as we have already seen, was to remain punishable, as under the laws of Draco, and those institutions of his being inflexible and unmitigated, the murderer was, consequently, an assured victim to the violated law.

" Si quis hominem sciens morti daret," to use the words of the old Attic law, "capital esto." (*z*)   So if any one should slay a homicide who went into voluntary banishment, and absented himself from the public games and sacred rites, he was to be punished with death as though he had put an Athenian citizen (*a*) to the sword. (*b*)   Again, if any one should have stabbed, or inflicted a malicious wound upon another, he was to be banished, and his goods were to be sold; and if after this, he were to return to his own country, capital punishment was decreed against him. (*c*) This was a similar offence to the act of "returning from transportation," which we visit here with the last penalty

Theft, (*d*) moreover, was punishable capitally upon some occasions, as in the cases of burglary, and kidnapping, and *cut-purses* also, were adjudged to death. (*e*)   Draco, indeed, had decreed death against every man who took away that which was not his own, as well as against the robbers of fig-orchards, (*f*) but these severities were abrogated by Solon.   However, stealing from the *Lyceum*, *Academia*, *Cynosurges*, or any of the *Gymnasia*, trifling as the theft might be, and stealing above ten drachms (g) out of the baths, or ports, were continued under the head of capital offences. (*h*)   With these exceptions, the law of Solon was, that he who stole should pay double the value of the thing he stole to the owner, and as much to the public exchequer. (*i*)

(*y*) See also The Laws of Theft, Potter, Ant. i. 179.

(*z*) Sam. Petiti. Com. in Leges Atticas, p. 508.

(*a*) The Athenian who came under the charge of murder lost his rights of citizenship till after his acquittal. " Accusatus cædis, ab illo die omnibus civitatis juribus abstineto " — Id. ut supra, 511

(*b*) Id. 510.

(*c*) Id 525, and see id , pp. 504-525 incl. , Liber Septimus , De Sicariis , Titulus Primus

(*d*) Theft was punished most severely amongst the Scythians (Univ. Hist. vi. 65) · but it must be remembered, that, in some countries, robbery is more cruel than the taking away even of life itself—it is the plunder of a skin of water in the desert.   The Hebrews, in the promised land, punished theft by compelling restitution —Ex xxii. 1, &c.

(*e*) Petit p. 532, 533 , Potter, i. 179.

(*f*) Petit. p. 534 , Potter, i. 179.

(*g*) Sevenpence three-farthings.

(*h*) Petit. p. 528 , Potter, i. 179.

(*i*) Petit. p. 527 ; Potter, i. 179.

Thus much for murder, theft, adultery, and drunkenness. There were, however some few other capital punishments, but it is observable, that part of these (which we are about to cite) were enacted by the successors of Solon

It was capital to divulge the Holy Mysteries,(k) to ease nature in Apollo's temple,(l) to propose the expenditure of the annual vote of 1000 talents for any other purpose than the defending of Attica against foreign invasions,(m) to recede from a promise made to the commons, senate, or judges, (n) to utter falsehood, under the pretence of being a discoverer of truth. (o)

Treason against the state was also capital, as the betraying of a garrison, ship, or army, &c (p) and so, again, was a desertion of the city for a residence in the Piræus (q)

And, it seems, that one other offence was punishable with death amongst the Athenians, concerning which no mention need be made, (r) and in the laws of the Gymnasia, we find, that none, excepting the schoolmaster's kin, were permitted entrance into schools, if beyond the customary age for sending youth thither, whilst the lads were in the school　The breach of this law was punished with death (s)

It is not our wish to detain the reader here with speculations as to the results of these capital inflictions.　The probabilities, however, are, that crime diminished greatly for some years after the legislation of Solon, and that the punishments decreed by the court of Areopagus, in conformity with the written institutions, were inflexibly exercised.　The reluctance to prosecute and convict, which held so much in the times of Draco, ceased under a more mild form of government, and, with the exception of that fearless struggle for political liberty which so early distinguished the Greeks, it seems reasonable to conclude, that the Athenians were in general obedient to the code which their legislators had prescribed for them

But, with the accession of Pericles to authority, the court of

---

(k) Petit. p. 33 , Potter, i 145 , Un Hist. vii. 379 in the note

(l) Petit p 7 , Potter, i. 145　A law of Pisistratus　The Athenians did this in the temple which Pisistratus had built, in contempt of the tyrant — Potter, ut supra.

(m) Petit. 382 , Potter, i 165.

(n) Petit. p. 430 , Potter, i. 169.　　　　(o) Potter, i. 182.

(p) Petit. p. 563 , Potter, i. 181.

(q) Petit. p, 561 , Potter, i. 182.

(r) Petit. p 468, &c. , Potter, i. 172.

(s) Petit p. 295 , Potter, i. 160　"The public judgments," (of the Athenians) says Dr. Rees in his Cyclopædia, tit. Athens, "were murder, malicious wounding, a conflagration of the city, poison, conspiring against the life of another, sacrilege — punished with death."

Areopagus was curtailed of its chief jurisdiction.   Pericles was incapacitated from being chosen a member of that court, and he, accordingly, formed a resolution to destroy its authority.   Ephialtes, his friend, procured a decree, by which most of the causes which the Areopagus had been accustomed to judge, were removed to a more popular tribunal, (*u*) and this " the wisest of the Athenians have looked upon as the first step to their ruin; for it gave the people such a dangerous notion of liberty, as rendered them ever afterwards ungovernable "(*x*)   After a time, the democratical influence became uppermost   accusations then grew frequent, condemnations common, "to be eminent, induced danger, to be low, contempt "(*y*)   It is allowed, that the Athenians were much degenerated in these turbulent days, they tore the sacred things from the temple of Delphos for the purpose of subsidizing the Phocians, (*z*) they offered no opposition to the grossest licentiousness, or the most unnatural lust; (*a*) they experienced in full the evils of a fluctuating government, and uncertain tribunals.   So far from maintaining their vote of 1000 talents towards the expulsion of their enemies, they made it capital for any man to propose the re-establishment of their army, or the conversion of the public revenues, towards the preservation of a military force (*b*)   Whilst, on the one hand, the laws of Draco had created neglect and insubordination by reason of their excesses, a departure from those of Solon, and from the unbending court of Areopagus, only served to introduce confusion instead of certainty, and licentiousness in the room of good citizenship   The same evils which accompanied the code of the severe legislator were ready to distract the republic at the moment when they abandoned a mild and prudent administration for doubtful tribunals, and a relaxed execution of the laws.

We have dwelt rather at length upon the criminal jurisprudence of Athens, and the institutions of Solon in particular, because the Roman law, the next main object of our enquiries, was founded upon the Greek code   From the Roman decrees European nations have largely borrowed, and our own country has been in some measure indebted to that source.   When we have considered the legislation of Italy, the chief springs of criminal law will have been disclosed   We shall have had the Jewish code, the Egyptian, the Athenian   Theseus, who spent some time in Crete, has been said to have improved the laws of his own land by the study of Cretan jurisprudence, and Epimenides, a philosopher of the latter kingdom, and contemporary with Solon, probably furnished the Athenians with fresh aids towards the accomplishment of their constitution.   To the Greek and Roman

(*u*) Univ. Hist vi 413   (*x*) Ibid.   (*y*) Id 528.
(*z*) Id. 511.   (*a*) Id. 529   (*b*) Potter Ant. i. 19.

laws, therefore, (viewing them as the basis of modern jurisprudence) we may add the institutions of Crete likewise (c)

LACEDÆMON.]—But we cannot proceed immediately to the far-famed regulations of the great Pagan empire, without adverting for a moment to the Macedonian punishments, and the laws of Lycurgus. The laws of the Spartan legislator, and their results, are most worthy of consideration, inasmuch as we find, upon a careful examination, that the principle of punishing with certainty, rather than extreme severity, has ever maintained a sway amongst nations. To be brief concerning the institutions of Sparta, we learn, that the life of a citizen was held to be of the chiefest value, and death, consequently, was but rarely inflicted. When it became necessary to deprive an offender of life, the execution was performed in the prison, *in order that the firmness of the criminal might not move the commiseration of the people* (d). The laws of Lycurgus were not written, but were transmitted by oral relation from family to family, and, it is probable, that the penalty of death was carried into execution on many occasions, more by reason of the bad character of the culprit, than the specific crime of which he had been guilty. However this may have been, the last great punishment was seldom resorted to, and the consequence of this judicious harmony of mildness and vigour is apparent from the fall of the Lacedemonians after their abandonment or neglect of the Lycurgic institutes. The Athenians degenerated when they became lukewarm in maintaining the precepts of Solon. Spartan independence was no more, when the code of Lycurgus ceased to be the beacon of the state (e)

MACEDON.]—Of the Macedonian punishments it is not necessary to say much, but we cannot forbear introducing a slight mention of them, because they seem to have been adopted upon the principle of certainty in their execution. Murder was capital, and so inflexible was the idea of Alexander the Great, concerning the constitutions of his country, that when he had killed Clitus, he insisted on submitting to death, though far from his

---

(c) See Mitford's Greece, i. 366, Univ. Hist. vii 4; Travels of Lycurgus into Crete, id. p. 228.

(d) See Rees's Cyclopædia, tit Lacedemonians, Beloe's Herodotus, vol. iii. p. 45.—It is not intended to advocate here the propriety of public executions, but it is incontrovertible, that the object of punishment ought to be the exciting of any other feeling than that of pity for the criminal. Diocles, the Syracusan lawyer, made a law that none should go armed into the council, on pain of death. Flushed with a victory, he forgot to lay aside his arms, and went in himself, but, discovering his error, he instantly slew himself. The people deified him.— Un. Hist. vii 585.

(e) See Polybius, lib. vi. c. viii. prope ad finem, Univ. Hist. 1747, vii 146, in the note.

own land, and could only be pacified by an acquittal, which the army, (who were the judges of those matters according to the Macedonian law,) awarded him (*f*) The verdict of the army was, that Clitus had justly perished Conspiring to take the King's life was also capital , and the fatal penalty extended not only to the culprit and his children, but to all those as well who were nearly allied to him Whence it was, that some of the kindred of Philotas, who rebelled against Alexander, stabbed themselves, and others fled into the wilderness (*g*)

ROMAN LAW]—As the Greeks were said to have borrowed the idea of their legislation from the Egyptians and the Cretans, so the Romans also, in their turn, reaped many advantages from the codes of other nations. Many of their lawgivers were acquainted with the manners of Lycurgus and Solon Numa was a Sabine, and the Sabines were the scholars of the Lacedæmonians (*h*) The Romans, moreover, were, in some measure, indebted to the Etruscans, a very ancient people, for some parts of their system of jurisprudence (*i*) But their early magistrates, before the tide of popular ascendancy arose, appear to have profited by the experience of those who went before them The list of capital punishments was small, the execution of them little less than certain Some of these, as the burying of the vestal virgins, (*k*) were, indeed, cruel, but the result of that severity only serves to confirm one of the main points of this essay, namely, that the rigour of a penalty will rarely, if ever, extinguish the crime where there is an adequate temptation In spite of the awful and irrecorable punishment, prosecutions were, at one time, instituted against no less than three of the devoted virgins for breaking their vows as priestesses of the rites of Vesta.(*l*) Tarquin was the author of the severe infliction referred to, (*m*) although the founding of the sacerdotal order is attributed to Numa. It was a law of religion, and obtained for many centuries in Rome, yet, notwithstanding this harshness, the institutions of Numa in general maintained a high character, and were much respected in succeeding times. The laws of Romulus, Numa, and other kings, especially those relating to general po-

---

(*f*) Q. Curtius, Crophius Antiq Macedoniæ, p. 14, part 1. § 6 , Un. Hist. viii. 399.

(*g*) Q. Curtius, lib. vi. , Potter Ant. 1. 347 , Un. Hist. viii. 399.

(*h*) Taylor's Elements of the Civil Law, 3d ed p. 3, citing Plutarch in Numa

(*i*) Un. Hist. 1747, vol. xvi 39. — A supplement to their twelve tables.

(*k*) They were buried alive, if found guilty of incontinence.

(*l*) Un. Hist. xii. 451. Their gallants were sentenced to be whipped to death. — Ibid.

(*m*) Un. Hist. xi. 328, citing Livy, Plutarch's Lives, 1. 184.

lity, were, indeed, regarded as the groundwork of the Roman code (*n*)

Besides this law of the vestals, (*o*) we do not meet with any capital pains on the subject of religion, for some centuries Even if a harlot touched the altar of Juno, her punishment was no more than the sacrificing of an ewe with dishevelled hair, in honour of the goddess. (*p*)   But in the reign of Constantius, a law was passed, condemning all persons to death who should pay any sort of worship, or sacrifice to idols (*q*)   Considering that the Christians had so lately been subjected to the most vehement persecutions, and that their religion forbade all kinds of tyranny, this edict of Constantius cannot fail to excite surprise   His father, Constantine the Great, had tolerated the Pagan temples, preferring to win the worshippers of idols by kindness rather than coercion (*r*)   But, like all severe punishments, this new penalty was disregarded.   Gibbon assures us, (*s*) there is the strongest reason to believe that " this formidable edict was either composed without being published, or was published without being executed "   The result of a different policy was as triumphant as it was consistent with reason   After the persecution of Julian, Jovian, his successor, proclaimed universal toleration, and Paganism instantly declined (*t*)

Murder. — Murder was long capital by the Roman law.   At first, indeed, Romulus appointed no punishment for parricide, thinking, with the Athenians, that it was impossible ; but an instance of that horrid crime having, at length, occurred after the lapse of centuries, it was decreed, that the offender (*u*) should be sewn up in a leathern sack and thrown into the Tiber   This was done amidst the execrations of the populace. (*x*)   The law was afterwards confirmed by Pompey the Great, whence it had the title of *Lex Pompeia* (*y*)   Romulus, nevertheless, held murder in great detestation, (*z*) and the memorable instance of the sur-

---

(*n*) Hooke's Roman History, i. 231, in the note.

(*o*) See also, in this law the note concerning the virgins, Kennet, p. 79, citing Plutarch in Numa, Adam's Ant. p. 297 ; Mœurs des Romains, p. 514.   And note, that the least disrespect towards a vestal was capital, as going under the chair upon which she was carried — Plutarch, ut supra.

(*p*) Aul. Gell. lib. iv. c. 3, Adam, p. 214, Cod. Theod. lib. xvi, tit. x. leg. 4.

(*q*) Un. Hist. xvi. 196 ; Gibbon, iii. 409.

(*r*) Gibbon, iii. 404, 405.   (*s*) Id. p. 408.

(*t*) Gibbon, iv. 230.

(*u*) Publius Malleolus, who slew his mother.

(*x*) Un Hist. xiii. 15.   (*y*) Kennet, p. 175 , Adam, p. 218.

(*z*) Un. Hist. xi. 293,   So poisoning also by women. — Id. 292.

viving and triumphant Horatius, proves with what inflexibility the criminal was usually treated. It is well known, that this young man slew his sister on his return from the defeat of the Curiatii, and that, in order to escape the execution of the sentence of death which had passed against him, he was necessitated to appeal to an assembly of the people However, he was made to pass under the yoke, and Tullus Hostilius, the king, was so struck, that he ordered expiatory sacrifices in order to pacify the anger of the gods. (*a*)

Treason. — Treason against the state (*b*) was also capital Valerius Poplicola ordained. that a person aspiring to the sovereign power might be slain without a legal condemnation, and impunity was promised to the slayer, provided the evil designs of the deceased could be proved (*c*) And the judgment against an offender, convicted of having had traitorous designs, was death.

Public Morals —The Roman lawgivers also allowed several penalties for violating the public morals to be capital, and as long as they had the feelings of the people on their side, (the moral sanction,) which was the case during the virtuous times of the republic, the law triumphed, and the general manners were incorrupt. Thus, the Roman matrons were celebrated for their chastity, whilst, at the same time, it was competent for their husbands to destroy them if they were guilty of incontinence — even if they drank wine (*d*) But no sooner had the public virtue abated, than the crime of adultery advanced, although the punishment was again capital (*e*)

Public Policy. — The ancient institution of the Romans concerning debtors, was a striking proof of the uselessness of extreme severity. If, after satisfactory establishment of the debt, and other formalities, the debtor were not redeemed upon the third market-day, the creditor was empowered to cause the sentence of death to be carried into effect upon him, or to sell him beyond the Tiber for a slave. If there were several creditors, they might share the debtor's body between them. This disproportioned penalty was so monstrous, that it was never put

---

(*a*) Id. 308, 309 As to the appeal to the people, see Un. Hist. xii. 115.

(*b*) Horatius was condemned for *treason*, through the policy of Tullus, who desired to shift the obloquy of sentencing a victorious conqueror from himself to the Duumviri. — Un. Hist. xi. 308.

(*c*) Un. Hist. xi. 367.

(*d*) Un. Hist. xi. 292 , Mœurs des Romains, pp. 137, 138 , Law of Romulus.

(*e*) See post, in the chapter. Seduction was punished after the same manner as the law of Moses the offender was compelled to marry the woman he had injured without a dowry, or to give her a fortune proportionate to her condition in life. — Mœurs des Romains, p. 202.

in force　The debtors were made slaves in the houses of their creditors during the continuance of their obligations, and as they were treated there with great cruelty, the sentence was finally altered to a public imprisonment (*a*)　The memorable story of the plebeian who appeared in the forum, loaded with chains, and torn with whips by a merciless creditor, is well known (*b*)

Other Capital Offences — Other capital offences, during the early days of Rome, were — the removing of a land-mark, (*c*) mutiny and cowardice in battle, (*d*) buying or selling a free-born citizen, (*e*) convening a clandestine assembly, (*f*) calling assemblies of the people at a distance from the city, (*g*) to which may be added a law of Romulus, which authorized any citizen to slay a party who had violated the close engagements between patron and client (*h*)　As soon as the people rose in superiority, their officers, ignorant of the principles of capital punishment, and of the moderation which their ancestors had gained by experience, immediately denounced offences against themselves, and the majesty of those they represented, as capital　To interrupt a tribune, when speaking, was punishable by giving bail to pay a fine, and, upon a refusal to do this, by *death*. (*i*)　It was capital also to leave the people without tribunes, or to create a magistrate from whom there should be no appeal　The offender was to be scourged and beheaded (*k*)　Menenius, the son of Menenius Agrippa, was charged with having connived at the destruction of the Fabii, and unanimously condemned to death by the tribes, and would have been executed but for the earnest interposition of the senate and his friends (*l*)

Capital punishment at length became obnoxious to the Romans, and a law was passed, at the instance of P　Porcius Læca, a tribune, that no one should bind, scourge, or kill a Roman citizen. (*m*)　Cicero refers to this when he exclaims, " O nomen dulce libertatis　O jus eximium nostræ civitatis.　O lex Portia, legesque Semproniæ." (*n*)　Thus, after several penal laws instituted by regal, patrician, and democratical governments, the

---

(*a*) Un. Hist. xi. 389, note (M), xii. 78, citing Livy
(*b*) Id. xii. 391.　　　　　(*c*) Law of Numa, Adam, p. 214.
(*d*) Un. Hist. xi. 449.
(*e*) Lex Fabia de Plagio; Adam, p 202.
(*f*) Lex Gabinia, confirming a law of the Twelve Tables, Kennet, p. 156.
(*g*) Adam, p. 202.　　　(*h*) Mœurs des Romains, Par. 1739, p. 117.
(*i*) Un Hist. xi. 407.
(*k*) Lex Duilia, Adam, p. 202.　　　　(*l*) Un. Hist. xi 442.
(*m*) Adam, p. 219, citing Livy, Cicero, Vernus, and Sallust, Lex Portia.
(*n*) In Verrem, Aul Gel. lib. x. cap. 3.

pain of death became odious and was repudiated. But this
happy condition did not endure. corruption reared its dishonest
and abandoned form ; tyrants advantaged themselves of the increasing depravity of the people, and then, imagining that violence would maintain their dominion, they had recourse again
to the capital infliction.

Sylla stands in the foremost rank of these restorers of capital
punishment Perhaps he was the first who returned to the old
system of taking life. But he renewed that system with re-
doubled horrors He was the author of a law which resembles
the perils of outlawry as they were authorized in this country
some centuries since. It was allowed to kill a person after proscription wherever he might be found. (o) Whoever harboured
or assisted a proscribed person incurred the sentence of death (p)
His proscriptions were infinite and their execution fatally certain He next directed that the lands and fortunes of the slain
should be divided amongst his friends, and their children were
declared incapable of honours (q) But his punishment for murder was only banishment —the *aquæ et ignis interdictio*. This
was the law, whether the death were accomplished by weapons
or poison, (r) and a 'similar penalty was ordained against false
accusers, and forgers, or persons guilty of the *crimen falsi*. (s)

The example being set, succeeding masters of Rome did not
hesitate to follow the beacon which the perpetual dictatorship of
Sylla had raised Mark Antony, when a member of the trium-
virate, decreed, that no one should thenceforward propose the
election of another Dictator on pain of death. And Augustus
Cæsar, on becoming emperor, (t) made no scruple of visiting
several offences with extreme rigour

We have now come to the times of the imperial dynasties, and
it will be observed, that unless when restrained by the voice of
the people, the emperors were skilful in devising such capital
punishments as might secure their own dominion, and strengthen
them in the corruptions which they were fostering around them.

Libel — Augustus, whose clemency has been so much celebrated
by historians, was the first to extend the crime of læse-majesty. (u)
Shortly before his death, he ordained, that the authors of all
lampoons, and satirical writings, which had the attacking or
blackening the reputation of others for their object, should be
punished with death (x) Such a proceeding did not indeed extinguish the high character of the emperor, but it shewed his de

---

(o) Un. Hist. xiii. 89.   (p) Adam, p. 200.   (q) Ibid
(r) Id. p. 201 , Kennet, p. 175
(s) Adam, p 201. And, indeed, several other offences. — Kennet,
p. 174.   (t) Kennet, p. 159
(u) Crimen læsæ majestatis.   (x) Un. Hist. xiv. 34.

fects as a politician   Though checked for a moment, the law
of libel was much violated in after times, and succeeding tyrants
were enabled to avail themselves of a bloodthirsty enactment to
wreak their vengence on those whom they hated, or had occasion
to dread.   The severity of the sentence arrested the prosecutions,
and deterred the magistrates from inflicting the penalty. Tiberius
mounted the throne soon afterwards, and immediately revived the
obnoxious law.   It was detested by all parties, and the prætor
even asked the emperor whether he should proceed against the
authors of libels as traitors , upon which Tiberius replied, that,
the law must be executed (y)   But notwithstanding this, life
could not be so wantonly sacrificed on the sudden. The emperor
forgave all the first convicts, and it was not until he had gained a
character for clemency through his dissimulation, that he ventured to spill blood for libel   The fates of Drusus, of Priscus,
and of the unfortunate jester are sufficient examples of the emperor's subsequent rigour. (z)   Caligula and Nero were not backward in enforcing this savage law of their predecessors, and the
former had the hypocrisy to execute some who had spoken ill of
Tiberius. (a)   At length the tide changed, and the sword of vengeance was directed against those persons who had assisted in
supporting the law of læse-majesty   For without informers there
would have been scarcely any prosecutions for libel and slander,
and as convictions multiplied, those persons who hoped to reap
benefit from the destruction of others increased likewise.   Titus
abrogated the law of majesty, and would neither suffer a prosecution for words spoken of himself, nor of his predecessors.   At the
same time he caused informers to be publicly whipped, and then
sold for slaves, or banished (b)   The accession of Domitian was
the signal for a temporary revival of the sanguinary ordinance, by
which many persons perished, (c) but Nerva again abolished it by
an edict as soon as he had been invested with the purple. (d) And
we find another condemnatory edict against this law in the time
of the great Theodosius.(e) However, the severity of the law against
informers was increased. Macrinus, the emperor, made perjury a
capital offence, and whether his accusation were true or false,
denounced the informer as an infamous person (f)   Aurelian (g)
and Dioclesian (h) pursued a similar policy, and Theodosius went
yet a step further, for not content with punishing a false accusation capitally, he ordained, that a party who should be proved to

---

(y) Un. Hist xiv. 104, citing Tacitus.
(z) See id. 108, 119, 167.   (a) Un. Hist. xiv. 283, 284.
(b) Un. Hist. xv 42.   (c) Id. 52, 76, 77, &c.
(d) Un. Hist. xv 107.   (e) Un. Hist. xvi 439
(f) Un. Hist. xv. 344.   (g) Un. Hist xv 461.
(h) Id. 507.

have informed thrice, should die, whether his statements had been just or untrue. (i)

Adultery. — Adultery, which Romulus had menaced with death, was again made capital by the Roman emperors Augustus was the first who renewed the system of severity against such as committed this offence (k) Domitian is said to have punished many adulterers of both sexes with death, (l) and Macrinus ordered the delinquents to be tied together, and burnt alive (m) Another crime, the punishment of which was at one time pecuniary, (n) and which was of a far deeper dye than adultery, was also made capital by Augustus Cæsar. (o)

Philip the emperor published an edict against it many years afterwards, (p) and by the Theodosian code unnatural offenders were ordered to be burnt alive in the sight of all the people (q)

Other capital sentences pronounced in the times of the Roman emperors were against coining, or the mixing of metals with a baser sort , by Tacitus, (r) against extortion by gaolors who were accustomed to gain money from their prisoners by ill usage (s) (a law of Constantine,) against magicians, astrologers, augurs, and pretenders to divination, by Julian who declared them enemies to mankind, and their offence treason ; (t) and against such of the equestrian order as should fight in the *Arena.* (u) (a revived edict of Augustus)

It is observable, that theft was not capital amongst the Romans It was visited by a pecuniary forfeiture, (x) but if a thief were found breaking a house by night, it seems that he might be killed by the owner of the house according to the laws of the Twelve Tables (y) A slave, however, convicted of theft was thrown headlong from the Tarpeian rock (z)

Results. — With respect to the results of these punishments, it is not easy at this distance of time to fix upon a very satisfactory conclusion.   It is clear, however, that the arbitrary laws of

---

(i) Un Hist xvi. 366.

(k) Lex Julia , Kennet, 175 , Adam, 208.

(l) Un. Hist. xv. 52.   (n) Id. 344.

(n) Lex Scatinia , Kennet, 175 , Adam, 220.

(o) Kennet, 175 , Adam, 220.   (p) Un. Hist. xv. 410.

(q) Un. Hist. xvi. 430.   (r) Un. Hist. xv 471.   (s) Id. 579.

(t) Un. Hist. xvi. 208. See, as to Witchcraft and Sorcery in the early times of the Republic, Ferguson, vol. i. p 228.

(u) Un. Hist. xiv. 33   Sea, on the subject of Capital Punishments in the early times of the Roman Republic, Ferguson, vol. i. p 68.

(x See Just. Inst lib. iv. tit. i. and ii.; Taylor's Civil Law, 3d ed. pp. 465, 466 , Adam's Ant. p 206.

(y) Taylor, p 468.

(z) Montesq. Esprit des Loix, lib xix. c. 13 , and see his chapter, " Des Loix des Romains à l'égard des peines," liv vi. c. 15.

treason and læse-majesty were ineffective. Both in the times
of the commonwealth, and in those of the imperial authority,
a succession of men, whom no penalties could daunt, was
never wanting, whether for the purpose of embarrassing the
government, or aspiring in their own persons to the sovereign
power The same consequences attended the severe edicts against
libel. It became impossible to execute them, so great was the
number of the offenders, and so obnoxious the nature of the punishment Augustus published his veto against *adultery*, and
menaced the criminal with the worst, but his own irregularities
were such as to weaken the effect of the very law he had been the
first to create (*a*)

With regard to the vestal virgins, whose fate was so awful, we
are informed, that from the time of Numa to that of Theodosius
the Great, eighteen only underwent the sentence due to their incontinence (*b*) It cannot be denied, that the excessive cruelty of
the punishment might have had some weight in lessening this
crime of sacrilege, (*c*) but notwithstanding this, we might be justified in accounting otherwise for the rarity of the offence. It is
quite certain that the people at large regarded this behaviour of
the vestals with the utmost indignation, even with superstitious
alarm. Their religion was outraged, their moral feelings were
violated, and the law itself was broken There was therefore,
the rare union of the religious, moral, and legal sanctions against
the offence. Can we wonder at its infrequency?

But we will not any longer detain the reader upon this point
He must be impatient, as indeed we ourselves are, to hasten towards the consideration of our own capital punishments.

It would be a waste both of time and of patience to attempt
even the feeblest outline of all the inflictions of death which the
human race have been emboldened, at different periods of history,
to execute. We have already enlarged upon the criminal codes
which the chief lawgivers of antiquity thought fit to establish, and
from whence Europe is said to have derived many of her present
institutions We have endeavoured to notice the results of such

---

(*a*) See Sketches of the Domestic Manners of the Romans, 1821,
p. 299.   (*b*) Mœurs et Usages des Romains, Par. 1739, p 514.

(*c*) " Pour elle, (the vestal) " on faisoit creuser une espece de caveau
dans un endroit de la ville proche la porte Colline, où apres y avoir mis
un petit lit, une lampe allumée, un peu de pain et d'eau, du lait et de
l'huile, on l'y faisoit descendre avec une échelle qu'on retiroit aussitot ;
ensuite on fermoit l'entrée de ce caveau, qui lui servoit de sepulture, et
où elle mouroit bientot de faim. C'etoit alors que la consternation re-
doubloit dans la ville, la superstition Romaine leur faisant croire que
l'etat étoit menacé de quelque grand malheur, toute la ville étoit ce jour-la
en deuil, les boutiques etoient fermées, il y régnoit une morne silence,
qui marquoit leur profonde tristesse."—Mœurs des Romains, p 514,
Sketch, &c., p. 104

punishments as we have had occasion to mention   The more
rational mode of bringing this chapter to a close, seems, therefore,
to consist in a brief allusion to such capital penalties in use
amongst modern nations as will serve to illustrate our own jurisprudence   and those also which have been adopted in countries
whose near neighbourhood to us renders their course of legislation a matter of local interest to us

It is well enough known, that when the Roman empire in the
West drew near its end, countless swarms of northern warriors
advanced from their desert regions, to share in the new invasion,
and partake of the spoil   The Visigoths seized upon Spain, the
Ostrogoths on Italy, the Franks on Gaul, the Burgundians upon
part of Germany.   Countries, however, quickly exchanged masters in the midst of this general dismemberment, so that the Goth
had hardly reared his empire, when he was menaced by the Sara-
cen and the Lombard, whilst the Lombard again was soon
obliged to surrender a short-lived dominion to the ambition of
the son of Pepin

But in the midst of these revolutions, good order and government were not entirely lost sight of.   The barbarians on the contrary, came to their new conquests prepossessed with the necessity of maintaining a system of law in their respective dominions   Theodoric, king of the Ostrogoths, ordered, that the Roman
law should be continued in Italy, (d) and Alaric, who reigned
over the Visigoths in Spain, directed, that the Theodosian code
should be abridged for the benefit of his subjects (e)   Yet the new
nations retained many of their own customs, so that the Roman
law was mixed up with an infinite variety of foreign constitutions.
The Germans, for instance, punished murder, not with death, but
by inflicting a pecuniary fine, or a compensation in great or small
cattle (f)   A similar usage prevailed amongst the ancient Anglo-
Saxons   Charles the Great, when he reviewed the laws of France,
took care to preserve the old customs and constitutions, to which
the people had been accustomed to pay a traditional reverence,
yet at the same time, he did not neglect to enforce the Salic code
which had then lately been introduced into the empire. (g)   The
Amalfitans, although they disregarded the authority of Justinian's
Code, were not backward in their admiration of the Theodosian,
and it is well known that the institutions of this people acquired
for them the applause of Eastern Europe. (h)

The Roman law then being taken, in some measure, as the
standard of legislation, notwithstanding the distant inroads of
strangers, we proceed to a very brief mention of the capital pu-

(d) Un. Hist. xix. 329.   (e) Mod. Un. Hist. xix. 351
(f) Un. Hist xix. 40.   (g) Mod. Un. Hist. xxiii. 142.
(h) See Rees Cycl tit. Amalfi.

nishments of other countries, and, as far as we can learn, of their results.

FRANCE.]—Although faint traces of the Roman institutions were observable amongst the Franks, yet they derived their principal code from the Salic, or law of the Salians, *(i)* a people who inhabited a part of Gaul contemporaneously with themselves—The system consisted, for the most part, in an accumulation of penalties, and a marked distinction between the punishments of slaves and freemen. If the party were too poor to pay the ransom required by the laws, and his relations were also unable to subscribe the penalty, the criminal was, on many occasions, condemned to die. Thus it was in the case of murder. Several solemnities were enjoined, and several appeals were made to the nearest of kin, in case the offender had not wherewithal to redeem himself; but these all failing, he was adjudged to atone with his life for the deed he had committed. *(k)* So it was, again, in the case of arson *(l)* So again, disobedience or misconduct towards a great officer or judge was punished in a similar manner *(m)* If a slave should slay another slave, or a person of the same rank with himself, the law ordained, that the respective masters of the two servants should divide the murderer between them *(n)*

If a slave should slay a freeman, he was to be delivered to the parents of the deceased, and this was the half of the composition for the murder. The master of the homicide was to pay the remaining half of the price which the law adjudged for a freeman's life *(o)* In the case of theft by a slave, the punishment was proportioned according to the sum which a freeman would have been compelled to pay under the same circumstances. Upon many occasions the number of stripes to be inflicted was regulated in this manner, but if the amount of the theft were so considerable as to call for a large fine on the part of a freeman, the slave was to die—[capitali sententiâ feriatur.] *(p)*

Our treatise will not be of sufficient limits to allow of an exten-

---

(i) Un Hist Modern, xxiii. 4, in the note. See Montesq. lib. xviii. c. 1. and c. 4 Esprit des Loix "Le pays qu'on appelle aujourd'hui la France, fut gouverné dans la première race par la Loi Romaine, ou le Code Theodosien, et par les diverses loix des Barbares qui y habitoient," Chap. iv. Leibnitz de Origine Francorum, sections 23, 24, 25, and 26.

(k) Leges Francorum Salicæ, by I. G. Eccardus, p. 105. See Hallam, i. 104, 105, 163 note.

(l) Id. p. 43   (m) Id, pp. 68, 96, 97.

(n) Leges Francorum Salicæ, by I. C. Eccardus, p. 71.

(o) Id. p. 72. "Sed si servus legem intellexerit, potent se dominus se obmallare, (i.e put in a plea,) ut ipse leudum non solvat. Id. Ib.

(p) Id. p. 81. See Montesq. liv. xviii. c. 3.

sive inquiry into the results of this system of forfeitures, but we
are assured, by comparing the testimonies of historians, that
crimes were not rare amongst the people of the middle ages.—
"Les familles faisoient la guerre," says Montesquieu, (q) "pour
des meutres, des vols, des injures" An infinity of perjuries (r)
was introduced by these monied compensations The price of
blood was contended for with a zeal which was only equalled by
the cupidity which prompted it. It was natural for men who felt
their innocence to execrate the false oaths with which they were so
often menaced The trial by battel suggested itself. But the
Salic law, unlike that of the Burgundians and Lombards, recognized not that species of proof. Charlemagne gave orders that it
should be introduced. A little before his time, Childebert, king
of Paris, had made murder and robbery capital offences (s) The
Salic law thus received a serious blow. (t)

Matters were then much changed. Every difference was decided by the sword. The test of crime was the weakness of the
accused, or the inability of the champion But this revolution
did not happen at once The original jurisdiction of the old
magistrates had undergone an alteration. A capitulary of Charlemagne ordained, that no man should be impleaded in the Hundred Court for his life, liberty, lands, or servants. (u) The Count
of the district was the new judge. (x) But complaints soon arose
against the new mode of administering justice, and special judges,
called Missi Regis, who held assizes four times in the year, were sent
from place to place (y) Then came *Le Combat judiciaire* This
was the close of the first era. The Salic law was yet in force
though much crippled by the institution of Childebert, the trial
by duel, and the capitularies of Charlemagne. The next era of

---

(q) Esp des Loix, liv xviii. c 17

(r) "Dans l'état des choses il étoit tres difficile que l'accusateur ou
l'accusé ne se parjurassent."—Representation made to Charlemagne.
Montesq. liv. xviii c 18.

(s) Hallam, i. 105, in the note Murder was punished in Burgundy
with death before this period. See Hallam, ibid note

(t) See Montesq liv. xviii. c 19

(u) Hallam, p. 192   (x) Ibid.

(y) Hallam, p. 193. Montesq liv. xviii c. 9, Montesquieu traces
the beginning of these petty jurisdictions, which were thus superseded
by the king's judges —"Les fiefs étant devenus héréditaires, et les
arrière fiefs s'étant étendus, il s'introduisit beaucoup d'usages auxquels
ces loix n'étoient plus applicables On en retint bien l'esprit, qui étoit
de régler la plupart des affaires par ses amendes. Mais les valeurs ayant
sans doute changé, les amendes changèrent aussi, et l'on voit beaucoup
de chartres ou les seigneurs fixoient les amendes qui devoient être payées
dans leur petits tribunaux Ainsi l'on suivit l'esprit de la loi sans suivre
la loi même." Esp des Loix, lib. xviii. c. 9.

French jurisprudence saw the triumph of the feudal system. The officers of *la haute justice*, the baron and the châtelain, were invested with the jurisdiction of life and death; the rules of evidence were resigned in favour of the judicial combat (z) at the accession of the race of Capet the Salic laws were silent. (a) The capitulars declined nearly about the same time, (b) and the customs of each place or district, (c) where the Count presided, usurped the authority of the ancient code (d)

Next came the establishments of Saint Louis People had become, in many cases, convinced of the folly of their judicial combat It would be hard, said Beaumanoir, that I should be compelled to fight for the proof of my relation's death, when the fact was seen by many persons in open day. (e) The number of these licenced duels proves that crime had not been diminished by their institution It was desirable to check the perjuries which throve under the Salic law, but the offender might escape under the new system from the consequences of the crime by a due display of valour and audacity. Louis ordained, that trial by battel should cease throughout his domains, (f) and although this prohibition extended no farther, its example was contagious, and the results were highly important. *Les Etablissements de S Louis* were founded upon the Civil Law which that monarch caused to be translated, (g) and thus there were two sets of laws coexistent in the kingdom, the Roman civil law, and the customary law The Etablissements soon gave way to the Roman jurisprudence which entirely superseded the code of Saint Louis, but the customs of the realm continued to maintain their local ascendancy At the same time the jurisdiction of the peers or vassals of the lord and of the bailiff declined, and in their stead the Parliament of Paris, (h) with its assistant tribunals assumed a power which shortly ripened into general dominion (i)

Thus we have, in effect, four eras of French jurisprudence up to the promulgation of the code Napoleon

1 The Salic Law. 2 The Feudal System. 3. Les Etablissements de S Louis. 4. The Parliament of Paris, with the accompanying edicts, ordonnances, and arrêts, which the French monarchs were enabled to put forth with a despotism nearly absolute

From hence sprang the establishment of the Marechaussée, or

(z) Hallam, pp 194, 195.   (a) Montesq liv. xviii c 9.
(b) Montesq. liv. xviii. c. 9, at the end.
(c) Droit Coutumier.   (d) Montesq. liv. xviii c. 12.
(e) Hallam, p. 199.
(f) Hallam, p. 198 , Montesq. liv. xviii. c. 29.
(g) Montesq. liv xviii. c. 38, 42.   (h) The Bed of Justice.
(i) See Montesq. liv. xviii. c. 39, and The Police of France, 1763, Part I

court for the punishment of prevotal crimes, all of which were
visited with death   Robberies on the highway, housebreaking,
with or without force, sacrilege accompanied by a breaking, sedi-
tions, popular commotions, unlawful armed assemblings, levying
of soldiers without the king's commission coining or uttering of
false money, were declared prevotal crimes, (k) and punishable
by hanging or the wheel (l)   Neither was there any unseasonable
delay in proceeding to trial, the prevot-general or his lieutenant
was accustomed to summon a tribunal immediately upon the apprehension of an offender, the *assesseur* prepared the evidence
forthwith, the *greffier* made up the record, the *procureur du roi*
prosecuted the case (m)   If acquittal ensued, the prisoner's custody had endured but for a short time; if convicted, his execution
speedily followed, for there was no appeal from the prevotal
court (n)

These establishments of the Marechaussée owed their origin to
the great increase of robberies by disbanded soldiers after the
peace of Utrecht (o)   Crime probably diminished after their ap-
pointment, but not by reason of the severity which accompanied
their sentences, because the same cruel punishments were in operation previously. The true causes of the decline of offences were
the rapid trial of the criminal, the certainty of punishment, (p)
and above all, the vigilance of the police, by which crimes were
prevented   This body of men was armed, and their being on duty
at stated times upon private notice given amongst themselves,
struck a terror into the disturbers of good order, and the plotters
of depredations (q)   The present establishment of the police of
England, proceeding upon the same principle, is likely to be
highly useful

We come now to the Code Napoleon   The principal offences
which it visits with death are, treason and rebellion, murder, forgery, arson, and under some circumstances which we shall mention presently, theft and perjury   There are some few other capital crimes which we shall not neglect to notice in their place (r)

Treason, or crime against the state, is divided into those acts

---

(k) Police of France, pp 37, 38.   (l) Id p. 22.
(m) Police of France, pp. 35, 36
(n) Murder was not one of the prevotal crimes, but it was capital, as
we have seen, and so was stabbing.
(o) Id. p. 25.
(p) Id. pp 17, 60. See Sketch of France, 1805, p. 45. If it were
admitted (which we do not) that the sanguinary punishment of the wheel
deterred persons from the commission of crime, it would not be an argument in favour of capital punishment in England, because we could
not resort to an infliction so cruel.   (q) Id. p. 31.
(r) Since this was written, the French have abandoned many of their
capital punishments.

which affect the exterior safety of the realm, and such as menace its interior safety. Capital offences of the first branch are—

     Bearing arms against France. (r)

     Inciting foreign powers to hostilities against France. (s)

     Treasonable negociations and treacheries (t)

     Betraying secrets of negociations or expeditions to foreign powers, (u)—or plans of fortifications, &c , (x)

     Concealing spies , (y)

Capital crimes against the interior safety are—

     To plot against the king's life, (z)—or the royal family, or

     To incite rebellion against the government, (a)—whether any act be done or not, (b)—whether any attempt made or not (c)

     To plot civil war, by exciting citizens to arm against each other, or

     To carry devastation, massacre, and pillage into one or more communes (d)

     Raising troops without lawful authority (e)

     Taking the command of a corps, fleet, port, town, &c without lawful authority,—or retaining any military command contrary to the order of government,—or keeping up troops after an order to disband or separate (f)

     Public officers obstructing the lawful raising of troops (g)

     Being at the head of armed bands for illegal purposes (h)

     Public officers plotting against the interior safety of the state. (i)

     Ministers of religion publicly pronouncing a discourse exciting a sedition or revolt which is punishable capitally (k) —the like, if done by writing, (l)—the like, if done by correspondence with foreign powers on matters of religion (m)

     Committing in the course of a rebellion any crime which is punishable capitally (n)

Murder is thus denounced " Every person guilty of assassi-

(r) The Penal Code of France, translated into English, 1819, p. 17, art 75

(s) P. C. 17, art. 76	(t) P. C. 18, art 77.
(u) P C. 18, art 80.	(x) P. C. 18, art. 81, & p. 19, art. 82.
(y) P C. 19, art. 83.	(z) P. C. 19, art. 86 , see art 97.
(a) P. C. 20, art. 87 , see art. 97.	(b) P. C. 20, art. 88.
(c) P. C 20, art. 89.	(d) P. C. 20, art. 91 , see art. 97.
(e) P. C. 20, art 92.	(f) P. C. 21 art. 93.
(g) P. C. 21, art. 94.	(h) P. C. 21, art 96.
(i) P. C. 28, art. 125.	(k) P C. 45, art 203.
(l) P C. 45, art. 206.	(m) P. C. 45, art. 208.
(n) P. C. 47, art. 216.	

nation, (o) parricide, infanticide, (p) or poisoning, (q) shall be punished with death " (r)

And this is so wherever it "shall have preceded, accompanied, or followed any other crime or delict " (s)

Malefactors making use of tortures, or committing acts of barbarity in furtherance of their crimes, are to be punished as guilty of assassination (t)

Chiefs, authors, instigators and inciters of rebellion or pillage are to be responsible for acts of murder, and punished accordingly, if the deed be done during the seditious or illegal assembly. (u)

And so it is if homicide ensue on the wilful destruction of buildings, bridges, &c (x)

If a child be exposed and abandoned in a solitary place, and death ensue, the offence is murder. (y)

In the two cases following the test of murder is made to depend upon the lapse of forty days between the stroke and the death — First, where a magistrate, in the exercise, or on occasion of the exercise of his functions, shall have been struck so as to produce effusion of blood, wounds, or sickness, and shall die within forty days, and the like in the case of a ministerial officer, or agent of the police force, or a citizen entrusted with a ministry of the public service during their respective employments, or on occasion thereof. Secondly, where any person shall have perpetrated the (z) act of castration upon another, and death ensues within forty days   The commission of that crime, where no fatal result happens, is punishable with perpetual hard labour. (a)

Murder, (b) however, is visited with a mitigated penalty in the following cases —If it be provoked by blows, or grievous personal violence. (c) In repelling, during the day, the scaling or breaking open of the inclosures, walls, or entries of a house or inhabited apartment, or the appurtenances (d) In the case of a

---

(o) Murder committed with premeditation, or lying in wait, art. 296

(p) Murder of a new-born infant, art 300

(q) Every attempt upon the life of a person, by means of substances which may occasion death, more or less quickly, in whatever manner such substances may have been employed or administered, and whatever may have been the effects thereof, art 301.

(r) P. C. 62, art 302   (s) P. C. 62, art. 304
(t) P. C. 62, art. 303.   (u) P. C. 63, art 313.
(x) P. C. 90, art. 437.   (y) P. C. 71, art. 351.

(z) P. C. 50, art. 231. " If the wounds are of that description which bear the character of murder, the criminal shall be punished with death," art. 233.   (a) P C. 64, art. 316.

(b) Murder, it will be observed, is used here indiscriminately with homicide.   (c) P. C. 65, art. 321.
(d) P. C. 65, art. 322.

woman and her accomplice caught in the act of adultery. (*f*)   If
it happen in consequence of castration after a violent outrage to
chastity, the revenge being immediate (*g*)   But parricide is never
excusable. (*h*)

In the following cases homicide is justifiable, or to use the
language of the code, it is neither crime nor delict.   When it is
ordained by the law, and commanded by lawful authority. (*i*)
When the actual necessity of lawful self-defence exists, or the
defence of another person. (*k*)

The two following cases are reckoned among those of actual
necessity of defence.—

"1st   If the homicide has been committed, the wounds occasioned, or the blows given, in repelling, during the *night*, the scaling or breaking open of the inclosures, walls, or entries of a house
or inhabited apartments, or of the appurtenances thereof.

"2nd   If the fact has taken place in self-defence, against the
actors of thefts or robbery, committed with violence." (*l*)

Theft.—The French have been tender of life in cases of theft
Under this head we include burglaries, housebreaking, and all
kinds of robberies.   In order to create a capital offence, five things
must concur—

1st. The robbery must be *by night*

2nd. It must be done by *two or more*

3rd. The criminals must have had *arms*, either apparent or
concealed.

4th   The *theft must have taken place*, "either by means of exterior housebreaking (effraction extérieure) or of scaling, or of
false keys, in a house, apartment, chamber, or lodgings, inhabited
or used for habitation, or their appurtenances.   Or by assuming
the title of a public functionary, or civil or military officer, or being
dressed in the uniform or costume of such functionary, or officer,
or by alleging a false order of the civil or military authority "

5th. The theft must have been committed with violence, or
threats of making use of the arms. (*m*)

Thus, in order to take life, there must be a conviction of *stealing in the night*, accompanied by *violence* or *threats of arms* in taking the property, and also by means of a *forcible or fraudulent
entry*, and there must be *more* than *one person* engaged in the deed.
So that a violent breaking, without a violent robbing, will not do,
nor will a forcible theft suffice without an illegal entry, and after
all something must be taken.   This is a great improvement upon
the old system, under which thieves who took the smallest article
upon the highway, or even attempted to do so, might have been

---

(*f*) P. C. 66, art. 324.   (*g*) P. C. 66, art. 325.
(*h*) P. C. 65, art. 323.   (*i*) P. C. 66, art. 327.
(*k*) P. C. 66, art. 328.   (*l*) P. C. 66, art. 329.
(*m*) P. C. 77, art. 381.   As to what shall be said to be an inhabited
house, see art 390.

broken on the wheel.   The crime of robbery has not increased in
Paris or in the country in consequence of mitigating the punishment   The moral sense of the French nation is in favour of a
severe penalty for violent robberies, but one short of death.   There
is one other offence which belongs to this part of our subject.
A theft effected by breaking of seals is declared to be punishable as a
theft committed by housebreaking. (*n*)   Therefore, if the five
circumstances concur, a breaking and stealing of the nature above
mentioned seems to be capital.

One word as to the *receivers of stolen goods.*   These persons
may be punished with death as being *accomplices* (*o*) in the crime
which their principals have committed, if, at the time of the concealment or receiving, they were cognisant of the circumstances
which induce the penalty of death. (*p*)   Thus, if a receiver be
aware of the violent entry and violent robbery, together with the
circumstances of its being a nightly depredation, and done in
company, he incurs the severest sentence of the law   Otherwise,
a receiver, who must be convicted of a *guilty knowledge,* is punished according to the offence of the principal thief

Lastly, "Those who, knowing the criminal conduct of persons
committing robberies or outrages against the safety of the state,
the public peace, or against persons or property, shall habitually
provide for them a place of retreat or meeting, shall be punished
as accomplices." (*q*)

Forgery, in which coining (*r*) is included, is not punished,
in respect of the quantity of offences with the same severity as in
England   The new Forgery Act by no means disproves this assertion.   In France, the violation of the standard coin, the seals
of the state, the public stocks, and the bank paper seem to be
the forgeries which the government there holds in the greatest abhorrence —It is capital

To *counterfeit* or *alter* the silver or gold coin legally current in
    France ; or

To take part in the issue or uttering of counterfeit coin, or
    in bringing the same within the French territory. (*s*)

(*n*) P. C. 53, art. 253.
(*o*) Accomplices are punishable as principals.
(*p*) P. C. 14, art. 62.   (*q*) P. C. 13, art. 61.
(*r*) " A crime which, like forgery with us, is punished ' sans remission.' "— Birkbeck's Notes of a Journey through France, p 55
(*s*) P. C. 30, art. 132.   But if, before the consummation of these
crimes, and before prosecution, the criminal shall reveal the original
authors to the authorities, he shall be exempted from punishment — or
even after prosecution, if he shall have procured the arrest of other guilty
persons.   But he may be placed for the remainder of his life, or for
time, under the superintendence of the high police.— Art. 138.

c 5

To counterfeit or falsify any *stock certificates* issuing from the public treasury, with its stamp,—any *bank notes or bills* authorized by law, or

To *make use of* any such counterfeited instruments, (*t*) or

To bring such into the French territory (*u*)

Arson —The crime of burning is punishable capitally when fire is wilfully set to buildings, ships, boats, warehouses, dock or timber yards, woods, underwoods, crops standing or cut down,(*x*) combustible materials so placed as to communicate the fire to such objects (*y*)

And if the injury be done to buildings, ships or boats, by means of a *mine*, the penalty is the same (*z*)   Lastly, To set fire to, or destroy by the explosion of a mine, any buildings, magazines, arsenals, ships, or other property belonging to the state, is capital (*a*)

Perjury and Subornation may be capital   For it is expressly provided, that if an accused party shall be condemned to a more severe penalty than hard labour for time, the false witness shall suffer the *same* penalty (*b*)   Subornation is regarded in a still more serious light   For if the false evidence be punishable with *perpetual hard labour*, or 'capital punishment, the suborner of such testimony is to die (*c*)

False Arrests are punishable capitally in three cases—

1st. If the arrest has been executed with a false costume, under a false name, or upon a false order of the public authority

2nd If the arrested, detained, or sequestered individual has been threatened with death.

3rd If he has been put to corporal tortures. (*d*)

Rape —It is worthy of serious attention that rape is not capital under this code; and it will be found upon enquiry that violation is not more common in France than here.   The fact is, that there the moral feeling of the people is against the crime, here the moral feeling is checked by reason of the severity of the punishment. —The French penalty is solitary imprisonment. (*e*)

Accomplices are to sustain the same punishment as their principals, (*f*) consequently, the offence of an accomplice may frequently be capital

Lastly, there may be a capital crime arising from the repetition

---

t) Of course *knowingly*.   (*u*) P. C. 32, art 139.

(*x*) "Whether the wood be in heaps or cords, and the crops in heaps or stacks."

(*y*) P. C. 90, art. 434   (*z*) P. C. 90, art. 435.
(*a*) P. C. 21, art. 95.   (*b*) P. C. 72, art 361
(*c*) P. C. 73, art. 365.   (*d*) P. C 69, art. 344.
(*e*) P. C. 67, art. 331   Not less than five, nor more than ten years.
(*f*) P. C. 13, art. 59.   Who shall be said to be accomplices, see art 60.

of offences against the laws   Thus, " if the second *crime* (g) be punishable by perpetual hard labour, he (the criminal) shall be condemned to the penalty of death " (*h*)

The proportion of capital punishments in France, as compared with England, are nearly as three to one.   Some years since, our statute-book contained about 166 of these awful denunciations They are now somewhat lessened, but the French code has little more than fifty, and the nation is already ashamed of these, for it has been seriously contemplated within the last few months, to abolish all capital penalties in France, some few very aggravated offences, perhaps, being excepted   It is to be hoped that we shall not be long after the French in this triumph of humanity and civilization   We *may* even precede them

A few words upon the results of capital punishment in France will close this short review of the subject as it regards that country.   And it may be asserted, that many enlightened and philosophical writers in France have declared, that the severe sentences of justice have, in their judgment, been productive of no beneficial effect   The words of Brissot cannot be too strongly admired.   He writes thus—" L'expérience de tous les siecles prouve que la crainte du dernier supplice n'a jamais arrêté les scélérats déterminés a porter le trouble dans la société " (*i*)

Again, he says, " La peine de mort n'a eu pour base que la fatale loi du talion, qui a égaré une infinité de législateurs   Il est bien singulier que cette loi, qui outrage l'intérêt social à un si haut dégré, ait été adoptée par les peuples les mieux policés "(*k*) Throughout the whole of Brissot's observations on the punishment of death (*l*) it is evident that he regards that penalty, not merely as cruel, but also as inefficacious.   Linguet speaks thus— " L'administration la plus douce, la meilleure ; la plus sage, la plus humaine, est—celle où l'ordre est rétabli aussi promptement qu'il a été enfreint." (*m*)

We quote in the next place the words of M Charles Lucas, Avocat. " Le rapport des exécutés à celui des accusés de crimes capitaux se trouve ainsi—

	Accuses.	Cond. à mort	Commués.	Exécutes	Acqms
En 1826,	915	150	28	110	431
En 1827,	876	109	30	75	460

(*g*) As distinguishable from *delict*.   (*h*) P. C. 12, art. 56.
(*i*) Theorie des Loix Criminelles, vol. 1. p 139.   He goes on — " L'exemple des Romains atteste cette vérité, elle est mise dans son plus beau jour par vingt années du regne de l'imperatrice de Russe, Elisabeth. — Id. ibid.
(*k*) Id. p. 151.   (*l*) Id pp. 137-162
(*m*) Conversation sur la Nature et l'Avantage des divers Gouvernements, p. 45.

" Voilà, dans le court passage d'une année à l'autre une progression assez effrayante, je l'espère, des nouvelles chances acquises au coupable d'échapper a la peine capitale inscrite dans la loi. Quand on songe que c'est en 1826, que la question de l'illegitimité et de l'inefficacité de la peine de mort a été soulevée à la fois par la publicité des concours et de la presse periodique, on ne peut trop sérieusement peser toutes les conséquences de ce fait, qui prouve, non seulement de la part de la société, mais de celle meme du pouvoir, une aversion aussi prononcée pour l'application de cette peine et une tendance aussi marquée vers son abolition. En effet, ce n'est pas seulement la société, comme on le voit, qui est intervenue, soit par son droit de grâce en préférant absoudre dans la triste alternative d'une condemnation à mort ou d'un acquittement, soit par son droit de commutation, en écartant telle ou telle circonstance aggravante pour arracher le coupable à l'échafaud, c'est le pouvoir lui-même qui a suivi le mouvement par l'extension remarquable qu'il a donnée à l'exercise de son droit de commutation."(*n*)

Again ;—" Quand donc la société dresse aujourd'hui l'échafaud en place de Grêve, le meutre qu'elle prépare et qu'elle consomme est doublement illégitime.—1°. Illégitime, parcequ'il n'est pas réclamé par le besoin de sa conservation, par le droit de sa défense; 2 Illégitime, parcequ'elle ne tue pas pour se défendre d'un ennemi, mais pour punir un coupable. que c'est comme châtiment qu'elle donne la mort, qu'elle fait acte de pénalité et non de conservation "(*o*)

In *Statistique Générale de la France* for *Departement du Mont-Blanc*, some information may be found on criminal matters under the head of " Histoire et Administration " The compiler of the Report attributes an excess of crime during some periods to the stormy condition of the country during the Revolution. He states, giving us the tables at the same time, that in 1801 and thenceforward,(*p*) offences were on the decline, but that in 1805 there was a slight advance Executions were extremely rare " Je ne crois point," says the author, " qu'il y ait eu aucune exécution à mort pendant l'an 10, l'an 11, et l'an 12, (1802, 1803, et 1804) "(*q*) " En général," he says in another place, " les grands crimes. ceux sur tout, qui attentent à la sûreté des

---

(*n*) Observations sur la question de la Peine de Mort —Revue Encyclopedique, vol. xli. pp. 581. 582

(*o*) Observations, &c. ut supra, Rev. Encyclop. vol. xli. p. 584. and see the work itself of M. Ch. Lucas, Par. 1828. Also Guizot, De la Peine de Mort, Par. 1829 The last edition of this latter work is reviewed in the 45th volume of Revue Encyclop. p. 451.

(*p*) The work was published in 1807.

(*q*) Statistique Générale Département du Mont Blanc, p. 390. M. De Verneilh.

personnes, sont très-rares. Il existe sur tous les points une es-
péce de *morale* publique, qui press et finit par chasser les mal-
faiteurs, et même ceux dont le séjour ou les moyens d'existence
donneroient lieu à des soupçons un peu graves "(r)   It is but
fair to add, that this author speaks in one place of an increased
number of capital executions for some years after 1789, (s) but
those who read the passage will be kind enough to remember,
that he sets down this increase of crime to the score of those
horrors and violences which plunged the whole land at that era
into scenes of blood   " Dépuis que les grands troubles ont
cessé," he continues, " le peuple s'est rapproché de ses anciennes
mœurs."(t)

Enough has now been said to shew that the sense of enlightened Frenchmen is against the punishment of death, that they
do not repudiate that punishment through any false notions of
humanity, but that they are enemies to extreme severity, because
of its inutility and inefficacy (u)

ITALY]—Three sets of laws have struggled for the mastery in
Italy at different periods   1. The Roman Law, or code of
Theodosius, 2. The Laws of the Lombards; and 3 The Roman
Civil Law, or the code of Justinian   These have been accompanied at various seasons by the fugitive or permanent institutions,
(as the case might be) of the rulers of that country, and also by
the local usages of each state, which have a parallel in the *Droit
coutumier* of France

At first the Roman Laws, or code of Theodosius, bore the ascendant, (x) but Evaric, the Goth, in the early part of the fifth century, introduced the customs of his own country, and caused them
to be put in writing, and the Roman law declined for a time. (y)
However, at the end of that century, Theodoric and the Gothic
monarch caused the Roman law to be again respected, though
he would not abolish the Lombard institutions, but preserved
them inviolable when they did not interfere with the code of
Theodosius (z)   Still, the Theodosian code could not very long
compete with the Lombard, at least, not in those districts which
the Lombards possessed, and which comprised the greater part
of Italy   Rotari VII, King of Lombardy, having caused the
laws of his country to be reduced again to writing, and King

(r) Id 391.
(s) Id. 390. " Quoique la peine de mort fût appliquée à un plus
grand nombre de cas dans la législation sarde, que dans notre législation
nouvelle."—Id. 389.
(t) Statistique Générale, &c. p. 390.
(u) See some sensible observations on the preventive police of France
in Morris Birkbeck's Notes of a Journey through France, pp. 97-99.
(x) Giannone Istoria di Napoli, tom. 1. p. 146
(y) See id. 190. et seq.   (z) Id. 214. et seq.

Grimoald, with other rulers, having made some farther improvement in them, the Roman law, although it had never been abolished, nor even treated with disrespect, began, for the second time, to decay (*a*) Even when Charlemagne overcame the Lombards, he caused their ordinances to be established as the law of the country, and also directed, that they should have force throughout Italy (*b*) This, therefore, was the triumph of Lombard legislation It was adopted by the Conqueror, (*c*) it was studied by the professors of the country, and it was carefully formed into a compilation for the use of the judicial tribunals (*d*)

But such are the alterations in human affairs, " le strane vicende delle montane cose," as Giannone expresses himself, that this law of Lombardy was soon destined to yield in its turn The code of Justinian, commonly known by the name of the Civil Law, which had lain hid for five centuries, began at length to be sanctioned and respected The Roman Emperor, who was deceived in his ideas of its early progress, (*c*) would now have regarded its gradual advances with the delight of a parent. The Lombard law, in fact, began to fall before that very code, which itself had like to have been strangled in its infancy. The Civil Law suddenly rose into great repute. In Naples it was at length received, though at first it struggled with the Lombard laws, with the constitutions of the Norman Kings, and those of Frederic, and with the approved customs of the realm Yet, notwithstanding all these, the jurists of the day held up the civil law to public admiration, and were eager in advancing its precepts, till at length the code of Justinian entirely triumphed, and the legislation of the Lombards became extinct (*f*)

We do not propose to detail here all the capital inflictions of the Theodosian and Lombard codes, but it is satisfactory to be enabled to say, that the spirit of both, especially of the latter, was inclined against capital punishment "Commenda Ugone Grozio," says Giannone, when speaking of the Lombards, " questo loro instituto di non spargere il sangue de' Cittadini per leggiere cagioni, ma solo per gravissime e capitali. Ne' minori delitti bastava, che per danaro si componessero, ovvero che il

---

(*a*) Giannone, i. 359. and see id. pp. 412. 433. 446.

(*b*) Id. i. 456.

(*c*) See id. ibid. and tom. ii. 286. where the Normans are mentioned as having left the Lombard laws untouched when they conquered Apulia and Calabria.   (*d*) Tom. ii. 289.

(*e*) On the contrary, it almost died with him. " Nulla dimeno l'autorità de medesimi quasi s'estinse insicome con lui."—Giannone, i. 337. and see id. p. 250.

(*f*) Giannone, tom. iii. p. 426. " Ed in progresso di tempo la loro forza ed autorità s'estese tanto, che finalmente vinse, e mandò in disusanza le leggi Longobarde."—Id. ibid, See also tom. iv p. 236.

colpevole passasse nella servitù dell' offeso, in cui s'era pec-
cato." (*g*)

Some offences, however, were capital, although upon a diligent examination, it will be found, that many of these were thus
severely sentenced under the institutions or capitulars of succeeding kings, rather than by virtue of the old Gothic code.
Thus Ruggiero I, King of Sicily, made it capital for any one to
falsify his letters, or seal, in Naples, which was under his dominion (*h*) Also, to cast false money, to receive it with a guilty
knowledge, or to be in any way accessary to that crime. (*i*) So
again, to clip the current coin, or to cut it in any way so as to
diminish its value (*k*) Again, to make use of false testimony,
to hide, take away, erase or obliterate the public wills (*l*) To
have, or sell poison, or medicines which had a pernicious effect
upon the reason (*m*)

But to return for a moment to the Lombard code. It was
capital to attempt expatriation without authority. (*n*) In cases of
murder, restitution might be made, only there existed the common distinction between a slave and a freeman, the former being
invariably sentenced to die. (*o*) And so it was if a slave were at
the head of a riot (*p*) For theft, the third offence was punishable
with death (*q*) And if the executioner should save the thief delivered over to capital punishment, his offence must be visited
with half the pecuniary loss occasioned by the robbery, and if
the same thief should again be caught in felony, he must suffer
his original sentence. (*r*)

There was another capital offence If a man were reprieved,
and he afterwards committed a new wrong, and then refused to
make amends under the plea of his being dead in law, it was declared that he should be remitted to his former sentence (*s*)

Another law of the Emperor Henry runs thus, — "Decet
Imperialem solertiam, contemptorem suæ presentiæ capitali
damnare sententiâ." (*t*) And this brings us just to observe, that
in several cases the king was expressly invested with the power
of life and death, so that the culprit lay entirely at his mercy. (*u*)

(*g*) Giannone, tom. i. p 450   (*h*) Giannone, tom. ii. p. 381.
(*i*) Ibid.   (*k*) Ibid.
(*l*) Ibid.   (*m*) Ibid
(*n*) Leg. Long. Lindenbrog, p 515.
(*o*) Id. 527 lib. i. tit. 9. vii., 528 tit 9. xv., 529. tit. 9. xx., 533.
tit. 9. xxxv., tit. 36. i.—p. 583.
(*p*) Id. lib. i. tit 17. ii. p. 543.
(*q*) Id. lib. i. tit. 25. lxvii. p. 571.
(*r*) Id. lib i. tit. 25. lxix. p. 571.
(*s*) Id. lib i. tit. 35. ii. p 583.
(*t*) Id. lib. ii. tit. 55. iii. p 656.
(*u*) Id. lib. ii. tit. 3. i. p. 590.

It will be easily seen from hence, that the Lombard laws, as they were originally composed, stood very clear from the punishment of death, and that the constant habit of compensating for injuries was the chief occasion of this lenity. The widrigild, or weregild, and the octogild, were atonements which entirely satisfied justice upon most emergencies (*x*)

THE CIVIL LAW —The code of Justinian, or civil law, was very merciful in respect of capital punishment. Several crimes, however, were denounced under the severest penalty. And first, treason. The undertaking of any offence against the emperor or the republic, was an offence of this nature. The very memory of the offender was to be held infamous (*y*)

Secondly, murder was punished with death, whether the crime were committed by means of deadly weapons, or by pernicious medicaments or drugs, or by the practice of odious arts of any kind. And all such as carried weapons, whether swords, clubs, or stones, &c., were menaced with the like sentence, if a murderous intent were proved.(*z*) The punishment of parricide is well known. The criminal was to be sewn up in a kind of sack with a dog, a cock, a viper, and an ape, and then thrown into the sea, or an adjacent river. He was thus deprived of the elements, his living body being shut out from the air, and his dead body from the use of the earth.(*a*) Adultery,(*b*) sodomy,(*c*) and rape,(*d*) were also capital.

In forgery, there was a difference between slaves and freemen. The former were condemned to die, the latter underwent the sentence of deportation.

The capital forgeries were the making or altering a forged will, or any other instrument, and the making, engraving, or counterfeiting the seal of another (*e*)

But it was capital to kill a slave, and the master was at liberty both to prosecute the murderer, and also to sue for damages by a private action for redress from the law Aquilia(*f*)

(*x*) See the Laws, passim, and Hallam's Middle Ages, 1. 105 With respect to the Theodosian Code, the reader may be referred to the edition of Maurilius cum perpetuis Commentariis Gothofredi. Lugd. 1665 , and Theodosiani Codicis Fragmenta, edited by Clossius. Tubing. 1824. As to the old Sicilian and Neapolitan Laws, see Codex Legem Ant. ex Bib. Lindenbrogi, p. 693, &c. where also the laws of the Burgundians, Visigoths, and others, may be found.
(*y*) Inst. lib. 4. tit. 18. § III. Lex Julia Majestatis.
(*z*) Inst. lib. 4. tit 18. § v. Lex Cornelia de Sicariis.
(*a*) Inst. lib. 4. tit. 18. § VI. Lex Pompeia de Parricidis.
(*b*) Inst lib. 4. tit. 18. § IV. Lex Julia.
(*c*) Inst. lib. 4. tit. 18. § IV. Lex Julia.
(*d*) Inst. lib. 4. tit. 18. § VIII. Lex Julia
(*e*) Inst. lib. 4 tit. 18. § VII. Lex Cornelia de Falsis.
(*f*) Inst. lib. 4. tit. 3. § XI.

Theft in general was not capital   But the offence of man-stealing was sometimes subject to the heavier sentence, according to the imperial constitutions (*g*)   And it was also provided, that if any judge should despoil the property of the church or the public during his continuance in office, he should be put to death.(*h*)

Such were, in comparison with our own, the *merciful* institutions of the Civil Law, and we shall find, as we proceed, that the lenity of the governments and states of Italy, which either adopted or recognized this code, had no effect in advancing the calendar of offences.   On the contrary, executions were rare, and public wrongs, *especially those not capital*, were not of frequent occurrence

Italy, as it is at present governed, remains subject to many masters   *Lombardy* is under the yoke of Austria, *Naples* belongs to the King of Sicily, *Piedmont* to the King of Sardinia, the Papal States are the territory of Mother Church; whilst Tuscany, Modena, Lucca, and Parma, are ruled by their own dukes, and there is, besides, the small republic of Marino

The author would gladly encounter the fatigue and labour of going through all the capital inflictions peculiar to these states, but he feels satisfied that the present occasion will not warrant so enlarged a view of the subject   A few general particulars, therefore, will close this head of Italy.   Lombardy, being the property of Austria, is subject to the code of that country which was so much improved by the Emperor Joseph.   The excellency of the institutions, civil, criminal, and ecclesiastical, has been highly extolled. (*i*)

Naples, after undergoing several changes,(*k*) at length became subject to the Philippine Code in 1598 (*l*)   It subsequently passed into the hands of the King of Sicily, who governed according to the order of his own laws.

Piedmont is regulated by the Sardinian Code; and, though we do not profess to enter into particulars, it may be observed, that the capital punishments are chiefly levelled against those who commit crimes with arms in their hands and with force

The criminal laws of the Church are peculiar to the Papal territories; they are not severe, as we shall shew presently.(*m*) The four dukedoms are governed by their own institutions.

(*g*) Inst lib. 4. tit. 18. x. Lex Fabia de Plagiariis.
(*h*) Inst. lib. 4. tit 18 lx. Lex Julia peculatûs.
(*i*) See Austria as it is, p. 204   Lond. 1828
(*k*) Alfonso, in 1443, sold the privilege of life and death to the Neapolitan barons.—Hallam's Middle Ages, i. 195.
(*l*) Giannone, tom v. 188.
(*m*) See Constitution du Pape Pius VII de sa propre volonté, tit. iii. De l Organisation des Tribuneaux Criminels.

Leopold, the Grand Duke of Tuscany, abolished the pain of death throughout his dominions in 1786, (n) but when the whole realm of Italy yielded to the ascendant of Bonaparte, the severer edicts were restored, and some crimes are, we believe, still capital in that state   The happy results of the abolition above-mentioned will be almost immediately adverted to   Lucca had long been under the influence of the heaviest sentences, but even there *simple* theft was not capital (o)   Now, after a survey of the various laws which have obtained at different times throughout Italy, it cannot be otherwise than gratifying to observe, that where capital punishments have been rare, crime has been scarce also, and that where, as in Tuscany, the severe penalty has been abolished altogether, crime has not advanced in consequence, but, on the contrary, has diminished   A writer upon Italy observed upon the rarity of capital punishments at Genoa   His observations are worthy of notice   " Les jugements à mort sont fort rares   Depuis six ans, on n'en a vu que deux, encore a-t'il fallu que le second eût été sollicité *par le peuple*   Le senat se fit forcer la main, il fut accablé de libelles et de placards pendant deux mois.   Peu s'en fallut que le coupable n'échappât; ceux qui le conduisaient au supplice le laissèrent évader ; mais le peuple le poursuivit, et obligea les gens de justice de le reprendre : il avait commis dix meutres ('p)

, Where should we find such a populace in England? The truth is, that the rarity of punishment gave death the popular sanction A man who had committed ten murders exasperated the people The law and the nation were in alliance   It is not so with us (q)

The writer goes on to speak of Tuscany, that very Tuscany whose duke destroyed the sanguinary calling of the executioner. " Il y a dix ans que le sang n'a coulé en Toscane sur un échafaud La liberté seule est bannie des prisons . le grand-duc les a remplies de justice et d'humanité." (r)   What was the consequence ?

" Cet adoucissement des lois a adouci les mœurs publiques ; les crimes graves devienent rares, depuis que les peines atroces, sont abolies, les prisons de la Toscane ont été vides pendant trois mois." (s)

Again he says, concerning thefts at Rome . —" Les besoins de

(n) Edict of the grand Duke of Tuscany for the Reform of Criminal Law in his Dominions, sect. li.—Warrington, 1789.

(o) See Lucensis Civitatis Statuta.—Luc 1539

(p) Lettres sur l'Italie, en 1785. tom 1. p. 67.   Rome, 1792.

(q) Thurtell would have been allowed to escape as far as the people were concerned

(r) Lettres sur l'Italie, tom. 1. p. 102.   (s) Ibid.

voler sont peu actifs et peu nombreux, et les peines contre le
vol ne sont pas sevéres."(*t*)   Yet, notwithstanding this lenity,—
Rien de plus rare à Rome que les vols caracterisés '(*u*)   At
Naples, also, he says .—" On le punit que très rarement, et
presque jamais du dernier supplice."(*x*)

Italian writers upon jurisprudence agree that the abolition of
death in Tuscany was productive of meritorious effects   Their
testimony, therefore, is in unison with that of the writer just
quoted   Guido Angelo Pozzi in his " Elements of criminal Law,"
published at Florence in 1815, has declared, that during the
suspension of the penalty of death, not one atrocious crime had
been committed.   He is cited by Carmignani, Professor at the
University of Pisa, in a work which has for its object the refuta-
tion of M Birnbaum's opinion on this subject   M Birnbaum(*y*)
had declared, that the abolition of the punishment of death had
produced such effects as to compel its re-establishment, and he
cited a work of Paoletti(*z*) in support of his assertions   Paoletti,
however, adds Carmignani, never could have expressed himself
in the manner attributed to him, because he was always opposed
to the severe mode of punishment (*a*) The probability, therefore,
is, that the Professor at Louvain was deceived by the obedience
which the Italian lawyers paid to Napoleon   The Emperor desired that death should form a punishment in the code of laws,
and it was so ordained.   Independently of the will of this moral
and political tyrant, the punishment of death stands condemned
in Italy by the concurrent testimony of the most able lawyers, and
the most careful experience   " Quali sono presso queste nazioni"
[several nations of Europe], says Filangieri, " le consequenze,
che derivano dall' abuso, che si è fatto della pena di morte? Si
è moltiplicato il numero di alcuni delitti più atroci, alcuni meno
atroci rimangono impuniti, si è indebolito il vigore della pena."(*b*)
Again , —" Per non veder un patibolo innalzato innanzi alla
porta della sua casa, per non esporsi alle publiche maledizioni,
il padrone nasconde alla giudizia il ladro ; si fa un delitto di ac

---

(*t*) Lettres sur l'Italie, tom ii p 163   (*u*) Id. p. 158.
    (*x*) Id tom. iii. p. 107   See an account of an execution in Italy—
Travels in Spain and Italy by Pere Labat, tom. vii. ch 1. Cérémonie
pour pendre un homme   (*y*) Professor at Louvain.
    (*z*) Un Ouvrage de droit Criminal, reprinted at Milan in 1804.
    (*a*) Revue Encyclopedique, vol. xli. p 590   " Paoletti était déjà
accablé sous les poids des ans et des infirmités "—Ibid   " Il mani-
feste assez clairment son opinion contre cette peine dans le dernier écrit
de sa carrière scientifique, sur la police, imprimé à Florence en 1822."—
Id. 591.
    (*b*) La Scienza della Legislazione, Tomo Terzo. Filadelfia, 1807,
p. 29.

cusar lo ; ed il furto rimane impunito sotto la protezione di quella legge istessa, che lo punisce colla morte."(c)

Filangieri, after declaring that death ought not to be adopted as a punishment in any other cases than than those of *Treason* and *Murder*, goes on to say, that the legislator may rest assured — " che un esecuzione di questa natura [that is, with torments] non sarà mai accompagnata dall' approvazione pubblica , che *un esecuzione non ratificata del voto pubblico è inutile*, (d) è che un esecuzione inutile è sempre ingiusta, perche l'oggetto della legge nel punire *non è di vendicare la società dell' offesa* ricevata dal reo, ma di liberar la da' nuovi mali, a quali la sua impunità potrebbe esporla,"(e) These words are remarkable . " L' esecuzione se ne faccia con tutti quegli apparati, che possono renderla piu imponente agli occhi del popolo ; ma che si cerchi nel tempo stesso di renderla quanto meno sia possibile tormentosa pel delinquente." (*f*)

SPAIN.]—In Spain, which fell under the dominion of the Visigoths, the capital punishments have not been by any means numerous. Treason and murder were, however, made capital at an early period The case of the famous General Paul, who nearly overturned the monarchy of the Visigoths, is an instance of the former (*g*) The Spaniards have always shewn a strong indignation against the crime of murder The case of the gentleman of Galicia, who was executed for killing a public notary, although forty thousand golden pistoles were offered for his ransom, may be cited as an example of this. (*h*) " Todo hombre," says the law, " que matare a otro asabiendas, que muera por ello " (*i*)

Treason is especially provided for in the code (*k*)

Perjury was declared punishable with death where the testimony of the false witness tended to convict another capitally, whether the accused person were actually executed or not (*l*)

The crime against nature was visited by burning and confiscation of goods (*m*)

(*c*) La Scienza della Legislazione, tom. iii. p. 30.
(*d*) Please to mark this, reader !
(*e*) Filangieri. Id ut supra, p. 33
(*f*) Id. p. 32. The 29th and 30th chapters in this volume are throughout well worthy of attention. See also Di Una Riforma D'Italia Villa-franca, 1770 pp. 321-354 and as to the laws of Corsica. Statuti civili e criminali di Corsica. Geneva, 1602.
(*g*) Univ. Hist. Modern, vol. xix. p. 436. See also vol xx. p. 389. There were some capital punishments in force against the Jews about this time. Id. vol. xix p. 414. note
(*h*) Mod. Un Hist. vol xxi. p 162.
(*i*) Leyes de Espana, Alcal, 1681., and see tit. 22 lib. 8. tit 23. Ley. 4   (*k*) Id Lib. 8. tit. 18.
(*l*) Id. Lib. 8. tit. 17. ley 4.   (*m*) Id. lib. 8. tit. 21.

In the several cases of burglary, (n) rape, and adultery, it was allowable for the injured party to take the law into his own hands, and to slay the criminal   These cases are put into the catalogue of excusable homicides (o)

Theft, however, it will be observed, was not capital, (p) neither in former times was robbery on the highway, (q) but latterly this offence has been deemed worthy of very heavy punishments, and the culprit has, accordingly, been broken on the wheel. (r)

Taking the results of these punishments for a moment into consideration, it is obvious, with reference to the last, that severity has gained no propitious end   Spain has been the scene of the most sanguinary attacks and robberies for many years past   The awful histories of midnight spoils and murders are frequently communicated to us by the various Chronicles of the times   How is this?   Let us quote Levae, one of the youngest advocates of a more lenient code—a distinguished Belgic writer.   " Dans tous les tems on a regardé la peine de mort comme le frein du crime, pourquoi, quand l'expérience en a prouvé l' impuissance et l'enefficacité, les gouvernemens ne chercheraint-ils pas un remède aux maux du corps social dans une autre peine? La crainte du supplicê n' a pu dompter les scelerats ' (s)

With respect to assassinations, as long as a temptation exists to allure the criminal, the penalty of death will be found sufficiently useless   When it was customary to hire mercenaries in Spain for the purposes of revenge, men have been found ready to shed blood to any extent.   One of two men hanged at Valencia, in the last century, confessed the perpetration of thirty three murders ; the other included in his catalogue a number not less than seventy seven (t)   " Criminal processes," says Mr Jacob, " are carried on with a degree of langour which is beneficial only to the perpetrators of enormous crimes, the murderer, even if the clearest evidence establishes his guilt, may, if he have money, remove his trial from court to court, may obtain a revision in each, and as long as his money lasts, delay judgment in a manner which, if it does not ultimately elude punishment, at least delays it till it ceases to have an effect on any one but the sufferer." (u)

(n) The crime of housebreaking, or criminal entries into houses, seems to have been common in Cadiz. — Pere Labat Voyages en Espagne, tom. i. p. 158.

(o) Leyes de Espana, lib. 8. tit. 23. ley 4. Id. lib 8. tit. 20, ley. 3.

(p) Id. lib. 8. tit. 11. ley. 7.   (q) Id. lib. 8. tit. 12. ley. 1.

(r) See Théorie des Cortes, Par. Marina. Traduit de l'Espagnol, Par. P F. L. Henry,

(s) De la Peine de Mort, par Adolph. Levae, Bruxelles, 1828. Rev. Encyclopédique, vol. xlii. p. 726.

(t) Bromley's Travels, p. 65.

(u) Jacob's Travels in the South of Spain, p. 291.

Thus, whatever reasons may be assigned, it is a fact, that Spain must be added to the list of countries which adopt capital punishments, but where, in return, no salutary effects ensue (*x*)

GERMANY]—We shall not enter at any length upon any more of the foreign codes   Germany has " The Capitulation of Election, and the order of criminal justice of Charles V. The Roman law , (*y*) the Lombard code of law; and the particular codes of each of the several states of the empire "(*z*) The criminal institutions, however, of Germany, as confirmed and settled by the ordinances of Charles V (commonly called the Caroline,) formed indeed a bloody code   Treason, (*a*) sedition, (*b*) blasphemy, (*c*) adultery (*d*) incest, (*e*) sodomy (*f*) were capital. So also were coining, (*g*) forgery (*h*) perjury, (*i*) false weights, (*k*) and false libels. (*l*) So again—rape, (*m*) the carrying off of women, (*n*) and the prostitution of children (*o*)

Murder—whether by poison, (*p*) parricide, (*q*) infanticide by exposure, (*r*) abortion—the child having had life, (*s*) or otherwise, (*t*) was punished with death. So it was, if death ensued in a tumult or quarrel, in consequence of a blow inflicted by the interference of any person. (*u*) Those who employed dangerous mentices which could not be justified by law nor equity were adjudged to die. (*x*) So were *dangerous vagabonds* (*y*)

(*x*) " Les seules lois authentiques, d'apres lesquelles la justice est administrée, sont consignees dans des codes publiés par leurs anciens Rois , tels sont *La Ley de las siete Partidos, et Ordenamiento Real, et Fuero-Juzgo, et Fuero Real*. Le principal, celui qui est de l'usage le plus habituel, est connu, sous le nom de Recopilacion. C est la collection de diverses Ordonnances isolees des Monarques d'Espagne, depuis les siecles les plus reculés jusqu'à nos jours "—Nouveau Voyage en Espagne par Bourgouin, tom. 1 p. 292. And see particularly p. 293. where it is shewn, that a revision of the Criminal Code was at one time contemplated in Spain   the quotation is too long for insertion here   See, with regard to the laws of Portugal, Ordenaçoes o Leys de Portugal, Lisboa, 1695. Quinto Livro   [A sanguinary code]

(*y*) That is, the Code of Justinian.

(*z*) Statistical Tables of Europe, p 15.   John Stockdale, 1800.

(*a*) Code Criminelle de Charles V. Vulgairement appellée La Caroline, 1767. Art 124.   (*b*) In some cases   Id. Art 127.

(*c*) Art 106   In some cases.

(*d*) Art. 120.   Perhaps bigamy in some cases, Art. 121.

(*e*) Art 117.   (*f*) Art. 116.   (*g*) Art. 111.   (*h*) Art. 112.

(*i*) Art. 107. where the false oath charged a capital crime.

(*k*) Art. 113. where the offence was frequently repeated

(*l*) Where the libel charged a capital offence.   Art. 110

(*m*) Art. 119.   (*n*) Art. 118   (*o*) Art. 122

(*p*) Art. 130.   (*q*) Art 131.   (*r*) Art 132.

(*s*) Art 133. See Art. 134.   (*t*) Art 137.

(*u*) Art 148.   (*x*) Art. 129.

(*y*) Art. 128. Answering to our Egyptians of former days, or gypsies.

Arson—was punished by burning the offender. (z)

With respect to thefts, they were made capable of some distinctions Sacrilege was capital; (a) so was highway robbery; (b) so was the entering of any place by *escalade*, or by *breaking*. (c) Such offenders were called dangerous thieves. The forcible entry alluded to aggravated offences, and made them capital upon occasions which would not have called for so severe a sentence without force   As in the taking of fish in an enclosed place (d)

The stealing of corn or other fruits of the earth by night or day might be a capital offence, according to the value of the damage done, or the mode of doing it, (e) but the mere stealing of fruit or vegetables was not so heavily punished (f)

The code also enabled the judges to pass a capital sentence where the theft exceeded five ducats, according to their sense of the circumstances of the case   As, the condition of the thief, the injury done to the person robbed, &c. (g)

A *third* theft, of whatever value, and however committed, was judged worthy of death (h)

There is an article which permits the judges to mitigate the punishment of theft in case of famine or want, but the most unequivocal testimony of distress was required (i)

Breach of trust was regarded in the same light as theft, and punished accordingly. (k)

Theft under the value of five ducats was not capital, (l) unless it were the third offence   Accessaries before the fact were punishable capitally, where the original offence was capital, and receivers were subject to the same penalty, but the mere concealment of offenders from the hand of justice was visited with a more lenient sentence (m)

Gaolers, who aided their prisoners to escape, were adjudged to suffer the same punishment as the convicts who were allowed to be at large (n)

Lastly, it was provided that the attempt to commit crimes should be punished with death, or otherwise according to the discretion of the judges (o) The following are the crimes which were deemed capital.

(z) Art 125.   (a) Art. 172.   (b) Art. 126.
(c) Art. 159.   (d) Art. 169. See Art 163.
(e) Art. 167.   (f) Ibid.
(g) Art 160   It is impossible to refrain from remarking, that our criminal jurisprudence is carried into effect according to these rules. They are all founded upon false principles, as will be shown hereafter
(h) Art 162   So is the law of Corsica. Statuti Criminali di Corsica. Geneva, 1602. p. 18. Sia impiccato per la gola.   (i) Art. 166.
(k) Art. 170.   (l) See Articles 157. & 158.
(m) Art. 177   (n) Art. 180.   (o) Art. 178.

Attemp's to commit lese-majesty, sacrilege, parricide, treason against the state, sedition. Other attempts to commit offences, however atrocious, as murder, were punished in a less severe degree.(p)

Other capitularies, decrees, or laws have been introduced from time to time into Germany, but the body of laws above referred to, is that upon which the criminal jurisdiction of the empire was chiefly exercised (q)

There is scarcely any country in Europe which has not its own particular code of criminal jurisprudence, and it is a pleasing fact, that in many places where the punishments are not severe, the moral character of the people is more elevated   In Switzerland, capital punishment is rare, but its inhabitants, at the same time, are celebrated for their honesty and humanity (r)   Each state or canton has been accustomed to its particular laws,(s) and it is proposed at this moment to abolish the punishment of death in Geneva, whilst the neighbouring district of Le Valais has already abrogated that penalty.(t)   Seventy years ago, these ideas of benevolence were entertained in Switzerland by men of the highest distinction.(u)   " L'horreur de voir un gibet à sa porte, et la crainte de la haine, et des malédictions publiques arrêtent la plainte des maîtres ; et l'excès même du châtiment a produit l'impunité d'un vol, qu'une loi plus modérée eut infailliblement réprimé."(x)   These were the words of M Servan, Advocate General at Geneva, in a discourse which he pronounced in the presence of his fellow-citizens.

In Russia, after a long career of severe penalties, the punishment of death was at length laid aside by the Empress Elizabeth. During her reign, which lasted for twenty years, there was not a single execution in her dominions, except in the rebellion of Regatcheff. It seems that this clemency did not increase crime, since Brissot writes thus —" L'expérience de tous les siecles prouve que la crainte du dernier supplice n'a jamais arrêté les scélérats déterminés à porter la trouble dans la société. L'exemple des Romains atteste cette vérité, elle est mise dans son plus beau jour par vingt années du regne de l'impératrice de

---

(p) Punition corporelle ou arbitraire.
(q) Although there are so many jurisdictions in that country as to make it a matter of extreme difficulty to point out the particular penal laws which are entertained by each state.
(r) See Les Loix et Statuts du Pays de Vaud.   Bern. 1716.
(s) Statistical Tables of Europe, p 67.
(t) Morning Herald, Saturday, August 20, 1831.
(u) See Discours sur l'Administration de la Justice Criminelle par M. Servan, Avocat Général, and especially pp. 123-133
(x) Id p. 126

Russie Elizabeth "(*y*)   On the other hand, Montesquieu gives an
authority against excess of severity in his chapter, "Impuissance
des Loix Japonoises"   In the case of Russia, it is to be observed, there was a superabounding clemency, in that of Japan,
an unrelenting system of cruelty   " On y punit de mort presque
tous les crimes," says Montesquieu (*z*)   The result is thus related by the philosopher.   ' Les relations nous disent, au sujet
de l'éducation des Japonois, qu'il y faut traiter les enfans avec
douceur, parcequ'ils s'obstinent contre les peines, que les esclaves
ne doivent point être trop rudement traités, parcequ'ils se
mettent d'abord en défense (*a*)   He sums up the matter thus —
" L'atrocité des loix en empêche donc l'execution, lorsque la
peine est sans mesure, on est souvent obligé de lui préférer l'impunité."

Concerning Sweden, Brissot has written thus.   "Dans la
diete tenue en 1778 en Swede, on a arrete, 1 la limitation des
peines de mort infligees par la loi contre certains crimes qui,
selon l'avis des ordres, seront punis en proportion de leur énor-
mité, 2 qu'à l'avenir aucun crime n'entrainera la perte de l'hon-
neur, à l'exception de ceux dont la bassesse et l'infamie sont la
base; 3 la fixation du tems de la prescription dans les affaires
criminelles, avec une restriction annexce, relative à des forfaits
plus graves."(*b*)

A few words upon American legislation will close the chapter,
and it is gratifying to record another instance of public feeling
against capital punishment   From the earliest period of our
colonial settlements in that quarter of the world, the penalty of
death has been discouraged.   Whatever may be the illicit or
corrupt practices of judges and lawyers there, it is quite clear
that the state of their laws involves them in a very slight degree
with the great question of life or death   Even in cases of murder, which is capital in many provinces in the United States,
prisoners seem to have every practicable advantage afforded
them (*c*)   In Pennsylvania, it is well known that the punishment

---

(*y*) Théorie des Loix Criminelles, tom. 1. p. 138.   See also p 146,
and id. note (67).   See the observations of the same author upon the
Pain of Death, id. pp. 137-154.   and as to the Punishments of the
Persians, id. 152. n. (72).   And moreover, Code Catherine, 1 e In-
structions pour la Code de la Russie —Traduit de l'Allemand, a Péters-
bourg, 1769   See particularly sect 202. et seq.

(*z*) Liv. 6. ch 13.   (*a*) Ibid.

(*b*) Théorie des Loix Criminelles, tom. 1. 146. n. (68).   And as to
the laws of Norway and Iceland, see Leges, Gula-Thingenses, Sive
Jus Commune Norvegicum, Hauniæ, 1817 , and Logbók Islend'inga
sive Gragas Codex Juris Islandorum Antiquissimus, qui nominatur
Gragas, Hauniæ, 1829

(*c*) The United States of North America as they are, pp. 169-173.

of death was not tolerated by the enlightened founders of that republic. "La république de Pennsylvania," says Brissot, "adopte dans sa legislation cette méthode si sage de détourner du crime par le spectacle des châtimens de longue durée et soumis à tous les yeux C'est l'unique moyen de rendre les punitions sanguinaires plus rares "(*d*) The same principle has prevailed ever since, and we find a late traveller applauding the penitentiary system established in that province, as the means of reclaiming a considerable number of convicted criminals "Here," says he, speaking of Pennsylvanian prisons, "is the best of all evidence, *demonstrative proof*, that brutal treatment, hangings, and gibbetings, are neither the most economical nor the most efficacious, as they are certainly neither the most humane, nor the most enlightened modes of punishing crime, or reforming society."(*e*) The same feeling has lately been manifested in Louisiana The general assembly there assented to a proposition made by the compiler of their code, M. Edward Livingston, that the punishment of death should be abolished.(*f*) The argument of that enlightened legislator upon the subject, will be found in the Revue Encyclopédique (*g*) It is well deserving of attention, both in respect of the theory as well as the facts which it contains The labours of M Livingston, which were successful, received an honourable mention at Geneva, in 1816, when it was proposed to abolish capital penalties in that city, and his country, Louisiana, was spoken of in terms of praise, in conjunction with Russia, under the Empress Elizabeth, and Tuscany, under Leopold (*h*) The great Doctor Franklin entertained the same decided objection to severity (*i*)

Thus we have endeavoured to treat in some degree of the punishments of foreign countries, as far as the question of life and death arises

I, We mentioned the capital offences which were recognised

(*d*) Théorie des Loix Criminelles, p. 146. (n 68).
(*e*) Fearon's Sketches, p. 158.
(*f*) Revue Encyclop. tom xlvii. p. 27, n. (1).
(*g*) Id. 24-42, and again 276-297.
(*h*) Revue Encyclop. tom xlvii. p 28. in the note.
(*i*) Id p. 288 in the note. In the 45th volume of this work there are similar good news from Egypt " Enfin, un des numéros reçus en Europe [Journals de Caire], annonce que la peine de mort a été abolie en Égypte pour tous les crimes, autres que les délits politiques et les vols commis par les kophtes, remplissant quelques uns des premiers emplois de l'état. Elle n'est pas même conservée pour les assassinats, et pour le crime de fausse monnaie. La peine substituée est celle de travaux forcés, dans l'arsenal d'Alexandrie, pendant dix, vingt, trente ans, ou pour la vie " tom. xlv. p. 204.

by ancient nations, the Jews, the Greeks, the Romans, and others.

II We adverted to the practice of modern states, the French, the Italians, the Germans, and other European kingdoms, together with the lenient institutions of America   We now hasten to give an account of the capital punishments in England, and of their results. These subjects will form the materials of the second chapter

CHAPTER II.

OF CAPITAL PUNISHMENTS IN ENGLAND

OFFENCES which are punishable capitally in England, are —

I Such as relate to the crown and government.
II Those which are injurious to religion and public morals
III Such as are committed against the person
IV The like against property

Of the First Class are,

High Treason —Treason against the king and government
Rescue, in cases of high treason
Mutiny.—Seducing soldiers and sailors to mutiny
Oath.—Administering, to commit treason or felony
Piracy —Putting force upon captains of ships
Rescue, in cases of murder.
Returning from transportation
Rioters.—Not dispersing after proclamation made.
Slave-dealing
Smuggling.
Stealing from the Post-office.

Of the Second Class are,

Arson, of churches, &c
Rioters —Pulling down churches, &c
Sacrilege.

The Third Class consists of

Abortion —Poisoning to procure, [the woman being quick]
Rape.
Attempts to murder
Bestiality.
Carnally knowing female children under ten years
Murder.
Shooting
Sodomy
Stabbing and wounding [which include the old offence, of cutting and maiming.]

The Fourth Class.

1. By larceny.   II. By malicious injuries

Arson and Burning [II.]
Burglary and housebreaking [I.]
False signals.—Making, to bring ships into danger [II.]
Forgery—of wills.—Powers of attorney to transfer stock at the
    Bank, India House, or South Sea House [I.]
Piracy [I.]
Robbery [I.]—By force.
    Extortion by threatening an accusation of an infamous crime
    Extortion by threats during tumult and riots.
Rioters.—Pulling down houses and other property [II.]
Stealing in a dwelling house, some person therein being put
    in fear [I.]
Wreck.—Plunder of [I.]

These being the offences at present subjected to the penalty of
death in England, it will be the object of this chapter to relate
the history of that severe sentence which the law has pronounced
against them, considering it with reference to each crime. We
shall then proceed, secondly, to detail the results of the punishments.

First, of offences against the crown and government.

Treason.—Treason in an extensive sense, means infidelity by
an inferior towards his superior In one more limited it is applied to certain offences against the king, his family, and government. In the earliest time, treasons, if not punished on the instant, as in the case of a vanquished rebel, were redeemable by
forfeitures Afterwards it came to be understood, that such
crimes, when committed against the person of the sovereign or his
royal majesty, were not clergyable at common law.(a) Then
the statutable definitions were made, independently of which
there were to be no treasons, and as these spoke universally of
acts done against " our lord the king and his royal majesty," it
followed, that the offence itself was capital

We have said that offences of this nature were capable of pecuniary compensation in very ancient times If the criminal
were poor, he lost his life without redemption; but, if he could
command a few pounds, his sentence might have been commuted
for the price at which the king's life was valued ;(b) or, in after
times, if he objected to, or was incapable of the payment, he

---

(a) Shakespeare notes the old distinction —" I do arrest thee of
capital treason "

(b) Leges Anglo-Saxonicæ, by David Wilkins, Leges Ælfredi (4),
p. 35.

might have demanded the triple ordeal.(*c*) And about the same period, an ordinance was made which allowed the accused either the ordeal,(*d*) or the amplest compurgation upon oath (*e*) Then came the laws of Canute, by which the party was condemned to die unless he should go through the triple ordeal,(*f*) and thus matters stood till the reign of William the Conqueror, who introduced the proceeding by duel in criminal trials (*g*)

In the reign of Henry I. it was declared, that whosoever should slay his liege lord, should be irredeemable He was to have his hair cut off, and to be flead alive.(*h*) This, however, was where the traitor actually took the life of his sovereign or lord paramount.

From hence until the famous statute of Edward III , the law of treason was changing, arbitrary, and uncertain At one time(*i*) it was called the raising of sedition against the king, or in the army, or the attempting to destroy the royal person, in which guilty acts aiders and abettors were included. These crimes came under the denomination of lese-majesty (*k*) Soon afterwards (*l*) grand or high treason was considered to be the compassing of the king's death, disinheriting him of his realm, falsifying his seals, counterfeiting or clipping his coin (*m*) But, inasmuch as great injuries done by one man to another, such as procuring the death of any one from whom seisin was derived, or bringing persons into those perils which would put them in jeopardy of their lives, members, or property, were accounted treason,(*n*) a still more extensive degree of confusion arose in respect of that offence Nor was this uncertainty by any means diminished in the reign of Edward the Second. The author of the Mirror speaks of three sorts of treason as recognised in that reign 1 The

---

(*c*) Id Liber Constitutionum Temp. Æthelredi, R. p. 110 , and this would have stood him in but little service unless he could have feed the priests.

(*d*) Juxta leges Anglorum, " et in lege Danorum per illud [Ordalium] quod eorum lex est " p. 123.

(*e*) Id. Concilium Ænhamense, p. 123. Reeves's Eng Law. i. 20, 21.

(*f*) Id. Leges Cnuti, (54), p. 142. and see id. (61), p 143

(*g*) Reeves, i. p. 82 See also id. p 195 Glanv. lib. 14. c. 1. Coutumes Anglo-Normandes par Honard, i. 575.

(*h*) Wilkins, ut supra. Leges Henrici Primi, p. 268. " Dampnetur ut diris tormentorum cruciatibus, et malæ mortis infortuniis, infelicem prius animam exhalasse, quam finem doloribus excepisse videatur, et si posset fieri remissionis amplius apud inferos invenisse quam in terrâ reliquisse protestetur."—Ibid.

(*i*) Temp. Hen. III.

(*k*) Reeves, ii. 5. citing Bracton

(*l*) Temp Ed. I.   (*m*) Reeves, ii. 273. citing Britton.

(*n*) Reeves, ibid citing Britton.

offences of devising mischief against the king in any way whatsoever, of ravishing his wife, or eldest unmarried daughter in his custody, or his niece or aunt, being heir to the crown   2. Falsifying the king's seal or money   3. Violating the ties of mutual relationship taken in a political sense, (as in the case of patron and client amongst the Romans), by taking life or member, lessening private security, &c (*o*)   And as though this broad sheet of treason were not sufficiently confounding, Home, the writer of the Mirror, places among the crimes of lese-majesty all misfeasances of the king's officers, treating them as breaches of allegiance to the sovereign, and so *perjuries* (*p*)

Armed with this spreading dominion over the relations of men, the monarchs of the time had no difficulty in establishing a treason against any obnoxious subject.   They were aided by the shifting manners of the age   The trial by ordeal had grown into disuse, the duel was on the decline, so that the matter was most frequently decided by the equals(*q*) of the party offending, and these, at first, formed neither an impartial trial nor an incorrupt tribunal

Again, upon a conviction, the king seized upon the lands and goods of the criminal, (for the Norman Conqueror had introduced forfeiture,) and the lord thus lost his territorial profits   In consequence of the multiplication(*r*) of constructive treasons, these bereavements became more frequent, and the barons persuaded the people, on the other hand, that their lives were daily in jeopardy   At length, in the reign of Edward III , the evil grew to such an extent as to command immediate redress   An accident hastened the crisis   "A knight of Hertfordshire forcibly detained a man till he paid him 90*l* , this was held treason, *because* he was in so doing, guilty of *accrouchment* (as they called it), or attempting to exercise royal power."(*s*)   It was in vain that the king answered the commons' application by saying, that the points of the treasons and accroachments were specified in the judgments themselves   neither the people nor the nobles were contented, and, accordingly, the sovereign yielded to a second petition, by ordaining the celebrated statute of the twenty-fifth of his reign (*t*)

These are the treasons enumerated by that act

1. To compass or imagine the death of the king, the queen, their eldest son and heir.   2. To levy war against the king in his

---

(*o*) The Myrror, cap 1. sect 4, 5, and 6.   Reeves, ii. 349.
(*p*) The Myrror, sect 6   Reeves, ii 350.
(*q*) Pares regno — for the nobles , or Sectatores, in the case of commoners.
(*r*) Killing the king's messenger, and misleading the king in council, had been adjudged treason.   See Reeves, ii. 451.   Luders' Tracts, i 59.
(*s*) Reeves, ii. 451.   (*t*) Luders, i. 11.   Reeves, ii 450. 451.

realm, or adhere to his enemies there, or elsewhere   3 To violate the king's companion, or his eldest daughter unmarried, or
the wife of the king's eldest son and heir —To warrant a conviction for these offences, it was required that a man should be
proveably attainted of open deed by people of his own condition

4. To falsify the great or privy seal,(*u*) or the king's money—
to bring false money into the realm for the purposes of merchan-
dize and payments

5. To slay the chancellor, treasurer, or judges, in their places
" And of such treasons the forfeiture of the escheats belongs to
the king, as well of lands and tenements holden of another, as of
himself "(*x*)

This and the statute 36 Geo 3. c. 7, (which we shall presently
advert,) are the principal laws which govern the offence of high
treason at the present day, and both authorise the infliction of
capital punishment for that crime   It is not necessary that we
should enter into a historical detail of the numberless treasons
which were declared during the interval   They were, however,
universally capital   The statute of Edward had pronounced,
that the parliament, in conjunction with the royal authority, shall
declare all future treasons   A compliant legislature stained the
statute-book of Richard, the next sovereign, with blood,(*y*) but
in the succeeding reign, these new creations were abandoned, and
the old standard was again adopted (*z*)   Upon the accession of
Henry VI, however, there was another successful attempt to
increase the catalogue of treasons   Escaping out of prison when
under a charge of treason; threatening letters, demanding money
upon pain of burning houses, carrying away cattle out of the
English counties by the Welch or Marchers, were declared to be
offences of this nature (*a*)   The sanguinary enactments of Henry
VIII. are too well known to need repetition,(*b*) and although by
comparison, the reign of his son and successor was not so deeply
tinged with legal carnage, several treasons were announced by
the parliament.(*c*)   It is, however, deserving of attention, that
the standard of 25 Ed 3. was set up in the beginning of Edward
the Sixth's government, and that a similar course was adopted at
the accession of Queen Mary, by repealing all previous laws
except the 25 of Ed. 3, relating to treason (*d*)

The Queen, however, caused certain acts, if done against her
or her husband, King Philip, to be declared treason, such as

(*u*) See the new Forgery Act, 1 Gul iv. c 66. and post, p 66. n (*k*)
(*x*) Reeves, ii 452. See id. iii. 116.
(*y*) Reeves, iii. 207.   And see his Chart of Penal Law.
(*z*) Id. 234.   (*a*) Id. 285 and see id. 408.
(*b*) Reeves, iv. 272, &c , and see id 257.
(*c*) Id 469, 475, 476.   (*d*) Id 468, 486.

preaching against the royal title, *the second offence;* writing, printing, overt acts, with the same intent, *in the first instance* (*i*) And it is observable, that the chief treasons of the three last reigns were writing or speaking against the rights of the sovereign   No one was more careful of her royal inheritance than Queen Elizabeth   It is true that the first germs of political freedom were discernible during the continuance of her dominion, but they sprang forth in spite of the arbitrary measures of the court, and not through any barrenness of severe laws.   For not only were the ordinary treasons declared, but it was also an overt act to utter by *speech, words,* or *sayings,* the criminal intention   And, moreover, to affirm by writing, printing, or express words, that the queen was heretic, schismatic, tyrant, infidel, or usurper, was high treason.   And so it was to say, that the queen had no power with the authority of parliament, to limit the crown, or that the then present statute was not good and valid (*f*)   Other treasons related to the Romish church   They were chiefly the receiving of bulls or other instruments, as instruments of absolution or reconciliation, and both authors and receivers were involved in the same jeopardy (*g*)   And the third offence of defending the power of any foreign prince within the realm, or doing any thing towards the maintenance of it, was treason. (*h*)   Jesuits and seminary priests were denounced in a subsequent year under the like penalties (*i*)   And the detaining any of the queen's towers castles, &c, or her ships, &c, burning her ships, or burning any of her houses, were declared treason. (*k*)

The principal treasons in the times of the Stuarts, were the conspiring against the royal person, embezzling the king's stores, and enlisting in foreign service   Then came the Act of Settlement, and the penalties consequent upon disturbing the Protestant order of succession, and as the parliament has been sparing in its declarations of treason during the last century, we are easily enabled to consolidate the whole according to the practice of the present day.

1. There are first, then, the Statute of Treasons, 25 Ed. 3. st. 5 c 2

II. Secondly, the corresponding with rebels or enemies out of England, or upon the sea. (*l*)

III. Thirdly, the treasons declared against such as should impugn the Protestant succession (*m*)

IV. Fourthly, the st 36 Geo. 3. c. 7, against compassing to depose the king, levying war for the purpose of putting any restraint upon him, or of intimidating either house of parliament.

(*e*) Reeves, iv. 489.   (*f*) Id. 104.
(*g*) Id. 105, 107.   (*h*) Id. 101.
(*i*) Id. 110   (*k*) Id. v. 106.
(*l*) See East's Pleas of the Crown, i. 77.   (*m*) Id. 90.

V. And by 7 Ann. c. 21, s 8, it was made treason to slay any
of the lords of session, or justiciary in Scotland, in the exercise
of their office

Now, with respect to the second class, the offence mentioned
there is punishable under the annual mutiny acts, and therefore,
proceedings upon that statute of Anne may be considered as obsolete.   Again, the firm establishment of the Protestant religion,
and the decay of the Pretender's family, have nearly extinguished
the third head of treasons, so that the two leading statutes upon
the subject are obviously those of the reign of Edward the Third,
and George the Third.   The following are the comments of Lord
Chief Justice Abbott upon these two acts, in the late trial of
Arthur Thistlewood

" You will have observed, gentlemen," (addressing the Grand
Inquest,) " that in each of the descriptions of offence that I have
enumerated, except the levying war mentioned in the ancient
statutes, the crime is made to consist in the compassing, imagination, or intention, (which are all words of the same import) to
perpetrate the acts, and not in the actual perpetration of them
But then it is further decreed by the ancient statute, that the
party accused of the crime shall be thereof proveably attainted of
open deed, and by the late statute, that the party shall express,
utter, or declare his intention, by publishing some printing or
writing, or by some other act or deed.   The law has wisely provided, because the public safety requires, that in cases of this
kind, which manifestly tend to the most extensive public evil,
the intention shall be manifested by some act of the party tending
toward the accomplishment of the criminal object proposed."(*n*)

PUNISHMENT.— We will advert for a moment to the punishment incident upon a conviction of high treason, not for the
sake of exposing its barbarities, but because the consideration of
it may assist us when we come to sum up the results of its severe
infliction.   The following seems to be the ancient judgment —
" To be drawn through the middle of the city to Tyburn, and
there hanged by the neck ," then, before death, to have the heart
cut out, the head cut off, and the body divided into four parts, to
be at the king's disposal (*q*)   The mercy of succeeding generations did not increase   Until a late period, the sentence was, to
be drawn on the hurdle and hanged, to be cut down whilst alive,
and to have the entrails taken out and burnt before the offender's
face, his head then to be cut off, and body quartered , both head

---

(*n*) Trials of Thistlewood and others, vol. i. pp, 5, 6.   See also
Trial of J Watson, vol. i. p. 4. charge of Bayley, J.
   (*q*) Reeves, iv. 175.

and body to be at the king's disposal (*r*) Townly was treated in
this manner, after the rebellion of 1746 ; but the executioner had
the humanity to dispatch him before the embowelling (*s*)

The punishment of women was, to be drawn to the place of
execution and burnt.

Thus stood the law until the year 1788 as to females, and until
1814 with respect to males Not that the sentence was invariably
executed with rigour. In Townly's case the executioner destroyed life before his operations Tne custom of previous
strangulation had prevailed in the case of women before the alteration of the law ; (*t*) and, in the very first instance, the strict law
of dragging a man along the pavement, had been exchanged for
drawing him on a hurdle (*u*) At length, in 1788, a distressing
scene occurred in London at the execution of a woman, who
fainted when brought to the stake , and the penalty was immediately changed to drawing and hanging (*x*) The sentence, however, touching males continued (*y*) In 1803, the words, " but
not until you are dead," were repeated to Despard and his asso-
ciates They were to be taken down again, and to undergo the
savage mangling permitted by the old law (*z*) But his Majesty
remitted the sentence, except hanging and beheading ,(*a*) and a
similar prohibition against anatomy has been issued ever since,
by the command of the sovereign For, although the law sustained an alteration in 1814, the quartering of the corpses of
traitors was still tenaciously maintained Sir Samuel Romilly,
struck with this, as well as many other sanguinary ordinances,
moved to moderate the punishment to hanging only, the offender
being previously drawn to the scaffold At first, he was defeated,
although the arguments in favour of his measure far outweighed
the appeals for ancient usages and the expressions of indignation
against traitors, which were sounded on the other side of the
House (*b*) But in the following year he again brought forward
his bill, and though sadly mutilated by an amendment, which is

---

(*r*) East. P. C. i. 137. Preface to Montagu's Debate in the House
of Commons upon the High Treason Punishment Bill. Other atrocities
still more shocking had been occasionally inflicted upon the half-living
bodies of convicted traitors.

(*s*) See State Trials, vol. xviii. p. 351. Montagu, ut supra,
pp. 8, 12.

(*t*) Colquhoun on the Police of the Metropolis, p. 40.

(*u*) Blackstone's Commentaries, iv. 92.

(*x*) London Encyclop vol. xxii. tit. Treason

(*y*) As in the case of Tyrie at Winchester, 1782, cor. Heath, J. Luders, i 170.   (*z*) See the Trial, p 268.

(*a*) Id. 269 , and Luders' Tracts, i. 169.

(*b*) See the Debate by Montagu.

now the law of the land, the system of embowelling, and of other cruelties, was for ever extinguished in law, as it had been before in practice (c) The remainder of this history is soon told The executioner was now empowered to hang, to behead, and to quarter the body, thus divided, to be at his Majesty's disposal In the case of Brandreth and others, who died at Derby, the Prince Regent mitigated the penalty to hanging and beheading; and when Thistlewood, Ings, and their party were put to death at the Old Bailey, his late Majesty made a similar order, and both the heads and bodies were forthwith privately buried. (d) The good sense of the legislature. it is to be hoped, will soon imitate the spirit of these gracious remissions, and erase from their statute-book, *at least*, every accompaniment of death (e)

RESULTS.]—Upon the subject of the results of capital pains in high treason, we shall not dwell long, for our purpose, in stating results, is in order to procure the abolition of the sentence of death, and, it is feared, that treasons against the King's person and government cannot be so leniently treated Nevertheless, the author will not shrink from boldly avowing his opinion—that life ought not to be taken, even upon this serious emergency, unless there be no other mode of preventing the criminal from injuring the government which he has already outraged. For the rapid stroke of military execution is the only true method of checking mischievous rebellion, *by way of example*, and that this is a sufficiently available remedy, in cases of imminent danger, the history of our country, by no means deficient in recent instances, amply shews. We do not destroy the offender from a principle of vengeance, but to deter others, and the slow progress of a trial (in the author's humble opinion), is not calculated to effect that object. In this view of the matter, a brief examination of the results of executions may not be inexpedient

The principle clearly discernible throughout the pages of our history, is, that men who deem themselves aggrieved by the existing authorities, act upon the impulse of feelings which are

---

(c) See the Debate by Montagu, and Chitty's Blackstone, p 93. n (19) Stat 54 Geo. 3 c 146 And see, on this subject, Luders, vol 1. Tract 11. on the Judgment in High Treason, p 149, and especially pp 166 172 Colquhoun, pp 38-40

(d) It would be not a little curious to enquire how far man has a right to deny his fellow-creatures Christian burial, admitting that to be a religious ceremony, but we will not pursue the subject in this place.

(e) It is utterly impossible that the practice of drawing a person to execution — and, after death, committing an outrage on his corpse, which God made perfect — can be sanctioned any longer.

entirely independent of consequences   The slavish fear of death
does come within their thoughts, the notion of future dishonour
or disgrace is far removed, because that which they do they think
is right   If we look to the transactions of former days, we shall
find that the chief commotions in our country have arisen from
disputes concerning the inheritance of the Crown—struggles for
religion—and rebellion against grievances

No execution, however sanguinary, has had the effect of deterring those who have, from time to time, considered their title
to the Crown as founded in justice, nor that portion of the people
who have been led to believe that the claim thus made, has been
just.   It was in vain that Henry IV shed blood upon the discomfiture of some malecontent lords at Cirencester.   In vain did
Richard perish beneath the hand of assassins   In vain was the
battle of Shrewsbury gained by the reigning prince.   Useless
was the capital punishment at Pontefract   Henry, throughout
his reign, was persecuted by insurrections, because the governing
idea abroad was that he had no right to the Crown   It needed
the kingly prerogative, too, to prevent the common people from
worshipping Richard Scrope, the archbishop, as a martyr.   The
imputed rights of the unfortunate Richard died not with his
successor.   A conspiracy was soon formed against Henry V. upon
the old pretence, and severity was again exercised against the
delinquents   A bloody and successful war with France smothered
awhile the flame which was about to rekindle   We need not
mention the ensanguined fields of York and Lancaster—they
are fresh in our remembrance   With the notion of right, on
either side, was allied that of fearlessness and perseverance.   The
battles of Saint Alban's raged in vain—Edward struck off the
heads of his opponents,—but that bloodshed did not save him
the battle of Tewkesbury.   The Duke of Somerset and the Grand
Prior of Saint John closed the march of death, but the spirit of
disaffection burnt as keenly as ever in the breasts of the conquered   An occasion only was wanting.   Warned by repeated
and narrow escapes, the Earl of Richmond still thirsted for that
which he deemed his just inheritance   Though there had been
twelve battles between the two Roses, the Earl still strove for the
Tudor dynasty   He was at length victorious, and became the
Seventh Henry.   But he was not destined to a bed of down.   He
had to struggle with the Simnels and Warbecks of the time, with
the lurking partiality of the people for the Earl of Warwick,
and, lastly, with the revolt of Suffolk.   Henry had not been
celebrated for his clemency; yet Suffolk and his accomplices
were ready in the day of trial   A similar contempt of consequences distinguished those who sought to place Mary Queen
of Scots upon the throne of England   The deaths of Norfolk
and Northumberland had no operation to prevent the Babington

conspiracy; and horrid as were the executions in this latter case, most unquestionably there would have been found fresh vindicators of the cause, but for the execution of Elizabeth's great rival. Passing over the Parliamentary troubles, (*f*) and the reign of Charles II, whose title was indefeasible, we come to Monmouth's rebellion, and the expulsion of James II. It needs but little acquaintance with history, to recollect the inflexible justice of the reigning monarch towards the natural son of Charles, and the soul-harrowing executions of Jeffreys Yet William, the king's nephew, scarcely four years afterwards, was in arms against his unbending uncle, and, in spite of those embittering recollections which still agitated the West, he possessed himself of Exeter, and was soon in a condition to advance upon Salisbury. But there were several who, through fidelity to their master, or the force of conscience, still held James's title to be paramount, and these were not deterred by the fear of death from taking the best measures in their power to restore the ancient sovereign To say nothing of the fierce struggles in Ireland — the conspiracies in which Sir James Montgomery, Lord Preston, and Ashton participated, the Lancashire plot, the assassination scheme for which Friend and Perkins suffered, the fate of Sir John Fenwick, sufficiently shew that men were not wanting who would hazard all for him whom they deemed their rightful Prince

The alarms which the Pretender and his son were constantly raising in England, during the reigns of the two first Georges, are the last which we meet with concerning the inheritance of the Crown They are, of course, familiar to all, but they establish this important fact—that, until time had thinned the ranks of the Stuart adherents, neither defeat nor death could quench the spirit which animated the cause. Whatever may be the signs of the present times, we have reason to rejoice that the insecurity or vacillation of the royal title is not among the evils with we have to deal.

Treasons on the score of *religion* have not been the more restrained by the inflexibility of executions. Long did the Papists confederate against the Protestant monarchs of the time, in spite of torture and of death The Gunpowder Plot was a creation of men who valued the restoration of their religion far more than their lives. It was in vain that Venner the enthusiast, the fierce leader of the Fifth-monarchy-men, perished by the hand of the hangman . scarcely had a year expired, when it became necessary to shed more blood, and six more of those deluded persons, heed-

---

(*f*) Cromwell, however, was exposed to perpetual insurrections in favour of the legitimate succession, which no executions could entirely quell.

less of the past, were drawn to the scaffold.   The Popish Plot (if such a plot there were) was characterized by an anxiety to restore the ancient creed ; and the Protestant Plot, as the Rye-house conspiracy was called, aimed at nothing less than the discomfiture of the Catholic priesthood.   Scenes of bloodshed were not spared the people   but whilst on the one hand the Catholic subject scrupled not to die for his religion, the Protestant, on the other, unawed by legal slaughter, submitted his neck also, with devotional zeal, to the executioner

Lastly, if we come to the consideration of those popular commotions which have been the result of real or imagined grievances, indifference to life, that well-principled foe to capital execution, will be found assuming a full and free dominion over the minds of Englishmen.   Revolt succeeded revolt in the reign of William I, chiefly through his oppressive conduct towards his English subjects   Some he put to death, some were banished or imprisoned, but the flame of rebellion burst out again almost on the instant, and fresh severities were exercised by the victor Scarcely, however, had these examples been made, when the Conqueror's own Normans swerved from their allegiance, and once more the scaffold streamed with blood.   The reigns of Rufus and the first Henry were less disturbed than that of their predecessor   but whoever will examine the history of their times, will perceive that clemency, and not severity, was the prevailing feature   Some were allowed to redeem their lives, which was the old Weregild, others were made prisoners, and restrained from further mischief; and, with the exception of William de Ardres, perhaps no man of note lost his life, in those days, for treason The clemency of Stephen contributed greatly to his ultimate success against Matilda   " The commendations due to his valour, clemency, and generosity, cannot be denied him," says Rapin (g)   Seventeen years of the reign of Henry II. were passed in safety from open treason, and when at length rebellion broke forth in the persons of his children, his victories were unattended by retaliation or severity   Of Richard's forbearance we cannot boast so much   The sedition of William Longbeard was punished with the loss of many lives, and the great conqueror of the Saracens was too prodigal of blood upon other occasions.   He died by the hand of one whose father and brother had perished by his own weapon.   Scarcely had he quitted the sceptre, when the Barons' wars broke out, and the English, as it were, again familiarized with savage scenes, were long before they returned to tranquillity.   It was in vain that John ravaged the kingdom, and in particular the lands of his rebellious nobles, fruitless were the confiscations of the great fiefs by Henry ; and

---

(g) Vol. i. p. 210

but for the better conduct of the young Prince Edward, the troubles of those times would not have been so soon appeased Those who might have treated the victory at Evesham, and the reduction of the Ely rebels with indifference, could not resist the forbearing manliness of Edward The Barons, far from entertaining resentments, or being exasperated by unwise executions, swore fealty with one accord, and invited the popular monarch to the throne of his ancestors

Would that his great example had been followed!

His son, absorbed in favouritism, was tempted to imbrue his hands in blood Urged by the Spencers, he assented to the death of fifteen Barons who had been taken in battle, but, far from having exhibited a prosperous example, a spirit of deadly revenge was instantly enkindled, which slumbered not till the monarch himself was cruelly murdered by assassins. Then followed the clement reign of the third Edward For the Earl of Kent's death he was not answerable, because he had not then assumed the reins of government, and if it be said that he directed the execution of the Earl of March, let it be added, that this man had condemned the Spencers without a hearing, that he had caused the death of Kent, the king's own uncle ; that he was considered the instrument of Edward II.'s murder ; and, lastly, that the people gave his condign punishment their sanction. But what were the occurrences in the next reign ? The Poll-tax was a grievance, and 100,000 men were instantly in arms they were crushed ; their leaders, Tyler and Jack Straw put to death, and the cruelties of Judge Tresilian, in Norfolk and Essex, have been compared to those of Jeffreys, but no sooner did the king pretend to absolute power, than the country rose again, and when, soon afterwards, the Duke of Hereford was induced to join the great conspiracy, the Londoners declared for him without hesitation

The supposed mal-administration of the government, in the reign of Henry VI , was the cause of Jack Cade's insurrection, and although much blood was shed on the scaffold, we have seen (*h*) that the people were not daunted, nor restrained from joining the standard of the House of York

It cannot be affirmed, by a careful reasoner, that the parade of an execution conduces to deter others from the crime. Witness the Cornish rebellion, in the time of Henry VII The conspirators said plainly that the king, if he should proceed to extremities, must hang three-parts in four of his subjects. His clemency in pardoning all who were engaged in the second treason, "*except* a few ringleaders who were hanged for an example," was very admirable, but the truth is, that the taking of these

---

(*h*) Ante, p. 61.

lives was an act of severity entirely gratuitous in respect of future benefits In the early part of the next reign, the Statute of Labourers gave offence, and an insurrection in Kent was the consequence foreigners became obnoxious, and a great multitude immediately began a work of destruction and murder the London apprentices were affronted in the time of Queen Elizabeth, and 300 of them quickly assembled at Tower-hill, with a trumpet and flag (i) there were disturbances by reason of the Inclosure Bill, in the reign of Edward VI. and because the Spanish match was unpopular, Sir Thomas Wyatt had no difficulty in mustering a very formidable array against Queen Mary's government The popular gatherings in the time of Charles II , for the purpose of pulling down all bawdy-houses the rising of Danaree and his party, with a similar design against all meeting-houses, and the violent proceedings of Lord George Gordon, in order to gain the repeal of immunities which had been conceded to the Catholics, may be mentioned also as instances of general commotions (k) It is true that the judges did not hold every one of these cases to be a treasonable conspiracy, but the majority of them was considered in that light, and the facts themselves illustrate our object most distinctly, because they prove that the infliction of death never deters an insurgent populace in the day of temptation.

Our most modern treasons have been those of Despard, Brandreth, and Thistlewood. The trial of Watson, also, is still fresh in the recollection of all The three first died by the hands of the executioner ; and it should be remembered, that Brandreth and Thistlewood were supposed to have added murder to their crime against the state Thistlewood, moreover, we may add, had been previously tried and acquitted with Watson , and who can say whether, had the punishment for treason been less than death, the jury might not, upon the former occasion, have passed such a verdict as would have incapacitated Thistlewood from the mischief to come? Thus we have demonstrated that the destruction of the traitor, or the agent of constructive treason, operates not as a warning to future agitators, but that, on the extreme contrary, it has sometimes caused an opposite effect, and bred the base appetite of revenge

If we shall be free hereafter from these blots in the shield of our general allegiance, it will be the result, not of the clemency or severity of the sovereign, not of the fear of death but, of universal instruction Education, political education alone can work the change Whether the intelligence proceed from the efforts of a Political Union, or whether it be disseminated (as it might be) in every

---

(i) See Luders's Tracts, vol. i. pp. 24-37.

(k) See Luders, i 45-51 , and p. 56.

National School in the kingdom under the patronage of Government — it is this alone which will teach men the true value of tranquillity, and the disastrous consequences of rebelling against their constituted head   In the same academy where the mechanic and the labourer reap their first rudiments of learning, let the golden economy of good order be also taught   The folly of unbridled lust, the furious phrenzy of a wavering and discordant multitude, the useless devastation of property, will then no longer be conspicuous   As reason advances, (and it is not now capable of retrocession,) the moral energies of man, subject to the law of peace, will be sufficient to overthrow all grievances   Thus directed, they will accomplish more liberty and union than millions of swords, and countless parks of artillery.

Rescue and Prison Breaking.

We should now have completed our remarks upon the subject of of treason, (k) were it not that the breaking of prison, with intent to procure a traitor's escape, and the rescue of a traitor, are of themselves acts of treason.

However, there is not much to be said upon this subject, for, although we have heard that, in very old days, men were occasionally hanged for a rescue, executions for this offence are by no means familiar to modern times (l)   For the sake of brevity, we will mention rescue in cases of murder, (m) voluntary escapes by gaolers, and breaking of prison generally, under this head; although we may lay voluntary escapes out of the question, because that offence was always within clergy, and clergy is now abolished.

As to the rescue of murderers, the capital guilt thereby created is by virtue of the statute, but there is scarcely any instance of a conviction   The particular provision upon this point was introduced into the statute of Geo. II as an additional mark of severity, — a statute which had for its chief object the diminution of sanguinary deeds

The rescuing of persons condemned to transportation from those who have received them according to the contract for conveying them abroad, is a capital offence, and so also is the aiding an escape of such convicts (n)

(k) In pursuance of the provisions of the new act, which repeals the punishment of death for forgeries in general, the falsifying of the king's seals is no longer a capital offence.

(l) By 25 Geo 2 c 37. s 9.   (m) Reeves, vol v. p 106.

(n) Four persons were convicted of a rescue, in 1821, probably for this offence, but I have not been able to find the particulars.—Parl Return, 1828, vol xx.   Rescuing from the *Penitentiary* is not a capital offence   There was, moreover, a conviction on the Suffolk circuit in 1770, Lent Assizes, entitled " being at large and breaking prison before execution ," and another at the Summer Assizes in the same year, en-

As to the breaking of prison, even the conspiring to do so was felony at common law, whether the party were confined on a civil or criminal account, provided the imprisonment were lawful But the stat Edw 2. *de frangentibus prisonam* confined the felony to cases of treason, and convictions which required a judgment of death. (*o*)   Still, as this was, at the most, a clergyable offence, it becomes unnecessary to consider it farther in this respect, because of the abolition of the benefit of clergy   Yet, breaking prison is a capital offence in some cases, by statute (*p*)   For example, a second offence of this kind, by persons confined at Millbank, is punishable by death. (*q*)   And in 1813 there was a conviction at the Huntingdonshire Spring Assizes, for an escape from the Bridewell in Huntingdon, but the prisoner was reprieved   In 1821, a similar conviction took place in Surrey, for an illegal breach of the Brixton House of Correction, but a doubt having been expressed, whether the offence were not merely a misdemeanour, the Judge declared, that he would look into the point, and we do not find that the convict was included amongst those who received judgment of death.   These capital convictions for breaking prison depend, therefore, upon the provisions of local acts.

There is one other capital offence relating to treason, which is that of *administering* an oath or engagement, " purporting or intending to bind the person taking the same to commit any treason or murder, or any felony punishable by law with death."   Persons aiding and assisting are equally guilty.   This statute was introduced by the Ministry in 1813, in consequence of the disturbed condition of the country, but the convictions upon it have been (if any) very rare, and, I believe it may be safely said, that there has not been an execution   In Ireland, the administering of oaths for *seditious purposes* was made a felony in 1810, punishable by transportation for life, or otherwise, as the court might direct. We will not dwell upon a crime which, *according to the testimony of our criminal records*, is scarcely in existence, and we may be fully assured, that upon a future *general* revision of our criminal code, the capital penalty above alluded to will be omitted in the new catalogue   However, perhaps it may be said with justice respecting the Irish act, that the severe punishment did not repress the offence.   I have not had an opportunity of consulting this last subject so as to be very accurate, but it certainly appears

---

titled " breaking prison before execution "   The last-mentioned person was left for execution , and indeed it is related that, in 1770, a desperate attack and rescue was effected at Aylesbury jail   See the Annual Register for that year, and the Parl. Returns, vol. viii 1819.

(*o*) Reeves, ii 290.

(*p*) See Russell on Crimes, ed. 1819, p 552.   (*q*) Id 581.

that for some years after the passing of the 50 Geo 3 there were
many indictments for the mischief in question, and a vast number
of acquittals, and, moreover, those convicted in general, met with
the extremity of the punishment permitted by the law *(r)*

We have now done with treason, and it will be remembered,
that the offences of Rescue and Prison-breaking were only introduced here for the sake of consolidation   As to Petit-treason, it
has been recently abolished as a substantive offence, and the acts
which formerly constituted that crime are now punishable as
murders   We proceed to consider the capital penalties consequent upon certain offences which threaten the security of the
state.

Mutiny

As long as it shall be necessary to invoke the aid of an army
either for the purposes of foreign struggles or the preservation of
internal peace, it is unquestionable, that a strict discipline must
be maintained   The same inflexible rule must be enforced in the
navy.   It is, of course, familiar to every reader that the punishment awarded by the law for mutiny is death, and the question
is, whether a sufficient regularity and obedience can be kept up
independently of that punishment   Now, a consideration of this
nature necessarily brings us in contact with the proceedings of
courts-martial, both naval and military, for the offences of mutiny
and insubordination are invariably punished by the Articles of
War   But for want of sufficient tables to lead the mind towards
an accurate judgment, the author is desirous of forbearing from
giving any opinion upon the expediency of the severe punishment
alluded to   Undoubtedly (assuming the proposition, that we
have a right to take life under any circumstances excepting in
personal self-defence,) the *immediate* execution of criminals taken
in the fact of mutinous conduct must have a tendency to repress
disobedience, but how far that heavy penalty, postponed as it
usually is for some time after the offence, has been productive of
benefit, or instrumental in checking crime, the author will not take
upon himself, in the absence of better proof, to determine   It is,
however, gratifying to find, that the general impression amongst
the members of courts-martial has been in favour of the prisoners
and of mercy, and also, that the writers upon this subject express a decided opinion that the infliction of death ought to be
very sparingly exercised   "I disapprove," says Lieutenant Adye,

---

(r) We may be allowed just to remark here, very briefly, that the same
great truth which identifies the penalty of death as being an unfruitful infliction is applicable to severe secondary punishments.   In proportion as
you have reason to mitigate laws, *(not mitigate sentences)* you soften the
character of the people

" of making capital punishments too familiar. For when a man,
after committing a trifling crime, finds that the penalty attending
it is the same as if he had been guilty of a more enormous one, it
is a strong inducement to a vicious mind to plunge deeper into
guilt " (s) And, M'Arthur, while he insists upon the lenity of
our martial laws, when compared with those of other nations,
condemns the 22nd Article against insubordination This law
awards death *absolutely* against any person who shall strike his
superior officer, or draw, *or offer to draw*, or *lift up any weapon
against him*, and the writer objects to its severity as being inconsistent with the " infirmities inseparable from human nature,"
and the " unguarded moments of passion, which, at times, no
prudence or circumspection can govern " (t) He, however, de-
fends the " *ultimum supplicium*" in cases of open mutiny, as being
" highly expedient, and not attended with that severity so frequently attributed to it (u)

Seducing Soldiers and Sailors to Mutiny
(37 Geo 3. c 70. made perpetual by 57 Geo 3. c 7)

The capital punishment for this offence owed its origin to the
famous mutiny at the Nore, in 1797 It is remarkable that Mr
Pitt, when he introduced the bill, had no idea of raising the crime
higher than an aggravated misdemeanour, leaving the punishment,
whether fine, imprisonment, or transportation, to the discretion of
the Judge Mr. Pitt expressed his doubts, after hearing a very
sanguinary speech from Sergeant Adair, " whether an increase of
punishment were likely to be attended with the success the learned
gentleman seemed to expect " He admitted, " that it would carry
with it more terror, but, whether the execution of it would be
more effective, he doubted." Mr. Perceval also proposed to re-
tain the offence in question within the benefit of clergy (x) Put
when the bill came into the committee. the Solicitor General of
the day (y) proposed the words — " guilty of felony without benefit of clergy ;" and the Minister, of course, offered no opposition
to the change. (z) Indeed, the feeling of the House seemed to be
very fully set in against any suggestion in favour of moderate punishment

---

(s) Treatise on Courts-Martial, p 132
(t) On Naval Courts-Martial, p 33.
(u) Id. p 32. See upon this subject, besides Adye and M'Arthur,
Sullivan on British Laws, Lond 1784, Liddel's Duties of a Deputy
Judge-Advocate, Lond. 1805, A Return of the Number of Persons tried
by General Courts-Martial, in the Army, from 1808 to 1820, Parl.
Papers, 1821, vol. xv p 169
(x) Parl. History, vol. xxxiii. p. 810.
(y) Sir John Mitford, afterwards Lord Redesdale. The bill was
prepared by Sir John Scott, then Attorney-General
(z) Parl. Hist. vol. xxxiii. p. 815.

The event, however, proved that Mr Pitt had not erred It will be remembered, that if the seduction of the soldier or sailor were completed, the offence would be no less than high treason, so that the bill in question was chiefly aimed at attempts and solicitations for the purpose of violating allegiance Now, the Minister, in answer to Mr. Sergeant Adair, had added his conviction, that instead of gaining practically, it would be involving the offence in technical intricacies, (a) if capital punishment were introduced, because it would be necessary to give a more definite description to the offence And it turned out that very few capital convictions occurred, as well as that in the instances where such results did happen, points were reserved for the consideration of the judges The case of Fuller, for seducing soldiers, and of Tierney, in Devonshire, for corrupting sailors, are the only examples which the author can find upon this subject, although there may be a few more In both instances points of law arose in favour of the prisoners, and it does not appear that either were executed But we need not dwell upon this crime, because it is one of those which the moral sanction of the people condemns — That is the chief reason of its infrequency in times of war No man will go about to entice others from their duty, unless he be urged on by a strong hope of reward, and a fair prospect of success. For the honour of our country it may be said, that whatever imperfections there may be in the military and naval services, (respecting which the author does not presume to offer any opinion,) there has been, with rare exceptions, a soul of honour in the soldier, a heart of oak in the sailor, — a singleness of heart in each, devoted to their native land

Riot Act.
(1 Geo 1 St 2 c 5. sect. 1 & 5. (b))

1 Twelve persons assembled, and not dispersing for an hour after proclamation made

2 Any person opposing the making of the proclamation

3. Twelve persons assembled, and not dispersing within an hour after a hindrance to the reading of the Riot Act.

There have been very few convictions for these offences under the Riot Act, and we shall, therefore, pass them over with a short notice They may be considered as a mean, (if we may use the expression,) between treason on the one hand, and the actual commission of riotous violence on the other In most cases, there has been either a constructive levying of war by persisting in

---

(a) Parl History, vol. xxxiii. p 810.

(b) The demolition of property, and of places of worship by rioters, will be treated of in subsequent parts of this chapter, according to the proposed arrangement.

such meetings, or an outrageous attack upon property. The crimes referred to are independent of both these extremes

There has been one conviction on the Oxford circuit, for the offence of remaining an hour after the proclamation. It took place in Staffordshire, in the year 1800, (c) but the author has not been able to ascertain whether the party was executed. And in 1821, two were convicted in Shropshire, (the Wellington rioters,) for the same offence, and one of these suffered. There seems, however, to be no good reason why the capital clauses upon this subject should not now be expunged from the statute book For we see how seldom it has been found necessary or expedient to have recourse to them, and also, how very frequently there have been riotous assemblies of the people in the teeth of the prohibition. It seems quite sufficient that a misguided multitude should be exposed to the fire or weapons of the soldiery, without this ulterior menace of the law Had the convictions been more frequent, it is obvious that their examples would have been disregarded, indeed, in all probability, not thought of. The numerous disturbances in various parts of the country since 1714, when the act passed, are sufficient proofs of this proposition Men, excited by a sense of real or imaginary grievances, would have come together, as they do now occasionally congregate, in utter defiance of the law and recklessness of the consequences They would never have known whether or not there were any capital penalty attached to their offence, and might have even died, like some of the *actual destroyers of* 1780, declaring with their last breath, their ignorance of having done any thing worthy of death Let us add, that a riotous assembly is of itself a misdemeanour at common law, and that *the day is fast approaching,* when it will be deemed a *greater disgrace and calamity to stand convicted of a misdemeanour, than it now is to ascend the scaffold* (d)

Piracy

There are three kinds of offences which may be tried under the head of Piracy

The first is, high treason, by committing hostilities at sea, under colour of a foreign commission, or by adhering to the king's enemy there in any other manner.

Secondly, Where mariners lay violent hands on their commanders, in order to prevent them from fighting in defence of the ships and goods committed to their trust

---

(c) And was probably connected with some meeting concerning the high price of bread.

(d) The curious reader may find some objections to the Riot Act of Gee. I., chiefly grounded upon its being an arbitrary statute —Observations upon the Riot Act, Lond. 1781, supposed to be by Allan Ramsay. The author says, that " you might as well make it felony to eat buttered peas, or wear leather breeches."

Thirdly, Piratical acts against *the subject*

It is with the two first of these offences that we have to do at present, the last being reserved for that portion of the work which treats of capital punishments in respect of property

And with respect to the first of these delinquencies, we must refer the reader to the remarks which have already been made upon the subject of high treason   If (admitting the right to take life,) a quick and striking example can be made of the sea-rovers and thieves who infest particular parts of the ocean, as, for example, in the cases of Major Stede Bonnet and his twenty-three companions, who were hanged *en masse* at White Point, in South Carolina, perhaps upon such an emergency some good might be achieved   But where prisoners are sent home to take their trials at the Old Bailey for the deeds which they have perpetrated at a distance, the force of example — the essence of punishment, is in a great measure, if not entirely, lost   For, unless you apply the effect of your penalty to the illegal passions of the mind at the time when the temptation arises, you fail in the great end of severe, or indeed, of any other infliction   Now, sailors at a distance from home, dissatisfied, perhaps, with their commander, and spurred on by the expectations of piratical freedom and booties, have no such friendly beacon before their eyes   They raise their lawless standard, seize their prey, are captured, and conveyed to England   The ancient system works again, the Judge of the Admiralty sits enthroned in his scarlet robes, the fatal verdict of guilty passes, and execution is awarded   The numerous hosts of ocean-depredators are striking instances of the inoperative quality of the punishment of death in this instance   The frequency of convictions also must occur to the considerate mind as a further proof of the proposition   And it should be added, that executions are by no means uncommon where the jury have pronounced their verdict against this class of criminals.

It may seem amusing to quote Robinson Crusoe in support of the usefulness of rapid punishment, but the annexed paragraph will probably be thought in point   "This is the sum of the story," said the gunner's mate to Robin, when the latter had just bought a capital vessel, which turned out to have been no other than a pirate   "You will all be seized as pirates, I can assure you, and executed with very little ceremony, for you know merchant ships shew but little law to pirates if they get them into their power" (e)   "Ask no questions," said Crusoe to his partner, "but all hands to work, and weigh without losing a minute." (f) And, "now," continues the traveller in his story,

(e) New Edition, by the Hydrographer of the Naval Chronicle, p. 380.
(f) Id. p. 381.

" I was embarrassed in the worst condition imaginable, for though I was perfectly innocent, I was in no condition to make that innocence appear, and if I had been taken, it had been under a supposed guilt of the worst kind; at least, a crime esteemed so among the people I had to do with." (g)

Now, if such a promise of summary vengeance had so strong an effect upon an innocent man, what consternation would it not strike into the guilty souls of a really mutinous and piratical crew ! They would be driven from ocean to ocean, sea to sea, strait to strait, till at length, prevention would stand in the gap, and punishment be no more heard of

As to the second offence, namely, the putting of force upon commanders, in order to prevent their fighting, it is of extremely rare occurrence, although there were some instances at the times when the statutes upon the subject received the royal assent

Lastly, the author is desirous of observing, that none of the above observations (and the remark will apply equally to all cases of high treason,) are intended to hold in cases where (h) *murder* has been perpetrated   That crime will be considered in a future page of this chapter, and the reader will be kind enough to refer thither for the comments upon that particular subject.

Slave Dealing.

We now come to another offence, which is so far piracy, as that the parties found guilty of it are to suffer as pirates, felons, and robbers   This is the trafficking in slaves *upon the high seas.* The offences enumerated by the statute (i) are—Carrying away, conveying, or removing the slaves   Aiding in those acts   Embarking, receiving, detaining, confining on board any such persons, of course, against their will, and *upon the high seas.* For elsewhere the dealing in slaves is punishable by transportation.   All the above mentioned acts are declared to be punishable as piracies, and consequently capital

The proscription which this statute denounces against man-stealers, affords us a striking instance of the perversity of human feelings   The very identical men, whose anger was kindled, *and most righteously*, against the cruelties of slavery, were the first to propose—no other than a punishment of death.   As if one species of barbarity (for such unquestionably was the slave-trade,) could be repressed by another equally savage, perhaps only distinguishable because it gained the sanction of the legislature.   These are stronger expressions than will be found in other pages of this work.   They are such as the author would shrink from upon most occasions, but the *life of man* ought not to be trifled with, and they must stand recorded.   There is the less excuse also, be-

---

(g) Id. p. 385.

(h) And be it remembered, that the crime of murder is a frequent companion of piracy.   (i) 5 Geo. IV c. 113

cause the Act to which we have referred is recent   The authors of the punishment had not to struggle with the prejudices of the people, the opinions of the judges, or the obstinacy of stiff precedents   They were free, free as the clear light of intellect could make them   but when they broke the chain of the slave, they left the stain of blood behind them. (*k*)

But we have in some measure extenuated a *sudden* example in cases of piracy, and the crime of man-stealing is piracy, therefore, some might say, how will the argument stand?   It will be borne in mind, that the piracies above treated of consist in adherence to the king's enemies, or the use of illegal force in the hour of battle, and, moreover, that in the latter instance, the punishment of death is not justified.

Now, with regard to the former, although even for treason, life ought not to be taken in cold blood, yet as long as the right of inflicting the last penalty (*l*) is entertained at all, a *rapid* example, and *instant* vengeance, (understand the word as stripped of all malevolent passions,) may be salutary to the state   For (and it is a proposition most signally applicable to the present day,) *a government must be supported, and the influence of the crown is now not too great.*   And those who go about the land declaiming against the government, who whet their tongues for selfish ends, and delude the poor idlers who listen to them, well know that they are preparing a scourge for their country, and that amongst the population they seek to mislead, order can be soon exchanged for anarchy.

But to return to the slave piracy bill   What have been its results?   An abolition of the traffic?   So far from it, that nefarious trade has thriven as surely, and nearly as openly as ever. Death has no bands to restrain cupidity, (*m*) but gold has a spell which blinds the victim of its enchantment.   It is a matter of notoriety, that a piratical dealing in slaves was carried on in neighbourhood of the Mauritius within a very late period, and that the conduct of a governor was questioned in parliament upon that subject   And the late trial at Bombay must be fresh in the minds of all   Yet even in that case, notorious as the traffic must have been, the conviction was for the minor offence only, and the offender incurred no heavier a sentence than that of banishment, or transportation to New South Wales for seven years. (*n*)

(*k*) See Parl Debates for 1824, New Series, vol x p. 1424.

(*l*) Ultimum Supplicium.

(*m*) The value of a slave, formerly, was between 20*l*. and 40*l*.   See the Report of the Committee of the Lords of the Council.

(*n*) There have been some proceedings for trafficking in slaves, at the Old Bailey, and on the Circuits, but, I believe, no capital convictions nor even a capital indictment

Smuggling.

The laws against smuggling afford us a very remarkable instance of the gradual advance and inefficacy of severity As soon as it became necessary to guard the revenue by a course of proceeding more methodical and consistent than had been the usage amongst our despotic monarchs of old times, it was soon observed that the vice of smuggling must be repressed At first, however, the legislature was content with prescribing forfeiture of the uncustomed goods, as a penalty for a breach of the new laws. And, accordingly, the statutes of Charles II , and Queen Anne, declared that the illicit goods, and sometimes that the ship should be confiscated Smuggling, however, increased, and the ordinary complaint of the day was, that the free trader sustained the most vexatious injuries It was then resolved, that the pains of felony should succeed, and that transportation should be the punishment for the illegal assemblies which had been productive of so much alarm and mischief. The chief contraband article at this period was *tea*, and, as we shall see presently, the profit acquired by the smuggler was enormous The minister of the day acquiesced in the appeals which were made to him for protection, and so convinced was he, that he did not hesitate in parliament to declare in favour of death or transportation " But," said he, " as our government always chuses to try first the mildest method, therefore the latter method of breaking these gangs is proposed by this bill."   Yet there were still some opinions on the side of humanity and sound policy, some who probably foresaw the future triumph of those great qualities, who felt, that in proportion as a country approximates to severity, her moral virtues must of necessity decrease   The bill, which only imposed transportation, was characterised by the advocates for mildness, as one of the most severe and dangerous ever passed by a British legislature, and, " I am afraid,' said one of the speakers, " it will be far from answering the end. While our numerous high duties continue," he added, "while there are such profits to be got by smuggling, it is in vain to expect we can entirely prevent it by the most se   laws we can make. They keep up [in France] a particula   of army called *Les Maltotiers*, for the purpose of prevent.   smuggling, yet smuggling is in that kingdom almost as frequent as in England, and their smugglers are much more desperate than ours, (o) for they march in little armies, are well armed and disciplined, and often engage in battle with the custom-house officers and their guard of Maltotiers " Notwithstanding this remonstrance, the act passed. This happened in 1736. And the prophecy against a decrease of smuggling was soon verified. Nine years had scarcely elapsed before the whole nation

---

(o) For instance, the smugglers at Lyons, in 1754.

was again in a state of ferment   The formidable bands of men
embarked in illicit traffic, so far from being broken, had become
more strongly organized , the smuggler was an absolute *nom de
guerre;* children were terrified at the mention of him, and women
fled to London in order to escape the gangs.   In this state of
things it was determined to legislate afresh, not with the mind of
philosophy, but of anger and mistaken zeal.   Two reports were
made by a committee appointed by the House of Commons, " to
enquire into the causes of the most infamous practice of smuggling."   Evidence was taken to a considerable extent, and it was
ultimately resolved, that the offence in question should be
punished with the most unrelenting vigour   Accordingly, smuggling was made a capital offence, and certain persons named, as
known contraband dealers, were declared attainted as outlaws,
unless they should surrender themselves within a given time (*p*)
But it is necessary to add, that about the same time, *the duty on
tea was lowered exactly one-half,* and a perceptible decline in
smuggling transactions was observed even before the passing of
the new laws   Now it was in evidence before the committee that
the tea consumed in England amounted to 4,000,000 of pounds
annually, and that 3,000,000 had been regularly run, or smuggled
It was also shewn, that a further reduction of six-pence per pound
would so much diminish the gains of the smugglers, as to lessen
the practice materially.   Indeed, some persons, who had been
concerned in the contraband trade, did not hesitate to affirm, that
the business would be altogether extinguished by such a reduction   But the parliament did not think fit to make this last reduction   They contented themselves with passing their capital
enactment, and propounding their charter of indemnity   They
had discovered, upon the production of accounts, that " smuggling still continued to a much greater excess than could have
been suspected, when the act of the last session passed,"(*q*) and
they feared, probably, to impair the revenue, at a time when
both France and Spain had assumed a menacing attitude towards
them   The result, therefore, was this   The severity of capital
punishment came into operation almost contemporaneously with
a decrease of the tea duties.   The question then, as to the consequences of these provisions now remains for consideration,
and, in order to elucidate the matter the more clearly, we must,
as usual, have recourse to a few tables

(*p*) It is recorded, that not one of these came in upon the King's
proclamation.

(*q*) Smuggling Laid Open, by Janssen   (Preface.)

I. Table of Executions in London and Middlesex, under 19 Geo II from 1747 until 1784.

	Ex		Ex
1747	5	1752	1
1748	8	1753	1
1749 (3—3*—& 1 for rescue)	7	1754	1
1750	6	1755-1784	0
1751 1 for rescuing a smuggler	4	Total	33

* Signifying that three persons were included in one charge. These were hung for breaking the Custom-House at Poole.

II Table of Executions in London and Middlesex, from 1749 to 1784 inclusive, for the like offence, *according to an official Table* Total 16 (r)

III. Table of Convictions and Executions on the Circuits, taken from the Appendix to the Report from the Committee on the Criminal Laws

	Con.	Ex.
Home Circuit, 1765—1814	2	0
Western .... 1770—1818	0	0
Oxford...... 1799—1819	0	0
Norfolk...... 1767—1819	0	0
Lancaster and Durham	0	0
Welch Circuits	0	0
Total.	2	0

IV Table of Convictions and Executions for Smuggling in London and Middlesex, from 1784 to 1826 inclusive.

	Con	Ex		Con.	Ex.
1784	1	1	1796—1799	0	0
1785 and 1786	0	0	1800	1	0
1787	1	1	1801—1804	0	0
1788	2	1	1805	1	1
1789—1793	0	0	1806—1826†	0	0
1790	2*	2			
1794	1	0	Total..	10	6
1795	1	0			

* Joint offence, shooting at a boat   † One was acquitted in 1807

V. Table of Convictions and Executions in England and Wales, from 1821 to 1826 inclusive

	Con.	Ex.
1821—1823	0	0
1824	1	0
1825	2	0
1826	1	0
Total.	4	0

(r) See Reports of Committees for 1819, vol. viii. p. 136.

Now, in reviewing these tables, the paucity of capital convictions since the Act of George II will strike the most careless reader. He will, however, be equally impressed with the fact of there having been several executions immediately after that statute. But the persons thus condemned, and as rigorously executed, were for the most part attainted smugglers, who died for refusing to surrender themselves, so that it became impossible to assume a decrease of smuggling because a number of outlaws were put to death under an *ex post facto* enactment. Indeed one of these unfortunate persons, who was hanged in 1752, declared, that he could not believe that there was any crime in smuggling, and he could not be prevailed on to think so, even at the gallows. Another had made the following appeal to his judge, some years before the introduction of the capital penalty :—" A smuggler," said he, " only steals, or rather conceals, what is truly his own, as being fairly purchased by him for a valuable consideration ; whereas the highwayman takes by violence what belongs to another." He thought he should have been treated with more lenity. He added, " Since I and my family must be ruined by this sentence, I will speak what I think upon it. the high taxes make living dear, dear living ruins trade, and the ruin of trade puts many upon robbing and stealing, and robbing and stealing brings them to the gallows "(s)

Further, an attentive reader will immediately set down the small number of capital convictions after this period, to the credit of that great reduction in the duties which has been mentioned. It no longer became worth while for the smuggler to hazard his liberty, and the chance of certain death in case of capture, to so great a degree as when his profits were more considerable. This circumstance, therefore, clearly accounts for a temporary diminution of the grievous offence which had so strongly attracted the attention of Parliament. But one might be led to suppose, from the above tables, that the mischief itself had been nearly extinguished. So far from it, there were not wanting men, and many men too, who, even for the smaller gain, were ready to venture their safety for the sake of the old traffic. Let us take a few instances. In the year after the sanguinary act passed, sixty persons, well armed, broke open the Custom-house at Poole, declaring that they were come for their tea, which, to the amount of 4,200lbs had been seized by the *Swift* privateer. Justice was done upon some of these men at the Old Bailey soon afterwards, but it was difficult to persuade the ringleader that he had done wrong. Nearly at the same time, thirty smugglers broke open the King's warehouse at Colchester, and carried off more than 1,500lbs of

---

(s) Gent. Mag for 1735, p 655. See also the pamphlet, Smuggling Laid Open, and Annals of Newgate, vol. III. p. 167.

tea. And the notorious murders of the custom-house officers happened nearly in the same year It was the common observation of the day, that the great mischiefs done by the smugglers of late, were owing to the decline of their trade, and that the illicit dealers were reduced to the greatest extremities A sufficient proof that the capital penalty had no merit in suppressing the evil Again, twelve smugglers, about the same time, broke open the gaol at Maidstone, and rescued a party of their confederates And for several years afterwards constant scuffles took place between the gangs and the revenue-officers For a time these marauders resorted to Boulogne, they spread throughout the coasts, they infested Scotland and the Isle of Man, (t) hovered about the west; and, disappointed of their usual traffic, hesitated not to engage in the most desperate enterprizes And this leads us to notice that the fewness of capital convictions, according to our tables, is not of itself a sufficient circumstance to warrant us in concluding that smuggling had declined For, upon attentively examining the records of the times, it will be found that many of the most atrocious offences of these days, and, indeed, of future years, were committed by men who had been smugglers The famous robberies in Suffolk, about ten years after the capital enactment, may be cited in confirmation of this statement. And further, it was very commonly the case that murder, or some serious injury, was committed during the operations of the smugglers. So that, although there be few indictments against persons for being found armed and assembled, under the Smuggling Act, the calendars will shew many convictions for murder, and shooting at revenue-officers (n) This being the case, it is clear that although the evil in question had been lessened by altering the duties, desperate men were by no means daunted at the idea of " felony without benefit of clergy," and the certainty of execution if they should be convicted (x)

However, after some years, it was found that the revenue again suffered a considerable loss from smuggling. The contraband traffic was now extended into other channels; and foreign lace, together with French cambrics, were as eagerly imported as the tea In 1779, the evil had so far advanced as to induce the government to interfere afresh Captains of ships and passengers

(t) See Letters concerning the Outrages in the Isle of Man, in the Tracts on Commerce, at the British Museum.

(u) As in the case of *Cephas Quested*, executed in 1821, for smuggling In the Parl Return for that year, there appears no conviction for assembling armed, &c., therefore he must be considered as classed amongst the malicious shooters

(x) If poaching were made a capital offence, the same results would follow, as long as the poacher could undersell the fair dealer.

were no longer permitted to bring over uncustomed goods   Penalties and forfeitures were imposed, and the utmost notoriety was prescribed to all retailers of tea, coffee, and spirits (*y*)   And it is not a little curious that, in the same year, a petition was presented to the House of Commons, from the London tea-dealers, complaining of the vast system of smuggling carried on by the prisoners of the King's-Bench and Fleet prisons. In 1782, it was thought fit to offer an indemnity to these dangerous robbers of the public purse, on condition of their serving in the navy, so that we have now proved to a demonstration that the existence of a capital law, the inexorable infliction of it, and the abstinence from prosecuting it, have had no reference whatever to the offence it proposed to exterminate.

But it will be asked, and naturally enough, how the smuggler could afford to make himself again so formidable upon the subject of tea, and how he could have contrived to redeem a trade already ruined by the wisdom of a former Parliament? The answer, we think, is satisfactory, and it supplies the only fact wanting to a perfect chain of evidence   In 1772, an extraordinary duty of one shilling had been laid upon all green and bohea teas, so that here was a fresh bounty to the smuggler of one shilling per lb, and he did not fail to profit by it. (*a*)

" The high duties which have been imposed upon the importation of many different sorts of foreign goods," says Adam Smith, " in order to discourage their consumption in Great Britain, have in many cases served to encourage smuggling, and in all cases have reduced the revenue of the customs below what more moderate duties would have afforded " (*b*)

The remaining history of this capital offence may be summed up very shortly   In 1779, the obstructing of revenue-officers was declared to be a misdemeanour, and this enactment virtually repealed the capital felony prescribed *in that respect* by the 19 Geo. II (*c*) Still there continued to be several offences for which the punishment of death was enjoined, and, we may add, enforced As the being armed and assembled, to the number of three, in order to export or land uncustomed goods; the rescuing such goods · the fact of aiding and assisting in the commission of those offences, and shooting at or maiming any officer   These crimes

---

(*y*) As by compelling them to paint their names and occupations upon their doors, &c.

(*a*) In 1784, also, a fresh arrangement was made respecting the duties on tea, and, upon reference to the fourth table, it will be found that a few examples of smugglers were made about that time. As the duties rose, or were reduced, in such a ratio has smuggling advanced or diminished.

(*b*) Wealth of Nations, iii. 365. See also, id. pp. 369—394.

(*c*) Russell on Crimes, ed. 1819, i. 166, note (i).

were all declared to be capital by the consolidating act of 1812
(52 Geo. III.), together with the shooting at any ship or boat belonging to the navy, customs, or excise. The refusal to surrender,
after an order in council, was also made a felony without clergy,
as before; and the parties refusing or neglecting, were declared
to be, *ipso facto*, attainted. Lastly, when the law in general
concerning the customs was, in 1826, concentrated in one act, it
became necessary to pass another bill for the prevention of smuggling. The capital felonies, however, were the same as those to
which we have just adverted, except that the omission or refusal
to surrender, was not included. So that, as the law stands at
present, the illegal assembling, and the outrages by shooting or
maiming, constitute the crimes for which the smuggler may be
capitally punished

We will now proceed to give the last table, namely, that from
1826 to the present time, which we have kept back until now for
a reason which will very shortly be self-evident

V.—Table of capital Convictions and Executions for Smuggling,
from 1826 to 1829, inclusive. (*d*)

		Con	Ex.
England and Wales	1826 (*c*)	1	0
,,	1827	16	0
,,	1828	0	0
,,	1829	0	0
London and Middlesex only..	1826	0	0
,,	1827	0	0
,,	1828	11	0
,,	1829	0	0
	Total....	28	0

We have kept back the foregoing table until now, because it
seems highly desirable that the singular increase of convictions
in the years 1827 and 1828 should be fully and manifestly shewn
This advance of trials for smuggling occurred just after the promulgation of the new act which preserved nearly all the old capital offences   And it happened also at a time when Mr Hus-
kisson's act for regulating the customs was, upon the whole, calculated to decrease contraband traffic   The chief employment
of the smugglers at this time, appears to have been the running
of spirits   In spite of the punishment of death with which they
were threatened by the law, they perpetrated the most daring attacks and outrages during these years of 1827 and 1828 (*f*)

(*d*) From an Official Return, House of Commons, 30th March, 1830
(*c*) The year when the Customs' Act was passed
(*f*) See, for a few instances, Annual Register, 1827, Hist. Chro
pp. 37, 75, and for 1828, p. 1.

Were they prohibited from assembling in armed numbers? There
was no end to their hosts and determined gatherings when a cargo
of geneva was to be "crept up," as the phrase was   Were they
menaced for firing into ships and boats?   Their discharges of
arms not infrequently alarmed the coast-guard, and brought upon
them a fresh army of enemies, whose attempts at capture they
were, nevertheless, resolved to resist in mortal conflict   Were
they forbidden to maim or assault revenue officers?   If ever
there were a post of danger, it was that of the preventive service,
whose people often died under the desperate hands of the routed
gang.

Circumstances may reduce the number of convictions, may
diminish, may even exterminate the smugglers, but we feel persuaded, that enough has been shewn to satisfy the country that,
in this respect capital penalties avail not   "The great evil of
smuggling," said Sir Henry Parnell, on the custom consolidation
debate, " arises wholly out of the system of protecting duties.
The bill now before the house, for preventing smuggling, would
be altogether uncalled for, was it not for this system "(g)

Post-Office

Whether the origin of posts in England should be attributed to
Edward VI, James I, or Charles I, it is not the design of our present undertaking to inquire   The revenue of the post-office appears
to have been an encreasing concern, and at length, owing to the
convenience of the management, as well as the general integrity
of the persons employed, people became willing to trust their
money, without apprehension, to the establishment above alluded
to   It is said, that at a very recent date, there were 544 deputy
postmasters in England, and that the general office in London
employed about 200 superintendants, clerks, and sorters, and
about 220 men in delivering. It is hardly possible to conceive that
frauds will not be occasionally perpetrated amongst a class of
persons so numerous, and so much exposed to temptation, and
it is surely a matter of congratulation that more robberies has
not been committed in this particular (h)   It was thought right,
however, in the year 1765, to make the robbing of mails, and the
stealing of bank notes and other instruments from letters, a capital felony.   In 1767, another act was passed, containing similar
provisions, but in some measure enlarged and amended, and in
1802 and 1812 two other statutes were made for the joint purposes of consolidation, and rendering the law upon the subject
more applicable.   We shall now give the tables concerning this
punishment, and then offer a few comments as to their results

---

(g) Hansard's Debates, New Series, vol xiii. p. 1242
(h) In 1774 the sorters in one department had been increased from
three to six or seven.

Table I.—Convictions and Executions in London and Middlesex, for Capital Offences against the Post-Office, from 1765 to 1832, inclusive.

Year	Con.	Ex.	Offence, &c.
1766	1	1	Stealing a bank note out of a letter at a receiving house in Chancery lane. An apprentice.(*i*)
1771	1	0	Stealing a bank note out of a letter. A *sorter* Escaped through an improper finding by the jury
1774	1	1	The like offence. A *sorter*
1779	1	1	Secreting a letter containing a promissory note A *sorter* Plea, guilty
1780	1	1	Secreting and stealing a letter containing a bill of exchange. *A supernumerary carrier*
1781	1	1	Stealing bags and letters from the *mail.*
1783(*k*)	1	0	Secreting and stealing a letter with bank notes. He was reprieved in consideration of a discovery which he made respecting the prisoners in Newgate
1785	1	0	Stealing a letter with a lottery ticket.
1786	1	1	Stealing and secreting a letter with a bank note A supernumerary *carrier*
1792	2	2	Secreting letters with bank notes 2 letter carriers.
1794	2	2	1 Secreting and stealing a letter with a bank note A *stamper* 1 Secreting a letter with a bank note A *sorter*
1795	2	1	1 Secreting and stealing a letter with a bill of exchange A *sorter* 1 The like offence A *sorter*, age 16 He was ordered for execution, but reprieved.
1796	1	1	Stealing a letter with two bank bills. A *carrier.*
1797	1	0	Stealing a letter with bank notes A *culler of the charges* (*l*)

(*i*) The first conviction on the act 5 Geo. 3. and, consequently, the first for stealing from letters

(*k*) In 1784 there was published a letter from a member of parliament to his disconsolate son, lately convicted of robbing the general post office. Lond Dodsley, 1s 6*d*.

(*l*) Before the letter carriers are called in.

Year	Con.	Ex.	Offence, &c.
1798	1	1	Secreting and stealing a letter with bank notes *Sorter* and *letter carrier*
1799	1	1	Secreting a letter with a promissory note for 10*l.* A *sorter.*
1800	2	1	1 Secreting and stealing a letter with a draft. The judges decided in favour of this man, because the draft was not stamped.
			1 Secreting a letter with a bank note Both *sorters.* (*m*)
1801	2	0	Pooley tried again for stealing only, under another section of the act. The judges again in his favour.
			1 Secreting and stealing a letter with bank notes Aged 14 Both *sorters*
1803	1	1	Secreting and stealing a letter with bank notes. *Clerk* and *collector, 8th division.*(*n*)
1805	1	0	Secreting and stealing a letter with bank notes *Examiner* Salary 210*l.* a-year. (*o*)
1809	1	0	Secreting and stealing a letter with bank notes. *Sorter.*(*p*)
1810	1	0	Secreting and stealing a letter with promissory notes *Sorter*, aged 20. and recommended on account of his youth (*q*)
1811	1	0	Secreting and stealing a letter with a bank note. *Letter-carrier.*
1812	2	0	1 Secreting and stealing a letter with a bank bill and notes. *Sorter.*
			1 The like; promissory notes only A *facer of letters* (*r*)
1813	2	1	1 Secreting and stealing a letter with bank notes. *Sorter* and *Carrier.*
			1 Secreting and stealing a letter with a bill of exchange. *Carrier.*(*s*)

(*m*) Note also, that two other *letter sorters* were acquitted in this year at the Old Bailey upon separate indictments.

(*n*) A *letter carrier* was acquitted in this year, and one also in 1804.

(*o*) It was a lottery ticket which tempted this prisoner to be dishonest In 1806 there was an acquittal of the man whose business it was to put the letters into the bag. In 1807 a letter sorter was acquitted.

(*p*) Another sorter was tried in this year and acquitted.

(*q*) There was also an acquittal in this year.

(*r*) A facer is one who puts the letters with the directions downwards, in order that they may be stamped.

(*s*) And one was acquitted for stealing a letter with a bank note from a receiving house. The latter was not employed in the post-office.

Year	Con.	Ex.	Offence, &c.
1814	1	0	Secreting and stealing a letter with a bank note. *Sorter (t)*
1816	1	0	Secreting and stealing a letter with a promissory note. A *stamper.(u)*
1817	1	0	Secreting and stealing bills out of a letter. *Sorter.(x)*
1819	3	3	Secreting and stealing letters with bank notes *Persons employed in the Post-office.(y)*
1824	1	0	Secreting a letter with a bank note. *Carrier*
1825	2	1	Secreting and stealing a letter with a bank note and promissory notes. *Sorter.(z)*
1827	2	1	Secreting and stealing letters with bank notes. *Carriers.(a)*
1828(b)	0	0	
1832	1	1	Secreting and stealing letters with bank notes. *Sorter.*

TABLE II.—Convictions and Executions at the Assizes, from 1765, as below.

HOME. *(c)*

Year.	Con.	Ex.	Year.	Con.	Ex.
1772	1	1	1804	1	0
1797	1	0	1811	1	0
1799	1	0	1812	1	0
1800	2	1	1813	1	0
1803	1	1			
			Totals	10(d)	3

(t) In 1815 a person indicted for secreting was acquitted

(u) In this year also one was acquitted.

(x) One, no bill found in this year. In 1818 a person not connected with the post-office was acquitted for stealing a letter with a bank-note.

(y) There was another case, but the prisoner was allowed to plead guilty to the minor offence.

(z) In the second case, the judges decided in favour of the prisoner (Sharpe). There was still another case, but the offender was allowed to plead guilty to the minor charge In 1826 there was an acquittal.

(a) In this year there was an acquittal, and there were other charges at the police offices.

(b) One acquitted in this year.

(c) Under the head " *Post Office, Mail Robbery,*" &c. Reports of Committees, vol. 8.

(d) In 1816 there was a commitment, but I believe no prosecution. 1817, nil.

WESTERN (*e*).

Years.		Con.	Reprieved.
1793	.... Mail robbery ...	1	0
1811	.... Secreting letter	1	0
1812	... Same..	1	1
1817	... Same........	1	1
	Totals ...	4	2

OXFORD (*f*)—*beginning at* 1799.

Year.	Con.	Ex.
1805 ..	.1	0
1810 ...	1	0
1816	2	Uncertain as to one—the other reprieved (*g*)
Total .	4	

NORFOLK.

Years		Con.
1791, Stealing a letter out the of P.O.	..	1, left for execution
1794, Stealing letters out of a bag of letters	1, reprieved.	
	Total ...	2

LANCASTER.

Years.		Con.	Ex
1801, Stealing letters by postman		1	0
1802, Mail robbery;	..	1	1
1811, Same	..	1	0
	Totals ..	3	1

DURHAM—*nil.*

MIDLAND (*h*)—*beginning at* 1805.

	Con.	Ex
1806, (One convicted of larceny only) .	0	0
1808, Secreting	1	0
1809, Two acquitted	0	0
1811, Mail robbery........ .	2	0
1812, One acquitted	0	0
1813, Stealing bags of letters	2	0
1814, Secreting	1	0
1815, Stealing a letter........	1	0
1816 (*i*) and 1817—*nil.*		
Totals .	7	0

(*e*) From the Official Returns, as above.
(*f*) From the same returns.　　　　　(*g*) Note of the author.
(*h*) From the Parliamentary Papers printed annually.
(*i*) There was a commitment in Yorkshire in 1804, but no prosecution.

NORTHERN. (*k*)
[*i e.* York, Newcastle, Appleby, and Carlisle.]

	Con.	Ex.
1806, One acquitted	0	0
1808, One acquitted	0	0
1813, Of larceny only	1	0
1814, One acquitted	0	0
1815—1817—*nil*		
Total . . .	1	0

TABLE III —Convictions and Executions for the like Offences, in England and Wales, from 1810 to 1818 inclusive; and the like from 1821 to 1829 inclusive (*k*)

Year	Con.	Ex.	Acq.	No bill.	Year	Con.	Ex.	Acq	No bill.
1810	2	1	0	0	1821	0	0	0	0
1811	3	1	1	0	1822	0	0	0	0
1812	4	0	0	4	1823	0	0	0	0
1813	3	1	3	0	1824	1	0	0	0
1814	2	0	0	0	1825	2	1	0	0
1815	2	0	1	3	1826	0	0	1	0
1816	4	0	2	2	1827	3	1	3	0
1817	2	0	0	1	1828	1	0	2	0
1818	0	0	0	0	1829	0	0	0	0
					Total . . .	29	4	13	10

Upon a review of these tables, it is suggested that the results are not in favour of the capital punishment. It appears that the severity of the law has been somewhat relaxed during the last ten years, and it is also evident that the offence of stealing letters has not increased. It is true, on the one hand, that the inspectors of the post-office may have been excited to greater vigilance: but then, on the other, the number of people employed has been much advanced,(*l*) and it was always a subject of surprise at the Old Bailey, that the sorters could so dexterously elude the scrutiny of former superintendants, It appears, further, upon a reference to the tables, that the chance of an almost certain fate had no effect towards extinguishing the dishonest principle, when a sufficient temptation presented itself to the offender's mind. If the object of severe justice be prevention, it must make us pause when we find a crime rather on the advance in the face of certain death; and again, when we see it diminish, notwithstanding less rigorous execution. This course of events is most providentially in favour of humanity, for even had the offence in-

---

(*k*) From the Returns, head, " Letters containing bank notes, secreting and stealing."

(*l*) In 1795 the sorters had increased from three to six or seven in London.

creased of late, it would not by any means have followed as a necessary conclusion, that the advocates for capital pains were justified. The truth is, that the evil under consideration arises from circumstances which are wholly independent of the capital punishment. The execution, therefore, is in effect, an act of vengeance, and if so, it will not be defended by any one in cases of this nature It is well known, that the persons who conduct the various arrangements by which we are enabled to receive our letters so punctually are, perhaps without exception, of unimpeachable characters previously to their admission as servants of the post-office Indeed, the situation has been frequently given as a reward for a life of good behaviour and integrity It is not likely, therefore, that the slavish fear of death should hold people in honesty, who have been accustomed to act rightly upon a far nobler principle. The truth must be told. A sore temptation intervenes, one, probably, to which they have never been yet exposed, and which they could scarcely have contemplated, and the prospect of realising a large sum without detection, has a greater influence on their minds than they have the courage to sustain. Thus, many classes of officers, from the examiner with his yearly salary, down to the carrier with his weekly pay, have been found dishonest. But the sorter and the carrier have been the greatest criminals, probably because they have had the greatest opportunities, and have been exposed for a longer time to temptation than others. It is in vain that the inspector takes his elevated place, and scrutinises the conduct of those who are employed in preparing letters for the post. The sorter, the stamper, the facer, the caller of the charges,—each of these in his turn has been found wanting; even the inspector himself has yielded on one occasion at least, to the allurements of dishonesty, whilst the carrier who waits without, has not been backward to violate the trust which has been reposed in him Yet it must be allowed, and it is with joy that we confess it, there are most numerous exceptions to these instances of fraud, and within the last three years, where one dishonest servant of the post-office has been detected, five hundred have been found cleaving to their trust, and uncorrupted by the thirst of gain. But not through the dread of death—for it has been almost demonstrated, that the terror of executions has failed to deter men from the evil of breaking letters. We must claim a higher ground for these honest servants, and affirm, that their steady and unshaken conduct has proceeded from the dear recollection of their unstained characters, and most of all, the fear of God. (*m*)

(*m*) As to the process of sorting letters in 1785 See the Sess. Paper, O B 1785, case 253. As to stamping in 1795, see id. 1795, p. 130 The mode of business with carriers in 1798, id. 1798, p. 97. Collecting, charging, facing, &c. in 1803, id. 1803, p. 256.

Returning from Transportation

The punishment of transportation was unknown to the common law, and therefore, this offence of illegally returning could only arise by statute. Blackstone mentions, that the exiling of criminals in this manner, was first thought of in the reign of Elizabeth, (n) but it seems that it did not come into full practice until the time of George I, and it is certain that we are indebted to that reign for the beginning of that class of capital penalties. In the early history of transportation, offenders were sent to America, but when the United States were severed from our dominion, it became usual to transport persons beyond the seas, (that is, beyond the asserted limits of our maritime sovereignty,) to Botany Bay. Nearly at the same time also, convicted felons, especially in bad cases, were allowed to transport themselves to Africa, or elsewhere, to serve his majesty, and the crown was also empowered to confine such persons on board of hulks, or floating prisons   This latter method saved the expence of transportation, whilst at the same time it made old ships available   The late acts upon this subject were passed during the last years of George the Third's reign. The summary of them is, that offenders may be sent to such places as the king, by the advice of his privy council, may appoint, either beyond sea, or elsewhere, (o) or to the general penitentiary at Millbank. If a party be adjudged to go beyond sea, his place of destination may be changed by order of the Court of King's Bench, or, if the matter arise in vacation, of any two judges. Further, if the king be willing to extend mercy upon condition, the offender may be forthwith ordered for transportation according to the terms of the condition. And the mutiny act warrants a sentence of transportation by the court, in cases of desertion, where they do not consider the crime as deserving of capital punishment—by the crown, in all other cases   The act of returning from transportation, or being unlawfully at large before the expiration of the sentence, is declared to be a capital offence under all these circumstances, excepting an escape from the Millbank penitentiary. There must be a *second* breach of prison, or escape, to authorise a capital infliction in the latter instance.

Transportation is for life, for fourteen years, or for seven years   Perhaps the first instance of the perpetual exile was introduced when felonious theft from the *person* ceased to be a capital crime (p)   It was declared also by a late statute that if a party

---

(n) Commentaries
(o) As, the Hulks. Formerly, a party could not be capitally convicted for escaping from the Hulks till his second offence. There was an execution in 1785 for the second offence.
(p) In the year 1808, although it had been usual to transport for life

be guilty of a second felony, he may be sent away for life, provided his former conviction be stated in the fresh charge against
him.   Accordingly, it has now become usual to transport for
life, and it may be observed generally, that this sentence of
banishment has commonly succeeded in lieu of capital punishment, and that the use of it in that respect is gaining ground.

The judgment for fourteen years is coeval with the introduction
of transportation under the statute of George the First, in 1718
It was adopted in the first instance against receivers of stolen
goods, and also as a commutation on the part of the crown for a
capital sentence   The same act declared that persons convicted
of offences within the benefit of clergy, might be transported for
seven years, and some misdemeanors were subsequently placed
under the same head of punishments   It has been thought right
to give this very brief outline, because the object we have in
view is to ascertain the nature of the temptation which seduces
convicts to leave the hulks, or to return from abroad in the face
of a very serious penalty.   With respect to the motives which
thus influence persons under sentence, it may be said that the
desire of visiting their native country acts powerfully upon many,
and to this may be added, the wish of retrieving their former
liberty   Criminals of this description not unfrequently complain
of hard usage at their respective places of confinement, but little
credit is to be attached to these statements, because order and
discipline are alone sufficient to raise discontent amongst convicts.   The facility of escape affords an additional inducement
for offenders to quit the hulks without licence, and it is a striking circumstance, that in proportion to the ease of accomplishing
the illegal act, so is the increasing criminality upon this particular occasion.   In several instances, money is the chief inducement to the commission of evil, and we contend (it is hoped
satisfactorily) that the punishment of death has no terrors to
countervail the prospect of gain.   Here, however, is a temptation
of a different nature, and this also, it appears, has an influence
entirely independent of the capital penalty

Now, with regard to the selection of convicts of this description
for execution, the old rule was to hang them, upon the principle
of their having abused the clemency of their sovereign, and thus,
having a second time violated the law, being unfit to live.   But
the modern course is, not to execute unless the prisoners have
been taken under circumstances which warrant the belief of their
being engaged in fresh acts of dishonesty or violence.   This new
principle has greatly diminished the number of executions, although it must be confessed that there are very many instances

---

in cases where the offender had been capitally convicted, and received
his Majesty's mercy *upon conditions.*

m former days of hardened and determined criminals who have returned home only to harass the public with fresh excesses

Not to fatigue the reader with too many tables, we will state the result of the punishment in this case very concisely —In London, as distinguished from Middlesex, from 1719 to 1755 inclusive, there were 25 convictions for those offences, and 18 executions   Of these, however, 9 convictions and 6 executions took place in 1720, the year after the passing of the Transportation Act , and from 1728 to 1739 there was neither conviction nor execution ; nor, again, from 1745 to 1753. (*q*)

In London and Middlesex there were 18 executions during the same period. (*r*)

From 1756 to 1817 inclusive, there were in London and Middlesex 184 (*s*) convictions, and 38 executions (*t*)

In 1818, 1819, and 1820, 3 convictions, but no execution (*u*)

From 1821 to 1832 inclusive (of September in that year), 29 convictions—no execution (*x*)

On the Circuits the numbers stand thus :

		Con.	Ex.
Home	1755—1814......	58	14
Western..........	1770—1818......	31	6—25 repr
Oxford	1799—1819......	10	0
Norfolk	1768—1818......	22	4 left for ex.
Lancaster	1798—1818......	7	0
Durham ..	1755 —(Lent)1819......	2	0
Northern (*y*)	1804—1817......	8	0
Midland..........	1805—1817......	13	1 (*z*)

And in *England* and *Wales*, including London and Middlesex, from 1810 to 1818, there have been convicted, for the offence under consideration, 77 persons, of whom 4 are said to have been executed , and from 1821 to 1829, 62 persons, of whom none appear to have suffered capital punishment

It will not be necessary to add much more upon this subject. The offence has not increased within the last seven years , and it is observable that, from 1821 to 1829, there have not been any executions; and yet, in this respect, there has not been an advance

---

(*q*) See the Parl. Returns, 1819, vol. viii. p. 148, &c.
(*r*) From my own MSS.
(*s*) This number is much swelled by reason of the carrying off of the Swift transport in 1783.   Twenty-five persons were convicted upon this occasion, and eight executed.
(*t*) Parl. Returns for the respective years.   (*u*) MSS.
(*x*) Parl. Returns, as note (*q*).
(*y*) York, Cumberland, Westmoreland, Northumberland.
(*z*) Parl. Returns, as note (*q*).

of crime. The truth is, that neither the Privy Council nor the Judges will sanction an execution, at the present day, for leaving the hulks,(*a*) or returning from beyond sea, unless the prisoner has been detected in the commission of a fresh crime. Thus, in the instance of the last execution for this offence, two persons, Finch and Tomlinson, were put to death in 1807. But it was supposed that they were the people who cut and wounded a watchman in St. Giles's, as they were attempting to rob the Watford carrier's cart, which, as far as one of the men was concerned, could not be true. For " the robbery took place in May, and one of the above unfortunate men did not escape from the hulks till June; so that both could not be implicated in that affair."(*b*) In reality, it was sworn at the trial, that Finch fired at the constable who apprehended him; and, perhaps, there might have been grounds for connecting the other man with the outrage at the carrier's cart. It is, moreover, observable, that both these men were convicted of the offence of returning, without more. A man had been hung in 1806 upon more plausible, though not less objectionable grounds. His name was Barnsley, or Beazley, and the course pursued with respect to him was, that after capitally convicting him for the return, he was tried for stealing a box of books from Pickford's cart, in Wood-street. He was convicted on this indictment, but not capitally, and he was subsequently executed, in pursuance of his sentence for returning. Objectionable as this decision on the man's fate seems to be, it was certainly more satisfactory to try him for his fresh crime. It was, nevertheless, rather hard to execute him, in reality for an offence which was not capital; and if it be said, that he had committed others, our objection arises—that he ought to have been tried for them. This is the difficulty which applies to the executions in 1807. Whatever may be the labours of the Council in coming to a conclusion in these painful cases,—however admirable their scrutiny, and humane their intentions, it is safer and better to exclude the admission of all testimony *against* the convicted party which is not reported as part of the evidence.

When we come to speak of Rape, and other offences which depend much upon the oath of a single witness, or upon circumstantial evidence, it is our intention to enlarge a little upon this point. At present, it is sufficient to protest against this mode of deciding a prisoner's fate. And the end is this · that as death has had no influence in deterring men from coming home, or escaping from prison, the severe penalty of the law should be changed for some other. It might be enough, in almost every case, to remit the offender to his former custody.(*r*)

(*a*) The majority of convictions has been for escaping from the Hulks.
(*q*) Jackson's Oxford Journal for August 22, 1807.
(*r*) In one of the Parl. Returns [1816, vol. xviii.] there is the state-

SECTION II.

Of the Punishment of Death in England for offences against Places of Religious Worship.

HAVING mentioned the capital punishments in England which relate to the crown and government, we proceed, secondly, to the consideration of those which the law denounces under the head of Sacrilege.   These are the burning or demolishing of any church, chapel, or dissenting meeting; and sacrilege, in the *limited* acceptation of that term, *i e* breaking and entering any church or chapel,(*a*) and stealing therein any chattel, or having stolen any chattel, breaking out of the same

As to the first class of crimes, namely, the arson and pulling down of sacred buildings, we have had, of late years especially, but few instances. The reason of this is plain . there have not been any sufficient inducements.   For there are not many exciting causes to occasion such evils as those of which we are now speaking A time of popular tumult may be productive of the most grievous outrages, as during the mob-tyranny of 1780, when the Roman Catholic chapels fell a sacrifice to vindictive ignorance. So again in the reign of Anne, when the design of the multitude was to destroy *all* meeting-houses   In this last case, the universality of the contemplated destruction was in favour of the dissenters since the law, which would have awarded a moderate punishment only for the burning of one hundred meeting-houses, construed the plan of burning all, into no less an attempt than one against the crown itself.

Again, the delusions of insanity can sometimes stir up a most mischievous incendiary   Such was Martin, whose object was to overthrow by fire an edifice no less celebrated and beautiful than York Cathedral   The injury which he really accomplished is well known to the lovers of architecture   But these violences and hallucinations are not the events of every year, so that it may be fairly concluded (and it is gratifying to record the fact), that executions for this species of sacrilege are very rare.

However, no sooner does the prospect of profit arise, than a new field is opened for the perpetration of evil   The same person who would not entertain a thought of burning a church, be-

---

ment of an execution at the Old Bailey in 1815 for this offence, but no such return appears in [1819, vol. viii] , and, although three persons were certainly convicted in that year, not one of them was included in the recorder's warrant.

(*a*) Observe, that dissenting places of worship are not included here, nor can they be implied.   It is a simple felony to rob such

cause the excitements of riot or of madness would not assault him, no sooner sees in his imagination the gold cup and silver plate, than he hesitates not to violate the sacristy, and seize the chalice. And, in truth, the people have not, it must be confessed, the brightest example before them. For the most venerable monuments of antiquity, even the Lady Chapel, at Saint Saviour's, are threatened from time to time by designs whose immediate or remote objects are either economy or gain. And it is rather singular, that if a noble ornament of the church is to be preserved, money must still be had to effect its safety. Money works for destruction, and pliantly enough, for restoration likewise. But to return Sacrilege, or the plundering of churches, has been held for many generations in great odium Alfred ordained, that larceny in a church should be punished by restitution of the value of the thing taken, by a fine also to the amount of the depredation, together with the loss of the hand which committed the offence The hand, however, might be redeemed by the king's licence, provided that the criminal would pay the price of his own life (*b*) Thus the law continued till the offence in question was made felony, and even then, if the ordinary chose, the party might have had the benefit of clergy. And when it is said, (as, for example. in Bacon's Abridgment,) the clergy was not allowed by the common law in cases of sacrilege, it must be understood to mean, that this privilege could not be had if the ordinary refused. (*c*) To proceed. at the juncture when Henry the eighth was humbling the clergy, and concerting those measures which ended in the Reformation, (*d*) it was determined to take away, amongst other things, their privilege of impunity in respect of several offences. A prior Act, (*e*) passed to try the temper of the people, had taken clergy from such as committed murder, or felony in any church. chapel, or hallowed place, but it lasted only till the next parliament, and persons in holy orders were excepted. (*f*) Now, however, this exception was omitted, and sacrilege became equally punishable whether done by clergy or layman. (*g*) Still, under this new statute, the criminal must have *broken into or out of* the church, in order to forfeit his clergy, so that it was reserved for the reign of Edward VI. to complete the sanguinary punishment upon this head In the first year of the reign of that monarch, clergy was withheld from all such as should feloniously *take* goods out of any church or chapel, and the law remained the same till the late enactments called Mr Peel's Acts, which restored

---

(*b*) Leges Ælfredi, apud Wilkins, c. 6. p. 36. See also id. p. 1. pl. 1, p 222. pl. 17.

(*c*) See Russell, ed 1819. ii. 962. note (*g*). East, P. C. 631.

(*d*) A D 1532.　　　　(*e*) A. D. 1513.

(*f*) Reeves, iv. 307.　　　(*g*) Id. 316.

the ancient law of Henry VIII   Consequently, there must now be a breaking either into or out of the holy place, and such an offence is capital by the present law   It needs scarcely to be added, that the body of the people were not much the better for the privilege of clergy, because of their ignorance of letters, so that, as far as they were concerned, sacrilege was a capital crime for the most part from the time when it was first made felony.(*h*) Having thus traced the history of this penalty, we proceed to detail some of the results.   These, however, may on the present, as well as many other occasions, be best ascertained by a reference to tables   For this purpose we have subjoined a few, from whence it will appear, that until the last seven years, sacrilege has not been by any means a common offence in England   In early days, indeed, we have heard of robbers of churches, (*i*) but owing to the privilege of sanctuary, many hardened persons have been restrained by their superstitions, (or, it may have been their religion,) from plundering the hallowed places to which they might safely fly in the hour of danger. By degrees, however, this feeling of veneration, which probably had its origin as we have just related, has declined, and, infected as it were with the advancing irreligion of the times, men seem not to scruple the breaking and robbing of churches in any higher degree than the plunder of a private dwelling   With respect to executions in London for this offence, there have not been more than two for a century; one of these took place in 1740, for robbing Saint Paul's, and the other in 1820, for breaking open Enfield church and stealing some black cloth, together with a surplice   In 1810, a great robbery was perpetrated at Saint Paul's, and the same church was attacked about the year 1783.

It may just be added, that the convictions at the Old Bailey, (to which we are about to refer,) were chiefly for small thefts, with the exception, perhaps, of Webbe and Hemingway, who were found guilty of robbing Enfield church, and for which offence Webbe suffered

Convictions and Executions for Sacrilege (*k*)

		Conv.	Er.
In London . .	1699 to 1755 inclusive	2	1
In London & Middlesex	1756 — 1829 (*m*) .	8	1
Home Circuit	1689 — 1718 . .	6	4

(*h*) See, upon this subject, Russell, p. 961, ed of 1819, vol. ii. p. 45. ed. of 1828.   East, P. C. 623-631.

(*i*) For instance, two notorious thieves were pressed to death for robbing Saint Martin le Grand, and three others hanged and burnt.

(*k*) From the Parliamentary Returns.

(*l*) In 1762, 1; 1797, 1, 1801, 1, 1816, 1; 1817, ..; 1819, 1; 1820, 2, total, 8.

			Con.	Ex.
————————	1755 — 1817	. .	5	3
Western . .	1770 — 1818	{ none under the head of sacrilege		
Oxford . . .	1799 — 1819	Lent Circuit	2	not asc
Norfolk .	1768 — 1817	. .	1	————
Midland . . .	1805 — 1817	. .	0	————
Lancaster . .	1798 — 1818	. .	5	————
Durham . .	1780 — 1818	. .	0	————
Northern York, Appleby, Carlisle, Newcastle. }	1804 — 1817	. .	1	————
England and Wales, including London and the Welch Circuits }	1810 — 1818	. .	23	————
	1821 — 1829	. .	52	————

Upon a review of these tables, we are inclined to attribute the
increase of sacrilege to the unprotected state of places of worship
accompanied by a decaying respect for them amongst the lower
orders, rather than to the rarity of executions for the offence —
Sufficient instances will be given in the course of these pages,
of the inefficacy of capital pains, some, indeed, have already been
introduced, and there is no reason why sacrilege should be an
exception to the ordinary experience upon this subject, assuming
that the severest sentence should be constantly inflicted upon
church plunderers. This, however, is one of the offences to
which we propose to revert again *in particular* in the fourth chapter, because it might be suggested, that a respect for the Most
High would require us to punish the violators of his temples with
the most condign visitation   It is a plausible, perhaps a natural
notion, but we still hope to show, in a future page, that the severity of the laws may be dispensed with, in this instance, without
erring in the least from the allegiance and love we owe to our
God.

SECTION III.

*Of the Punishment of Death in England for crimes against the
Person.*

WE come, thirdly, to a class of very grave offences, amongst which
murder stands in sad pre-eminence. The reader will remember,
that homicide, shooting, stabbing, poisoning, crimes against the
persons of women, and those against nature, together with *attempts
to murder*, shoot, or stab, are classed in this catalogue. We will
begin with

MURDER.]—It is well known that, amongst the Anglo-Saxons, homicide was punished by a compensation to the relations of the slain, called the *were*, and a fine to the king, or lord of the district where the killing happened, called the *wite*.   Like the Franks, our ancestors would have thought the loss of one citizen ill repaired by that of another (a)   This recompence, however, was estimated according to the rank or fortune of the individual who perished, so that the payment for slaying an eorl was far greater than that for a slave's death; and the jurisdiction where the offence happened was also a matter of consideration, so that a killing within the king's city incurred a larger public fine than the same within a lord's sovereignty (b)   And the place, moreover, independently of the jurisdiction, formed a feature in the inquiry, as, for instance, an open grave, where feuds often arose   For a death on such a spot a separate fine was prescribed.   The *were*, in some reigns, depended much upon the rank or property of the deceased, the *wite* upon the place where the misadventure occurred, but in others, the *were* seems to have been uniform, and the *wite* variable, according to place, wealth, or quality (c)   We call it *misadventure*, because the distinction between murder, manslaughter, homicide *per infortunium*, and justifiable slaying, were not as yet established.   And it is well understood, that the word "*murdrum*" was, for some time, taken to mean the fine imposed upon the vill, or hundred in default of the vill, rather than the deep deed with malice *prepense*, as we hold it at the present day   This being the case, we will take a very cursory view of the fines above alluded to, and then proceed with our history.   Thus, if one slew another in the king's city, he was to pay 50s.(d); if in an earl's, 12s.(e), ostensibly, because of the breach of the peace   If the death were at an open grave, 20s. were payable.(f)   Then, as to persons   The death of a freeman was redeemable by 50s.(g), of a guest, according to circumstances—80s., 60s, or 40s (h), a ceorl, 6s. (i)   These were the *wites* in the time of Ethelbert   The *weres* seem to have been uniform, namely, 100s.,—at least in this reign. (k)   But if a slave should kill another, he was to forfeit all which he had (l)   In the reign, however, of the Kings of Canterbury, the servile class were treated with less regard, for homicide by a slave was punished by the delivery of the slave, which

---

(a) Hallam, Mid. A 1. 104. See, as to the more ancient punishment for murder, Henry's Great Britain, 1. 214.

(b) See Turner's Anglo-Saxons, 4to. 11. pp. 240, 241, &c.

(c) Id. p 241.   (d) Wilkins, p. 2 pl. 5.

(e) Id. pl. 13, p. 3.   (f) Id. pl. 22, ib.

(g) Id. pl 6, p. 2.   (h) Id. pl 26, 27, pp. 3, 4.

(i) Id. pl. 25, and see also pl. 20, p. 3.

(k) See id. pl. 21, 31, 7.   Sharon Turner, 11. 241.

(l) Id. pl. 85, p. 7.

was equivalent to his execution, and a fine of 300s upon the master, if an earl were slain; 100s. if a freeman. (*m*)   If the murderer escaped, four times the value of the murdered person were required from the owner of the servant, in the case of an earl, and twice as much in the case of a freeman, together with purgatory oaths that the offender could not be apprehended (*n*)   But if any one should slay a slave committing theft, half the value was to be paid to the owner (*o*)   And, moreover, it was declared, that if a layman were caught in the act of stealing, no *were* should be required for his death (*p*)   Nevertheless, King Ina subsequently exacted an oath, under these circumstances, that the criminal was killed while flying for his theft, and it was also necessary that the slayer should not conceal the matter, upon pain of compensation (*q*)   And even a wandering stranger might have been treated thus as a thief, unless he cried aloud, or blew a horn.   Oath, however, was to be made, as above, and no secresy entertained.(*r*) The *were* had now become payable according to the rank or riches of the deceased, in the same manner as the *wite*, and thus we are brought to the days of Alfred, merely adding that, in Athelstan's reign, these *weres* were more regularly computed (*s*)   There was now an interval between the eras of compensation; (*t*) for as these money retributions prevailed, on the one hand, for many years before the time of Alfred, so they revived again after his death, and continued for several reigns, until the introduction of the trial by battel   Alfred, who founded many parts of his legislation upon the law of Moses, drew the first distinction between wilful murder and involuntary homicide, and decreed that the criminal who killed another wilfully (*sponte*), should die.   The words are, " morte moriatur," " let him die the death."(*u*)   Such a person might be taken from sanctuary, in order to expiate his offence.(*x*)   But if the killing were accidental or unintentional, the *were* and the *wite* became the measure of punishment, provided that the slayer sought an asylum or sanctuary, (*y*)which corresponded with the " Cities of Refuge," in very old days.   The *wite* and *were* again applied where death happened in consequence of the owner's neglect to keep in a dangerous ox (*z*)   The same rule

---

(*m*) Wilkins, p. 8, pl. 1, 3.
(*n*) Id. ibid.   See also Leges Inæ, pl. 74, 76, p. 26.
(*o*) Id. p. 12, prope ad finem.   (*p*) Id. p. 12.
(*q*) Wilkins, Leges Inæ, pp. 17-20. pl. 16, 35.
(*r*) Id. p. 18, pl. 20, 21.
(*s*) It is said that forty days were allowed for the payment of the *were* and *wite*.—Turner, ii. 242 , and see Wilkins, p. 3. pl. 23.
(*t*) Henry's Hist. of Great Britain, ii. 296.
(*u*) Wilkins, p. 29. Leges Ælfredi, pl. 13.
(*x*) Ibid.   (*y*) Ibid.
(*z*) Wilkins, p. 30, pl 21.

was enforced where a loss of life took place in consequence of the violence of a predatory band (turma)   If the guilty person were not avowed, the whole band were fined (*a*)   And, with respect to thieves, Alfred ordained, that if any one should kill a burglar breaking his house by night, he should be guiltless.   But if the killing took place after sunrise, it lay on the slayer to shew that there was a necessity for taking life, for otherwise he himself was to die.(*b*)

Soon after the death of Alfred, we find that the old method of estimating men's lives was again resorted to (*c*)   Athelstan, indeed, declared homicide to be capital, yet he permitted the accused to deny the fact, and to make compensation after a conviction by the triple ordeal (*d*)   And Edmund ordained, that the relations of the murderer should no longer be in dread from the hostility of the deceased's kindred, but that the slayer should bear his own fault (*e*)   Yet, notwithstanding these improvements, this rule of recompence continued, and so we find it in the laws of Ethelred, (*f*) and in the Senatus Consultum de Monticolis Walliæ.(*g*)   We may add, that in these last reigns it was declared, that whoever should perish in opposing the laws of Christ or of the king, should have no recompence made for his death (*h*)   And also, that persons killed in attacking houses should be unrevenged (*i*)   And finally, with respect to the Anglo-Saxon penalties, although Canute included murder amongst his five inexpiable crimes,(*h*) yet we find a law concerning the *murdrum*, or fine in cases of murder, amongst the ordinances of Edward the Confessor, whence it appears that the value of a man's life (capitis æstimatio) was still duly apportioned (*l*)   The clergy, however, had assumed an authority about this time by no means insignificant.   Whatever crime a man might have committed, it was very competent for him to gain absolution from the priests, and frequently an honourable escape from the ordeal then in use.(*m*)   In the time of Edgar, the hierarchy prescribed certain ecclesiastical penances for homicide, which were ostensibly promulgated under the king's name.   These were fastings and lamentations, and, in some cases, perpetual grief for the offence (*n*)   And, in the North, if any man should slay another within the walls of holy

---

(*a*) Id. p. 40, pl 26.
(*b*) Id p. 30, pl. 25.   (*c*) Id. p 53.
(*d*) Id. Leges Æthelstani, p. 57. pl. 6.   Turner, n. 266
(*e*) Id. Leges Eadmundi, p. 73, pl. 1.
(*f*) Id. p. 105. pl. 5.   (*g*) Id. p. 125. pl. 5.
(*h*) Id. p. 123.
(*i*) Wilkins, Leges Cnuti, p. 142. pl. 59.
(*k*) Id. p. 143. pl. 61.   (*l*) Id. p. 199, pl. 15.
(*m*) See id. p. 142, pl 53.
(*n*) Id. pp. 89, 90. pl. 6-15 , and see p. 72, pl. 3 , p. 134, pl. 6

church, he was to redeem his life (*o*) If a priest committed homicide, he was to lose his order (*p*)

We now come to the times of the Normans and here that may be said which is familiar to every reader of history, namely, that the Conqueror abolished capital punishment throughout his dominions. In its stead he substituted mutilation, a grievous exchange, but still his commands were explicit " Interdicimus etiam ne quis occidatur, vel suspendatur pro aliquâ culpâ "(*q*) The *weres* for homicide continued (*r*) And the same law prevailed throughout the days of Rufus and Henry I., only that, in the latter reign, there might be judgment of life and member, if the *were* and *wite* should be left unpaid,(*s*) and in cases of death by poison, or in church, the offender was to be delivered up to the relations of the deceased, to abide their mercy or justice.(*t*) The same ordinances also, concerning priests in cases of homicide, and the like ecclesiastical penances, which we have above noticed, remained in force (*u*) There was, however, one exception if any one, dreading lest he should be compelled to serve his father, or mother, or any of his kinsfolk, were tempted to slay the person whose servant he was to be, his life was declared to be forfeited, according to the Salic law, although he might still undergo the ordeal of nine heated ploughshares (*x*) Thus we see how gradually the offence of homicide became more the subject of punishment than of bargain, and how ineffectually the ordeal operated to accomplish that purpose is sufficiently well known. In the reign of Henry I , also, distinctions in homicide began to be recognized As, if the deed were done through covetousness, dispute, drunkenness, or by procuration So, again, if the death took place in self-defence, or by the hands of justice (*y*) These distinctions do not appear to have been yet resolved into the offences of murder and manslaughter , but the new ideas and changes upon the subject led to important results For, by degrees, all homicides came to be considered as irredeemable by a money compensation , and as there existed contemporaneously the trials by ordeal and battel, men resorted to the one or the other to vindicate their cause. And so, again, as the term felony

---

(*o*) Id. p 111.

(*p*) Id p. 115. and p. 142, pl. 38.   The distress of Archbishop Abbot, who killed a keeper in the time of James the First, will be recollected here. Some subsequently appointed bishops objected to be consecrated by him.   (*q*) Wilkins, p 229. pl. 67.

(*r*) Id. 221. pl. 8 ; 224. pl. 26 ; 228. pl. 53.

(*s*) Id. 264. pl. 68 ; 265. pl. 70.

(*t*) Id 267. pl. 71. If the relations thought fit, he might still redeem his life by paying the were, wyte, and manbote.—Ibid.

(*u*) Id. 263. pl 66 , 268. pl. 73.   (*x*) Id. 278. pl. 89.

(*y*) Wilkins, 267. pl. 72

came to be applied rather to the crime itself than the forfeiture (which was the original acceptation of the word), homicide, or murder, being attended by a confiscation of property, was denominated felony. (z)   These observations apply to the state of things in the reign of Henry II, when Glanvil wrote; and we learn from that author that, in his time, there were two kinds of homicide   the one secret, the other manifest, or done before a witness (a)   Both these were frequently tried by appeal; for the ordeal *per judicium Dei* was fast declining, and in the early part of Henry III.'s reign, orders were given to discontinue the fire and water universally. (b)

Gradually, again, did the trial by battel decrease and yield to the inquiry by the country.   The last mode of trial, so familiar to our own days, was encouraged in some measure by Henry II ; (c) and when Edward III came to the crown, very serious efforts were made to promote the appeal to a jury (d)   However, it was not until a much later period that the battel was wholly neglected, and almost all are aware of the celebrated appeal, in our own times, which led to the abolition of the old rite by an act of parliament Finally, in the reign of Henry VIII., murder was made felony without benefit of clergy. (e)   In early times, as we have before said, ignorance of reading produced the same result as a more modern statute denying clergy; but at length robbers and murderers did " bear them bold of their clergy, and live in manner without fear or dread ," so that it was found convenient to punish these mischievous men, and at the same time to humble the ecclesiastical authorities   Accordingly, the crime of murder, *with malice prepense*, was subjected to the severest punishment of the law.   And this leads us very briefly to inquire, how the legislature and the judges came at length to draw distinctions in cases of homicide.   There having been some attempts to make these discriminations in the time of Henry II. (as we have related), it was soon afterwards understood, that the killing of a person might be adjudged of in four ways.   First, as a matter of justice Secondly, of necessity   Thirdly, of accident, unaccompanied by negligence, and, fourthly, of free will, or where one, " of certain knowledge, and by a premeditated assault, in anger or hatred, or for gain, killed any one, *nequiter et in felonia*, against the king's peace. (f)   If no one saw the deed, it was called *murdrum*, as in Glanvil's time. (g)   These were the chief distinctions, although there were some few others, which will also be found in the book which we have cited in the note. (h)   And further, the legal im-

(z) Blackstone, iv. 97   See also Reeves, ii. 153.
(a) Reeves, i 198   (b) Id. ii. 24.
(c) Wilkins, p. 330. pl 5.   (d) Reeves, iii. 134.
(e) Id. iv. 307, 316.   (f) Id. ii. 10.   (g) Ibid.
(h) Id. pp. 10, 11, iii. p. 118, iv. 176.   Perjury, if it had the ef-

punity for killing a thief or housebreaker still cont,nued, provided
the death could be shewn to have arisen from necessity (i)

The same legal differences again prevailed in the days of
Henry VI and Edward IV   Felonious homicide, it was said,
must be with malice prepense; and that which happens against a
man's will. cannot be done *animo felonico* (j)   And thus we
come to the reign of Henry VIII, when clergy was taken away
from murder, upon which the offence, which we now call *manslaughter*, almost immediately came into notice   For, to relate
the matter very shortly, when the statutes of Henry VIII, and
Edward VI excluding clergy had passed, the judges no longer
held, as before, that an acquittal of the murder was sufficient to
discharge the prisoner from the whole indictment.   They considered that a felony still remained, (k) and this was no other than
our " manslaughter "   Accordingly, if the convict could not read,
he was still liable to be hanged, and executions for manslaughter
consequently took place. (l)   Thus it is that we have heard of
men being hanged, in former times, for *chance-medley*. However,
in the reign of Elizabeth, it was resolved, that one who had been
acquitted of murder, and found guilty of manslaughter, should be
burnt in the hand and imprisoned, (m) and thus the controversy
ended.   The difficulty is said to have arisen because manslaughter
and felonious homicide were considered at one time as synony-
mous; and so manslaughter included murder, the former being
the generic term. (n)   It need scarcely be related that this is not
the case at present, a common verdict by jury being—" Not
guilty of murder, but guilty of manslaughter." (o)

Poisoning, which had long been looked upon as a very bad
species of homicide, arrived about this time at its highest degree

---

fect of procuring a judgment of death (and subsequent execution, Russell, ed. 1819, 621), was deemed homicide in the reigns of Edward I.
and Edward II., Reeves, ii. 276, 353. , so was poisoning, id. 276.

(i) Id. ii. p 11. See also vol. iii p. 119.
(j) Reeves, iii. 409.   (k) Id. iv. 536
(l) Id. p 393, 538.   (m) Id. v. 220.
(n) Id p. 221.
(o) The truth seems to have been this —First of all, a verdict of not
guilty was not necessarily an acquittal of the *murderer*, because that was
an offence done *clam et secreté* , nor vice versá   But secondly, when the
word "murdravit" by degrees had crept into indictments, an acquittal
of a charge " quod murdravit" was a discharge of the whole, because
murder was the common name for homicides   Thirdly, however, when
the benefit of clergy was taken from murder *with malice prepense*, (and
it seems that these words were not usually inserted in the old indictments), murder again acquired a definite legal meaning, and then it was
that not guilty of murder, did not, of course, imply not guilty of the
felonious homicide.

of detestation.   For in consequence of the villany of the Bishop of Rochester's cook, who is said to have destroyed seventeen persons, an act was passed declaring the offence to be high treason, and punishable by boiling to death. (*p*)   In the reign of Edward VI this crime was again reduced to felony,(*q*) and so it remains to this day.

We have not much more to add concerning the history of the law of murder.   At the accession of James I the well-known statute of stabbing was passed, which subjected offenders to the guilt and consequences of wilful murder, if the deceased died within six months next after the stab or thrust.   This, however, was deemed to be a harsh law, and was accordingly soon rendered inoperative, for the act stated, that malice afore-thought needed not to be proved . but the judges held that there must be malice (*r*)   The act was expressed in very general terms, and had very few exceptions; yet the judges held that many cases were not within its meaning, although they came within the letter, and were not covered by any of the exceptions. (*s*)   Thus the sting of the statute was extracted by the skilfulness of the judges   Then again, towards the end of the reign of the same monarch, the concealment of the death of a bastard child was declared to be evidence of its murder against the mother, unless she could prove by one witness, that the infant had been born dead.   This act, however, was considered to be far too severe, and, together with the statute of stabbing, has been repealed.(*t*)

From this time until the reign of George II , the law of murder seems to have been untouched   But about the year 1752 there happened to be, from various causes to which we shall by and by advert, an increase of this serious crime ; and parliament imagined that, by marking the punishment in a more signal manner than before, they should effect a diminution of the offence   Accordingly those provisions, which are so familiar to all, were introduced, and they remained, until very lately, the law of the land.   Sentence was to be passed immediately after conviction ; the execution to take place the day next but one afterwards, unless Sunday ; the body of the murderer to be dissected . and bread and water to be his only aliment to the hour of his death.   Such were the striking features of a law which had for its object the decrease of violence and outrage.   It was also competent for the judge to direct that the body of the criminal should be hung in chains, but this custom had been long discontinued, probably because it was

---

(*n*) Reeves iv. 282.   See also id ii. 276 ; and Wilkins, Leges Inæ, p. 26 pl 77 , Leges Eadgari, p. 92 pl. 39.
(*q*) Id iv. 470
(*r*) And, therefore, the common law would have done as well.
(*s*) Russell, ed. 1819. pp. 708, 709.   (*t*) Id. p. 618.

discovered that the exhibition answered no other end than that of annoying the unoffending inhabitants of the neighbourhood (u)

Lastly, it has been declared by Lord Lansdowne's Act for consolidating offences against the person, that murder shall be capital; but as no alteration in the law was created in that respect, it is not necessary for us to pursue the subject further in its historical detail

And now (by the late Anatomy bill) the dissection of murderers is abrogated, and the judge is empowered to direct that the criminal shall be buried at the foot of the gallows, or hung in chains It is surprising that an antiquated custom, barbarous in its nature and detail, should have been revived in an age which pretends to intelligence Such a mark of disgrace, however, cannot continue. The power of hanging in chains was exercised in the North upon a late occasion, but the feeling of the inhabitants, and the sense of the press, were manifested in a strong manner against the execution of the sentence; and the bodies thus shockingly exhibited, have since, we believe, been taken away by friends or relations

RESULTS]—We therefore proceed according to our plan, to point out the consequences of the capital punishment for murder , or perhaps, *in this instance*, it might be more proper to say,—the history of the crime itself And here we must beg to observe, that the statement of these results is not made with the same view as most of those which will be found scattered throughout these pages There are many who consider that, whatever lenity may be hereafter shewn in amending our laws, murder should, at all events, be punished with death Many there are who view this matter as a religious question, and would deem a departure from severity, as a crime against God himself. Others might be disposed to insist upon the continuation of the present law as a measure of political expediency ; and, finally, the public at large are friendly to the capital penalty in many of those cases which the judges hold to be murder. There is, therefore, the popular sanction on the side of execution upon several occasions. Consequently, although the author reserves to himself the liberty of making a few observations in a future chapter, he is desirous of saying, that the object of the following details and tables, is rather to invite a calm and impartial discussion, than to promote at once the abolition of the present capital punishment for murder. Not but that it may possibly appear that the crime itself has not been at all affected by this great penalty—that is not the question to which

---

(u) It was by no means uncommon at one time for the inhabitants of a place to petition the judge that he would abstain from ordering a body to be hung in chains in their district.

we now allude—because there are many, very many, who regard murder as a substantive offence, and quite independent of the number of criminals · that, therefore, is the point to which we request a careful and discriminating attention (*x*)

But to pursue our narrative of the results it is indeed true that " blood hath been shed ere now i' the olden time ," and that savage deeds were committed by our early ancestors, even the worst kind of homicides, as Chaucer has it

" Mordre will out—that we see day by day."

Yet there is reason to believe that secret murders were not more common in those times than at present. The land was sometimes full of blood ; but the carnage arose chiefly from the deadly feud which the law in a manner winked at (*y*)—the *fæhthe* or "enmity which the relations of the deceased waged against the kindred of the murderer " (*z*) Drunkenness, also, must have led to many fierce encounters amongst the Anglo-Saxons One of their kings, in order to check this propensity, ordained that the cup should never be filled beyond a certain mark or point, but this restriction was soon abandoned   " To drink was the common occupation of all orders in this they spent their nights and days ; (*a*) and it is a common record, that the Saxons feasted bravely in the night before the battle of Hastings This was another cause of the felonious homicides which so often happened   Then, again, the violent acts of their chiefs, and of the nobles, promoted the fruits of an evil example, which extended far beyond the sovereignties of the Norman race.   The murders of Edward the Martyr, of the second Edward, of Richard II , of Henry VI., of Tracey, by Edwin the Forrester (*b*) of Prince Alfred, by Godwin, (*c*) of Becket, of Prince Arthur, by John, (*d*) were circumstances by no means tending to extinguish a thirst for blood, when ambition, or covetousness, or revenge, excited the temptation. Accordingly, the early periods of English history, although perhaps not

---

(*x*) As far as the personal opinion and humble efforts of the writer are concerned, it is probable that he will, in the fourth chapter, suggest with great diffidence, that executions, even for murder, *upon circumstantial evidence*, should be dispensed with, and, accordingly, that if death be inflicted, it should only accrue in cases of *open, deliberate* slaughter.

(*y*) Till the reign of Edmund I., when this species of personal hostility began to be discouraged by the government.

(*z*) Turner's Anglo-Saxon. ii. 487 8vo.

(*a*) Berington's Henry the Second, p. 604.

(*b*) Henderson's William the Conqueror, p. 110.

(*c*) As it has been supposed.

(*d*) " Pessimo mortis genere, quod Anglo *murdrum* appellant."— Matthew Paris For instances of the *crimen sacrum, vel regule*, see Buck's Richard III. in Kennett's Complete History of England, i. 573.

stained with more secret assassinations than our own, abound, nevertheless, with feats of open massacres, bold maraudings, in which robbers spilled blood like water, (e) daring attacks upon houses, (f) which provoked the hazard of life as a necessary consequence, and deeds of revenge, which served as matters for boasting rather than concealment. (g) Thus there were in those days many grievous assaults, which deserved punishment equally with the silent and unseen murder. And although there was a sufficient readiness to take the life of an assassin during these times of the Saxons, Normans, and Plantagenets, yet (if we except the doctrine of Alfred) it arose rather from a principle of revenge and retaliation than a calm desire to do justice For, as Edward II. declared respecting Gaveston's death—" Till now I have kept my hand from blood and fatal actions; but henceforth I will act my passions freely " " *Blood must have blood,* and I will spend it freely, till they have paid his wandering ghost their forfeit " (h) The result, therefore, of the capital punishment for murder, as far as the day of the last Plantagenet, seems to have produced no greater abatement of violence than during the exactions of the *were* and the *wite.* And we may just remark in passing, that, according to the Saxon law, if any one lent his weapons to another to kill with them, both were made responsible for the *were.* (i) Indeed the circumstance of a penalty being awarded against any one who should importune the king to pardon a murderer, (k) shews that the offence was by no means uncommon in the days of Richard II It was no longer allowed to redeem the consequences of a deadly feud, and the relations of the slain accordingly felt that the pardon of the sovereign was a grievous denial of justice Edward III. had previously extended his mercy to the Lord John Clifford of Lwyas, for the murder of Sir John Copland, and it was not unusual to purchase a charter of pardon from the Crown. (l)

The disturbed condition of the country during the heavy wars of York and Lancaster, was not likely to have diminished the catalogue of violent crimes From the outset, indeed, of Henry the

---

(e) See Johnson's Lives of Famous Highwaymen   Reign and Death of Edward the Second, by E. F. 1680, p. 43.   Hayward's Lives of Norman Kings, p. 282

(f) See the Records of the Times, published by the authority of parliament.

(g) For the part which the clergy bore in these murders, see Henry's Great Britain, iii 366.

(h) Reign and Death, 1680, p. 32.

(i) Turner, ii. 486. 8vo.

(k) Life and Reign of Richard the Second, 1681, p. 141.

(l) Barnes's Edward, iii. p. 626.

fourth's reign, to the fall of the last Yorkist monarch in Bosworth field, deeds of blood were constantly perpetrated.

The waggeries of Prince Henry and Sir John Falstaff might have gone no farther lengths than those of theft and terror, but there were many daring spirits, who, to robberies on Gad's Hill, would not have hesitated to add murder in case of the least resistance   In fact, it is related of Sir John himself, that he and some of his comrades hanged the public executioner on his return from Kingston, as a person dangerous to their profession. (*m*) And, upon another occasion, being stopped on the road by a brother cut-purse, he bound his man hand and foot, pinning a paper to his back, at the same time, with an account of his crime. And, accordingly, the thief was soon discovered, and at the next assizes convicted and executed. Some light also is thrown upon these times by the circumstance, that one of our monarchs was much found fault with for hanging a cut-purse without bringing him to trial (*n*)

These cut-purses were commonly murderers, as, for instance, the famous Thomas Dun, (*o*) who, after many bloody deeds, was brought into the market-place at Bedford, and, " without undergoing the trouble of a formal trial," was put to death in a most barbarous manner (*p*)   Not to detain the reader, we may just add, that murders amongst the great had by no means diminished, as the fate of Henry the Sixth, Edward V.—of Gloucester, Suffolk, and Clarence, sufficiently testify   And, (as we shall see by and by more particularly,) where it was not judged fit to destroy life at once, revengeful persons had recourse to the most desperate mayhems

We turn with pleasure, *in these respects,* to the reigns of the Tudors and the Stuarts, because whatever might have been the vices of those sovereigns, the crime of wilful murder came, at all events, to be more discountenanced than at any previous period Henry the Seventh, it will be remembered, was the first prince who invaded the ancient privilege of benefit of clergy, an immunity which had been productive of many abuses   He was very rigorous in cases of murder, for when one Grame had been convicted of killing his master, a special act of parliament was passed to prevent the offender from claiming his clergy.   And another law was forthwith made, debarring all lay persons from their clergy, who should prepensedly murder their lord, master, or sovereign immediate. (*q*)   The same monarch also ordained, that an indictment might be preferred within a year and a day after a homi-

---

(*m*) Lives of Highwaymen, p. 7.   (*n*) Id. p. 8.
(*o*) Thence *Dunstable.*   (*p*) Lives of Highwaymen, p. 27.
(*q*) Reeves, iv. 157.

cide, as well as an appeal (r)   And we have already stated, that the benefit of clergy was taken away from murder generally, in the next reign   Nevertheless, the legal murders committed by Henry VIII were not calculated to soften men's hearts, and the horrible death endured by Rouse the cook, for poisoning, (s) was obviously an act of cruel vengeance rather than of preventive justice   The strange act of legislation for punishing " malicious strikings by reason whereof blood was shed," in the king's palaces or houses, (t) affords us another example of deliberate barbarity. It seems, from these circumstances, that great disorders and violent actions still prevailed in the country, that the government had now become sufficiently enlightened to strive at their suppression, but that the law was made an engine of retaliation instead of prevention (u)   And although the severe act against poisoning was repealed in the reign of Edward the sixth, yet it is well known, that throughout his and his sister Mary's administration, the whole country was full of bloodshed and persecution, to say nothing of the sway of martial law, the worst of all tyrannies if unduly executed (x)   It was now well established, that a person convicted of murder would assuredly undergo his sentence Yet the temptations to which human nature is subject still prevailed, and the reign of Elizabeth was noted for murders and outrages   In 1571, this evil was attributed to the multitude of rogues, vagabonds, and sturdy beggars, so that the parliament decreed the apprehension and whipping of all wandering persons, and further, that they should be " burnt through the gristle of the right ear, with a hot iron of one inch compass for the first time so taken " (y)   It will be allowed, that this was not precisely the just method for civilizing the poor. The alarm, however, was not imaginary, for the parliament complained of the daily happening of " horrible murthers, thefts, and other great outrages." (z)— And, indeed, the fate of one Arthur Hall, a merchant, and of George Sanders, another wealthy citizen, both of whom were murdered under circumstances of great atrocity, might have well justified this terror (a)

(r) Bacon's Henry VII in Kennett, vol 1 p 594.
(s) He was boiled to death in Smithfield in Feb. 1530   Mrs. Thomson's Hen VIII. II. p. 213   (t) Reeves, IV. 304.
(u) It is said, that not less than 70,000 persons perished by the hands of justice in the reign of Henry VIII.
(x) See Hayward's Edward VI. in Kennet, II. p 295, and in the time of Elizabeth. Aikin's Elizabeth, II p. 387   In the reign of Mary happened the dreadful murder of Thomas Arden, a gentleman of Feversham, by his wife and other persons   they were convicted in 1551.— Celebrated Trials, Lond. 1825, 1 134.
(y) Stow's Annuls. 1631, p. 672.   (z) Id. ibid.
(a) Id pp. 672-675.   See also Lives of Highwaymen, p. 134. Life of Thomas Wynne.

We will not detain the reader. The usual complement of murders will be found throughout the reigns of the Stuarts, and we propose to subjoin *tables* from the revolution, (or a few years afterwards,) which will still more accurately develop the results of the capital punishment for this crime In the reign of James I. there were several " monstrous murthers," (*b*) not to mention the death of Sir Thomas Overbury ; and during the succeeding sovereignties, the world was frequently astonished and abashed by the discovery of some unprecedented deed. Sir Edmondbury Godfrey's name is but a mere unit in the catalogue (*c*) Execution also continued to be done for acts of murder with much inflexibility, and although James I. thought fit to pardon the Earl and Countess of Somerset, he was not by any means so merciful to the Lord Sanquhar, who suffered for the assassination of the fencing master. (*d*) Cromwell's resolution in putting the brother of the Portuguese ambassador to death for a murder, is well known, and Judge Hale's fearlessness in ordering the soldier for execution, is also a matter of historical record. Mr. Francis, the lawyer of Gray's Inn, met with no remission of his punishment when he thrust his tuck (*c*) into Dangerfield's eye, and the Marquis Palœotti, surprised as he was at the result, found that the destruction of his servant was an inexpiable offence in the canon of the English law. (*f*) We need not add Earl Ferrers But it is a sad reflection, that amidst this improved justice, and this rigid determination to fulfil it, there should have been many executions of innocent persons for murder. Such, nevertheless, was the case, and we shall take an opportunity hereafter of adverting more particularly to the facts, when we come to suggest some objections to the entertaining of *circumstantial* evidence in capital cases.— We now proceed to the tables to which we have alluded, it being of course understood, that murder was almost invariably punished capitally from the commencement of the years referred to.

All the tables will have an especial reference to the year 1752, when the aggravated penalty for the crime was introduced, and to the returns from London and Middlesex, we propose adding columns, stating the probable exciting *causes* of the respective offences, and the *places* where they were committed. In the first case, it will be ascertained, whether the heavy judgment pronounced upon murderers has had the desired result of repressing the evil, and in the others, a guide may, perhaps, be afforded to the legislator and the moralist in the prosecution of any future endeavours on their parts to amend the law or diminish the offence.

(*b*) Stow, ut supra. pp. 870-884.
(*c*) See the State Trials of this period, and Johnson's Lives of Highwaymen.
(*d*) State Trials, 8vo. 11. 743   Celebrated Trials, 1825, 1. 266.
(*e*) A short narrow sword. Stocco, Ital   (*f*) Cel. Trials, 111 372.

PART I.

CONVICTIONS AND EXECUTIONS FROM 1689 UNTIL 1752, WHEN
THE MURDERERS' ACT WAS PASSED.

Table I.—Sundry Executions of Criminals, convicted at the *Old Bailey*, from 1689 to 1730 inclusive, for Murder (g)

	Ex		*Causes*	*Places*
1689	 1		Unknown.	
1690	 3	⎧1	Attempt to escape..	Salisbury Court
		⎨1	Malice against a turnkey	Newgate
		⎩1	Robbery (3 persons).....	A house.
1691	 3	⎧1	Drunkenness	A house of ill
		⎨1	Unknown (2 men.)	[fame.
		⎩1	Bastard	
1692	 2	⎧1	Passion	A house.
		⎩1	Malice	In a coach.
1693	... 4	⎧3	Unknown.	
		⎩1		
1694	 2	..2	Robbery	House
1696	5	⎧1	Quarrel	Highway
		⎨3	Robbery	A house
		⎩1	Quarrel	Highway
1697	 6	⎧1	Robbery	House
		⎪1	Drunkenness	Unknown
		⎨2	Unknown	
		⎪1	(Wife) jealousy.	
		⎩1	(Bastard child.)	
1698	 3	⎧1	(A child) unknown	
		⎪1	Robbery—Drowned in the....	Thames
		⎨1	Shooting a woman, under the idea that she had conspired against the Government ...	Street
1699	 2	⎧1	Dispute with his wife, having committed bigamy	House.
		⎩1	Accessary to the above	
1700	5	⎧3	Robbery	Tavern.
		⎨1	The same	Highway
		⎩1	Play-house quarrel	Tavern

(g) MS. We do not profess to give the whole, but such only as we can ascertain. Note also, that many of the murders committed about this time were done by *swords*, and that, but for the common use of those weapons, on several occasions, blood would not have been shed.

	Er.	Causes.	Places.
1701 2	1	Bastard child.	
	1	Malice, and he committed robbery afterwards......	House.
1703 4	1	Passion ....At a fair.	
	1	The same...... ....The street.	
	1	The same (his wife) ....Highway.	
	1	The same.. ....Tavern.	
1704 3	1	Passsion ....Street.	
	1	Interrupted in committing burglary	Street.
	1	Attempt to escape apprehension Street	
1705 2	1	Passion ....House.	
	1	Robbery ....Street	
1706 .... 1..1		Jealousy	
1707 .... 1..1		Burglary	House
1708 5	1	Drunken quarrel ....Guard Room in the	
	1	The same ....House. [Tower.	
	2	Bastard children.	
	1	Unknown	
1710 ....1. 1		Robbery	House
1712 .. 5	1	Malice, poison by a girl of 14 ..House	
	2	Attempt to escape .... In the Old Bailey	
	1	Bastard child. [Court	
	1	Murdered a boy in a fit of sullenness..............	House.
1713 3	1	Robbery ....On the River.	
	2	Attempt to escape .. ..Clerkenwell-	
1714 2	1	Unknown ....House [Bridewell.	
	1	Robbery ....House.	
1715 ....1..1		Drunkenness ....Fleet Prison.	
1716 4	3	Robbery ....Street	
	1	A quarrel ....House.	
1717 4	2	A drunken quarrel ....Street	
	1	Quarrel with a fellow servant ..Kitchen	
	1	Robbery ....Garden.	
1718 . 6	1	Passion ....Street.	
	3	Robbery ....Highway	
	1	Robbery ....Street -	
	1	Revenge ....House.	
1719 5	1	Drunken passion ....House.	
	1	Passion ....House.	
	1	Revenge—poison. (Died in Newgate)	
	1	Unknown (his wife)	
	1	Drunken frolic ....Street.	

	Er.	Causes.	Places.
1720	1 ..1	Quarrel, (special commisson)	Abroad.
1721	1..1	Robbery	House.
1722	5	2 Robbery . ...Street. 1 Robbery ....Highway. 1 Revenge .... House 1 Passion (his wife) ....House.	
1723	4	1 Passion ....On the River 1 A brawl in the street 1 Quarrel in the street (about a girl) 1 Passion ....House	
1724	1. 1	Hatred to his wife (appeal) ...House	
1725	2	1 Hatred to his wife ....House 1 Passion .... House	
1726	4	1 Quarrel ....Tavern 3 Murder of a husband by his wife and 2 others, through hatred. 1 died in Newgate } House	
1729	1. 1	Malice (appeal) ....House.	
1730	2..2	Robbery ....Highway	

Total, 106

Table II.—A regular List of Criminals executed for Murder at Tyburn, from 1731 till April 15, 1752, when the new Act passed

	Er.	Causes	Places
1731	5	1 Threatened by a woman whom he had got with child .... } Highway. 1 Robbery ....Highway. 1 Malice . ...Gaming-house 1 Quarrel .. . .Ale-house 1 Quarrel ....House.	
1732	3	1 Hatred to his wife .. ..Out of a window. 2 Riot, and murder of a man who stood in the pillory, at Seven Dials for perjuries against innocent persons.	
1733	5	1 His wife, passion, ...House 1 His wife (habitual brutality) ..Street 1 Robbery (by a woman—three murders) .... } House. 1 Soldier shooting his corporal, passion, ... } In the Tower. 1 Attempt to escape	

	Ex.	Causes.	Places.

1734 .   3
- 1 (Bastard child)
- 1 (His wife, drunkenness and habitual brutality.). . ... } House
- 1 Murdering a butcher's boy in Hungerford Market, through drunkenness

1735 5
- 1 Bastard child
- 1 Robbery ....House.
- 1 Revenge .... House
- 1 Passion (his wife) ....,...Shop
- 1 Passion in his .... House

1736 . 1
- 1 Murder of a watchman in Bunhill Fields, smuggler interrupted.

1737 ... 6
- 1 Bastard child
- 1 Soldier for killing a watchman in Westminster, sudden passion
- 1 Quarrel (his wife) ....House
- 1 Murder of a man in Newfoundland (through malice)
- 1 Murder of a fellow servant, in a passion, ... } Work-shop.'
- 1 Passion and brutality, his wife House

1738   . 3
- 1 Bastard child.
- 1 His wife, dislike,............House.
- 1 His wife, quarrel, .,.........House (h)

1739 4
- 1 His wife (drunkenness) . .... Baldwin's Gar-
- 1 Wife (brutality) . .. .House   [dens
- 1 Husband (brutality)..........House.
- 1 Bastard child.

1740 3
- 1 (Drunkenness,) butcher for the murder of another butcher } Clare-market.
- 1 (Drunkenness and passion,) a woman with whom he cohabited .... } House
- 1 (Drunkenness and passion,) a young woman .... } House.

1741 .... 1 Robbery....... .... .House.

(h) In this year, 1738, one man, who would have been hanged for the murder of his wife, died in his cell, and also a man, who had been convicted of killing a sheriff's officer, died in Newgate.

	Ex.	Causes.	Places

1742 4
- 1 Wife, quarrel .... House.
- 1 Murder of a negro, through passion .... } Rag Fair
- 1 A Woman with whom he cohabited, quarrel, ... } House.
- 1 Robbery ....House

1743 ... 1 Bastard child.

1745 3
- 1 Murder of his apprentice, cause unknown
- 1 His wife, passion, ... House.
- 1 His wife, quarrel .... House

1746 .. . 4
- 1 Robbery .... House
- 1 Brawl .... House.
- 1 Quarrel . ...Public-house.
- 1 Wife. jealousy .. ..House

1747 2
- 1 Revenge .... House.
- 1 Robbery .. ..Street.

1748 . .. 1 Brawl .... Highway

1749 .... 1 Jealousy .. ..House

1750 .. . 1
- 1 Soldier, for a murder in Tothill-fields, in a sudden brawl.

1751 1
- 1 His wife, drunkenness and passion, ... } House.

1752, till April 15, when the new act passed .6
- 1 A child, through a sudden impulse, ... } House
- 1 Robbery ... . House.
- 1 Quarrel ....Street
- 1 Robbery .... .Highway.
- 1 Quarrel ....House
- 1 Strangling an infant, cause unknown, ... } House.

N.B.—See a list of convictions and executions for murder, in *London* only, as distinguished from Middlesex, from 1699 till 1752, in the Parliamentary Papers for 1819. Vol viii p. 146 This table extends to 1755.

Table III.—A List of Convictions and Executions on the Home Circuit, from 1689 till 1718 inclusive.

	Con	Ex		Con.	Ex.
1689	22	18	1695	2	0
1690	7	5	1696	20	15
1691	0	0	1697	4	4
1692	2	1	1698	5	2
1693	2	0	1699	5	4
1694	7	7	1700	1	0

	Con.	Ex.		Con.	Ex.
1701	1	1	1711	2	2
1702	0	0	1712	5	4
1703	1	1	1713	1	1
1704	3	2	1714	8	7
1705	4	2	1715	4	2
1706	1	1	1716	5	4
1707	2	1	1717	3	0
1708	3	0	1718	0	0
1709	1	1	Total	123	87
1710	2	2			

PART II

Table IV.—List of Persons hanged at Tyburn, for Murder, from April 1752, when the new Act was passed, to the year 1755 inclusive.

	Ex.		Causes	Places.
1752	3	2	Robbery	Highway
		1	A woman with whom he co-habited, in a fit of passion,(i)	House
1753	6	2	Robbery	Highway.
		1	Revenge.	
		1	His wife (passion.)	
		1	Robbery ....,....	Highway.
1754	4	1	Of a man sent to watch the prisoner, and who detected him stealing greens, ...	Chelsea
		1	His wife	Unknown
		1	A turncock for the murder of a paviour	Unknown.
		1	Murder of a man at Barnet ..	Unknown
1755	3	1	Murder of a child by a woman in a workhouse.	
		2	Murder of the husband by a wife and her paramour	

Table V.—Capital Convictions and Executions for Murder, in London and Middlesex, from 1756 till 1832 inclusive.

	Con.	Ex.	Causes, Places.
1756	2	2	1 Wanton assault on a man at his own door.
			1 His wife, he having formed a connection with another woman—in a house.

(i) Being the first who suffered under the new act.

	Con.	Ex.	Causes, Places.
1757	1	1	Bastard child.
1758	1	1	Hatred, in house
1759	1	1	Soldier for stabbing a man with whom he was fighting in the street
1760	5	4	1 Bastard child.
			1 Revenge—in a house (*k*)
			1 His wife, unknown.
			1 Unknown.
			1 Killing a sheriff's officer who arrested him, in a house.
1761	6	5(*l*)	1 A painter who struck a woman in her own house, and then murdered her, for fear she should accuse him
			1 Bastard child
			1 His wife, passion, in a house.
			1 His wife (*m*)
			1 Quarrel in a house.
			1 Of a master by his apprentice — quarrel about wages—in a house
1762	2	2(*n*)	2 Women for the murder of their apprentice, at home—brutality.
1763	4	4	1 Robbery in a house.
			1 A Portuguese sailor—quarrel in a house.
			1 By a woman unknown
			1 Unknown (Name, Sinderbury.)
1764	2	2(*o*)	1 Jealousy, in a house
			1 His reputed wife, unknown
1765	3	3	1 Bastard child
			2 Robbery in the street.
1767	4(*p*)	3	1 Starving his wife in her own house—brutality.
		(*q*)2	Robbery on the highway
			1 Murder of her apprentice—brutality—in a house
1768	6	6	1 Drunkenness.

(*k*) Poisoned himself — verdict, Felo de se.

(*l*) In the Parl. Return three, which is evidently a mistake.

(*m*) This man was pardoned , the first since the passing of the new act

(*n*) The Parl. Return has a blank here, which is wrong, for the notorious Metyards were hanged in July for the murder of their apprentice.

(*o*) The Parl. Return has only one execution.

(*p*) The Parl Return gives four executions but the fact is, that one of the robbers was reprieved.

(*q*) One was reprieved

	Con.	Ex.	Causes, Places.
1768			1 A woman who murdered a child through a sudden impulse Drowned in the Thames.
			1 Robbery on the highway
			1 Passion by a woman, in the street
			2 Brawl between the coal-heavers and the River sailors.
1769	3	1	2 Riot at the Brentford election (r)
			1 Murder of a woman with whom he co-habited
1770	8 (s)	6	2 Sudden affray with a watchman in the street (t)
			2 Robbery on the highway.
			1 Quarrel, his reputed wife, in the house
			3 Robbery on the highway.
1771	8 (u)	8	2 Passion, in the street
			2 Revenge against a man for giving evidence, in the street.
			4 Jews, Burglary
1773	2	2	1 Robbery on the highway.
			1 Her husband — sudden passion — in the house.
1774	1	1	Bastard child.
1775	2	2	1 Bastard child
			1 Quarrel in the house.
1776	6	6	1 Attempt to escape apprehension, in the street.
			1 Murder of a woman, with whom he co-habited — passion — in the house
			4 Smugglers
			1 Murder of a custom-house officer, in the street.
1777	2	2	1 Passion, in the street
			1 Robbery in a house.
1778	1	1	Murder of a woman with whom he had co-habited — passion — in a stable
1779	1	1	Jealousy — a clergyman — Covent Garden Theatre (x)
1780	1	1	His wife — passion — in the house.
1782	1	1	Robbery — on the highway.

(r) Both pardoned.
(s) Parl. Return — Con 6. Ex. 4.
(t) Pardoned on condition of transportation.
(u) Parl. Return — Con. 9. Ex. 9.
(x) In this year there was a special verdict

	Con.	Ex.	Causes, Places.
1783	3	2	1 Quarrel in the house.
			1 Quarrel between two neighbours (y) in the street.
			1 Drunkenness — jealousy — in the house
1784	1	1	Robbery—in the street
1785	1	1	His own son, barbarity — in the house-
1786	5	5	1 Malice — in the house
			3 Attempt to rescue a man taken for picking pockets — Holborn.
			1 Robbery — in a house.
1787	2	1	1 Robbery by a servant — in a house.
			1(z) Sudden impulse — in a house
1789	2	2	1 His wife, intent to marry another — on the highway
			1 Robbery—on the highway.
1790	5	5(a)	3 Robbery—on the highway
			1 Murder of a child — sudden impulse in a house.
			1 Murder of a woman with whom he cohabited — passion — in a house
1791	3	3	1 His wife — passion — in a house
			1 His wife — quarrel — in a house
			1 His wife — quarrel about other women In a house
1792	2	2	1 Brutal attack in the street
			1 Drunkenness, in a house
1795	1	1	Murder of a watchman in the street, sudden passion.
1796	5	5	1 Robbery, in a house
			2 Murder of a beadle — brawl in the street
			2 Robbery, in a house.
1797	3	3	2 Robbery, on the highway.
			1 Quarrel, in a house.
1798	1	1	His wife—quarrel — in a house
1799	4	3	3 Murder of a Bow-street patrol, by the Irish, in a tap-room.
			1 Riot in the street Reprieved.
1800	1	1	Drunkenness, in a public-house.
1801	2	2	1 His wife — passion — in a house.
			1 Impulse of bad feeling—Chelsea Hospital.

(y) Pardoned on condition of two years' imprisonment in Newgate

(z) Reprieved on the ground of insanity. He was convicted, and had sentence of death passed on him. The Parl Return gives only one conviction for this year, which is evidently incorrect.

(a) Parl. Return, four executions; but it will be found, that all the five persons were executed

	Con.	Er.	Causes, Places.
1803	2	2	1 His wife and child (cause unknown) Drowned in the Paddington canal
			1 His wife — brutality — in a house
1804	1	0	Killing the Hammersmith Ghost—in a lane
1805	1	1	His child — passion — in a house.
1807	3	3	2 Robbery, on the highway.
			1 Murder of a man with whom she cohabited — in a house.
1811	2	2	1 Drunken scuffle, in a public-house
			1 His wife — passion — in a house
1812	1	1	Revenge — House of Commons.
1813	2	2	1 Robbery, in a field
			1 His wife — passion — in a house.
1814	3	3	1 Shooting a woman to whom he pretended an attachment, brutality — in a house.
			1 The like, sudden impulse — in a house.
			1 Robbery, in a house
1815	1	1	Murder of a woman in Portugal
1816	1	1	1 A Spaniard, drunkenness — public-house.
			1 Stabbing a man in a brawl, in a public-house
1817	1	1	Bastard child.
1818	3	3	1 His wife — jealousy — in a house
			1 His wife — passion — in a house
			1 Revenge — a woman with whom he had lived nine years, having married another man — in a house
1819	1	1	His wife — jealousy — in a house.
1822	1	1	Quarrel with a woman with whom he cohabited — in a house
1824	1	1	Murder, by using a scythe in a passion—in a field.
1825	1	1	His wife — connection with another woman — in a house.
1826	1	1	Murder of a man by an Irishwoman in a passion, because he wanted to soothe a quarrel between her and her husband — in a house
1827	1	1	1 Murder of her husband, by poison — cause unknown — in a house
1828	1	1	Bastard child.
1829	1	1	Brutality to her apprentice.
1830	1	1	Murder of a policeman to prevent apprehension — in the street
1831	3	2	3 Burking—2 executed.

1832   5   3   1 Burking—a woman
includ-   1 Setting his house on fire, whereby several
ing Sep-   persons were burnt to death
tember.   1 His wife—brutality.
               2 Robbery on the River Thames (*b*)

The following seems to be a summary of the motives which have excited these sad deeds.—

Cases since 1689

Attempts to escape apprehension, and rescue . .	13
Arson	1
Brawls—which education and good manners have lessened	9
Brutality—absolute—lessened by education .	12
Burking	3
Drunkenness—decreased by education .	20
Hatred—principally husbands towards their wives	9
Impulse, sudden	9
Jealousy . . .	8
Infanticide—lessened by an increasing hatred of the seducer, and by the arts of economy which encourage legitimate and prudent marriages	18
Malice	19
Passion and quarrels—lessened by education, which prescribes self-command, and by the disuse of offensive weapons .	76
Riots, public	2
Robbery and burglary—lessened by the increased vigilance of the police, and consequent security of the highways	48
Wanton assaults . . .	2
Murders of wives by their husbands	47
————— husbands by their wives	7

Table V.—A List of Persons convicted and executed for Murder, upon the Circuits

	Year.	Con.	Ex
Home	1689 to 1718 . .	123	87(c)
————	1755 — 1817 . .	129	108
Western	1770 — 1818	133	117
Oxford	1799 — 1819 (Lent Circuit)	49	Not known
	Convicted and left for Execution		
Norfolk	1768 — 1818 . .	46	

(*b*) Reprieved.
(*c*) In 1689 there were, Con. 22, Ex. 18, and in 1696, Con. 20, Ex 15.

			Con.	Ex.
Lancaster	1798 — 1818	. . .	11	11
Durham	1755 — 1819	(Lent ass)	11	6
Northern(c)	1804 — 1818	. . .	13	13
Midland	1805 — 1817	. . .	20	5(d)

Table VI.—England and Wales, independently of London and Middlesex. List of persons committed, against whom no bills were found, and who were not convicted, executed; prosecuted; and acquitted, upon charges of Murder, from 1821 to 1830.

Year.	Com.	No Bills, &c.	Con.	Acq.	Ex.
1821	71	19	23	29	22
1822	85	24	24	37	18
1823	60	13	12	35	11
1824	73	28	17	28	15
1825	94	21	12	61	10
1826	57	12	13	32	10
1827	65	19	12	34	11
1828	83	15	20	48	17
1829	47	7	13	27	13
1830	65	21	16	28	14
	700	179	162	359	141

Attempts to Murder.

The next class of crimes to which we are desirous of directing the attention of our readers, is that which comprises all *attempts* to murder, together with those injuries to the person which are commonly effected by guns, sharp instruments, and other offensive weapons. The first may be taken thus:—

1. Shooting
2. Stabbing, wounding, cutting and maiming
3. *Attempts* to shoot.
4. *Attempts* to drown, suffocate, or strangle.
5. Administering, or *attempts* to administer poison

We will endeavour to consider these offences together, for, with few exceptions, the same malignant principle which prompts the commission of one, will be found present at the perpetration of the others. And it should be added, that this cardinal test of guilt is common to all the deeds in question, namely, that if death ensue, murder must be the consequence. So that whenever it

(c) York, Carlisle, Newcastle, Appleby.
(d) From the Parliamentary Returns.

G

happens, that a shooting or stabbing, or other mischief takes place, if the law will not hold the criminal guilty of murder should fatal results be the consequence, he cannot be said to have incurred any of the capital pains prescribed by Lord Lansdowne's statute in respect of the five mischievous acts above enumerated.

Our ale-loving ancestors were very prone to brawls and quarrels, which naturally arose out of their long and deep carousals The monarch lingered at his cups with his favourite nobles, and the meanest of his subjects strove (as far as money would permit) to follow his great example One is not surprised, therefore, to hear of mutilations and woundings, of eyes struck out, ears cut off, teeth uprooted, limbs crippled Injuries such as these were so common, that a pecuniary standard was fixed for them in like manner as for life itself. The Visigoths, the Longobards (Lombards), the Swedes, the Danes, almost all the barbaric tribes had established this kind of compensation for wounds, and the Anglo-Saxons settled their own respective retributions with much precision and nicety (b) The weapons which they usually employed in the heat of quarrel were the lance, the sword, and the dagger, and so eager were they to avenge their wrongs, that it was thought expedient to make fighting in the king's palace a capital crime (c) The offence was redeemable, however, in general, by a penalty. They would also use their fists upon occasion, so that the custom of deciding quarrels by boxing might well be denominated by a learned Chief Justice, a good old English method. Alfred, who imitated the Mosaic law, made an alteration in the measures of compensation for these injuries of stabbing and wounding Following the theocratical legislator, he ordained that an eye should perish for an eye, a tooth for a tooth, a hand for a hand ; that there should be burning for burning, wound for wound, stripe for stripe.(d) Yet his retributive justice was so far tempered, that these mischiefs might still be atoned for by pecuniary awards.(e) William I , and Henry I , also established certain prices for each kind of wound, (f) and the latter monarch made a distinction between cases where blood was shed, and mere blows without drawing blood.(g) The ordeal and duel succeeded to these times of compensation, and we find that appeals of mayhem *(de plagis et mahemia)* were not uncommon in the thir-

---

(b) See Wilkins's Anglo-Saxon Laws, p 4. pl. 23-71.   Turner s Anglo-Saxon History, ii. 489.
    (c) Leges Inæ, apud Wilkins, p. 16. pl. 6.   Leges Ælfredi, p. 36 pl. 7   Leges Cnuti, pl. 56.   See also Wilkins, pp. 111. and 272 and p. 244, pl. 13
    (d) Wilkins, p. 30, pl. 19.   (e) Id p. 44. pl. 40
    (f) Id. p. 221, pl. 12 & 13.
    (g) Id. p. 281, 2, pl. 93 & 94

teenth century. But in the case of a duel, if the appellor were
injured in such a manner as that he could not defend himself,
the offender was obliged to put his guilt or innocence to the issue
of a trial *per probos et legales homines*,(*h*) and then if they found him
guilty, the common law judgment, *membrum pro membro*, prevailed, unless the criminal could redeem himself by a payment of
money. By degrees, however, this punishment became obsolete,
partly, perhaps, because the increase of knowledge was unfavour-
able to retaliation, partly, because " upon a repetition of the
offence, the judgment could not be repeated."(*i*) But the statute law took cognizance of these savage attempts, whilst the ancient ordinances of the land were reducing them to aggravated
trespasses The tongue and eyes seem to be the first members
which claimed the protection of the legislature, and the occasion
was a practice which prevailed in the reign of Henry IV., of cutting out the tongue, and putting out the eyes of persons in order
to prevent them from giving evidence The course was, to beat,
wound, imprison, and maim the victims, and then proceed with
the mutilation in order to abolish the chance of testimony which
might otherwise be given against the perpetrators (*k*) This barbarity was now made felony, and it may be added, that it was
the only capital felony in existence concerning mayhems, if we
except *castration*, which the best writers consider to have been,
even at common law, an act punishable with death. (*l*) It was
capital for the most part, because of the ignorance of the people
at large, who were unable to claim clergy through their inability
to read.

In the reign of Henry VIII, the ear came to be considered
worthy of notice, and it was enacted, that whoever should cut off
an ear, otherwise than by authority of law, should forfeit treble
damages, and 10*l*. to the king. The harquebuss was now well
known, but it does not appear to have been used much for the
purpose of malicious shooting.(*m*) The sword, and latterly, the
pistol, were the chief instruments employed for robbing on the
highway, while the short dagger decided the sudden quarrel or
affray at home. We have no concern here with the statute of
stabbing That act, which was made for the express end of repressing beats between the Scotch and English, had no operation
unless the injured person died within six months, and after all,
it was merely declaratory of the common law. We may, therefore,
go forward to the days of the Coventry act, and it will be observed,

---

(*h*) Reeves's History of the Law, ii. 34, 35.
(*i*) Russell on Crimes, ed. 1819. p. 841.
(*k*) See East, Pleas of the Crown, i 393.
(*l*) See 4 Black. Com 206
(*m*) Hollinshed relates, that the regent of Scotland was murdered
by a harquebuss during the minority of James the Sixth

that in consequence of the extension of the benefit of clergy, the statute of Henry IV. was in effect no longer a capital felony In 1664, a Mr Bacon was convicted of lying in wait to kill Sir Harbottle Grimstone, and was sentenced to fine and imprisonment, to find sureties for life, and to acknowledge his offence at the bar of the Court of Chancery (n) In 1669, a desperate attack was made upon Sir John Coventry, according to the new scheme of lying in wait, and notwithstanding his brave defence, his nose was slit to the bone by the persons who attacked him. This outrage was done through a spirit of revenge, and as Sir John was popular in the House of Commons, an act was soon passed making it felony without clergy to maim or disfigure by this sort of ambuscade (o) The tongue. eyes, nose, lip, every member, in fact, came now under the protection of the statute law, but the intent, it will be noticed, must have been to maim or disfigure. Next came a statute of Queen Anne, passed because of the murderous assault made by De Guiscard upon Mr Secretary Harley in council The attempt to kill, as well as the unlawful assaulting, striking, or wounding a Privy Counsellor in council, were accordingly declared capital felonies Hard upon this followed the Black Act [9 Geo I], so called from the black faces of certain marauders in Waltham forest, although, in these days, we might have suspected that the name had been awarded it in respect of its numerous capital felonies. Guns were now sufficiently used to warrant a provision against malicious shooting, and that offence was now deprived of clergy, or to speak more properly, was made a new felony, and expressly debarred of that privilege.

The next enactments upon this subject were, one in 19 Geo 2, by which the shooting at a ship or boat belonging to the customs or excise was made capital; and another in the 26th of Geo. 2, which inflicted the pain of death upon all persons who should beat or wound shipwrecked mariners, with intent to kill them. It had for its object the restraining of those cruel deeds which sadly distinguished the inhabitants of our coasts, and the motives which prompted it were certainly humane, although the principle of destroying violence by severity is daily receiving a shock amongst those who reflect upon the infirmities of our nature The crime, however, of lying in wait still conti-

(n) East's Pleas, &c. i. 411.
(o) Filangieri (Scienza della Legislazione), tom. iii p. 337. seems to have fallen into a mistake in supposing that the plea alledged by Coke and Woodburne upon this statute was allowed by the judges. Coke urged, that the primary intention of their assault was to commit murder, and, consequently, that the lesser charge of cutting could not be sustained, but the judges overruled his objection, and execution followed. Filangieri argues, however, as though this suggestion of Coke had been held available, and thus appears to have committed an error in his stricture upon our laws in this respect.

nued, and in 1765, the well known case of Carrol and King occurred.   These men were convicted and executed for slitting the
nose of Mr. Kerby, a barrister, and from thenceforth it was no
uncommon circumstance for thieves to use the knife   Mr Kerby
had seized a boy who was picking his pocket, and it had been
arranged that the two prisoners should stab any person who might
attempt any resistance   At length these injuries by robbers became so grievous, that in 1782, the Recorder received a letter
from Mr. Secretary Townshend, directing him to report without
delay all cases of plunder attended by cruelty.   This was done,
and the return acted upon.   It is rather surprising that, considering the temper of the times, an act like that which passes under
the name of Lord Ellenborough's Act, should not have been
thought of sooner.   For to convict under the Coventry Act, there
must have been a lying in wait, and to convict of a cruel assault
on the highway, there must have been a taking of some property,
however small.   However, in 1803, a year in which there were
fewer convictions for robbery at the Old Bailey than for many
previous, when the diminution of that offence had become perceptible through the increased vigilance of the police, it was
deemed proper to introduce a bill little less sanguinary than the
Black Act.   It recited that, " divers cruel and barbarous outrages
had been committed of late, with intent to rob, murder, maim,
disfigure, or disable."   It then declared, that all persons shooting
at, or attempting to shoot ; and all persons stabbing, or cutting
others with the purposes before mentioned, or with intent to do
grievous bodily harm, or again, to resist lawful apprehension, or
who should administer poison with intent to murder, should be
guilty of capital felonies.   And this statute with its various inter-
pretations, remained the law of the land till Lord Lansdowne's
late act, which repealed all the previous provisions upon the subject, including, of course, the Black and Coventry Acts   Between the time of passing Lord Ellenborough's Bill and the
enactment to which we have just referred, there were very few
additions to the criminal law upon this point.   In 1812, indeed,
it was declared capital to fire at a ship or boat belonging to the
customs or excise, but this was no more than the re-enacting of a
similar clause in a repealed statute, and in 6 Geo. 4, a provision
of the same kind took place.   With these, and perhaps one or
two other exceptions, the history of personal injuries by shooting
or stabbing, may be carried forward to the bill of 1829. Attempts
to drown and strangle were added to the catalogue of deadly
crimes by the new legislative measure, but the original offences
punished with death by Lord Ellenborough's Act were, without
one omission, re-cast in the mould of the severest penalties.   It
now only remains that we should state the results of these stern
ministrations, and here, as in many other cases, we shall borrow
our principal aid from tables.

Results.

It is not our wish to detain the reader here with a detail of the disputes and broils of early days. Enough has been said under the head of murder to illustrate the effects of the punishments for personal injuries, because, as the greater number of wounds nave been inflicted with a design to take life, and as the same exciting causes will be found to have prompted those evil deeds, the consequences of severe penalties may be judged of almost as closely in the one case as in the other. Again, on the other hand, where the most deadly injury has not been intended by the stroke, there has been an indifference as to human life, a total want of care as to the consequences of the blow; and it will further be remembered, that in very many convictions for *murder*, it has appeared in evidence, that the intent to kill the person hurt has been absent. Thus, in unison with this last position, is the custom of foreigners newly come to this country, whose habits of assassination do not, perhaps, extend so far (on most occasions at least,) as the destruction of life. It seems, according to the various testimonies given at the Old Bailey, that the Portuguese, the Spaniard, the Lascar, inflict their wounds with a carelessness, which intimates rather the action of momentary revenge, than a desire to extinguish existence altogether. And the end of the argument is this—a man has often used a weapon hastily, without meaning to kill, but the party has died, and the murderer has perished on the scaffold. A man has not unfrequently struck with a deadly design, and the person has not died, whilst the criminal has sometimes forfeited his life, sometimes has been reprieved. Therefore, the results of capital punishment have operated equally in the cases of murder and of wounding, inasmuch as the offender who gives the blow is almost invariably without foresight as to the results of his act.

We will, however, mention a few facts very briefly. During the ancient carousals of the English, there were frequent stabbings, and deeds of vengeance; as the centuries advanced, these outrages seem rather to have been augmented by the violent conduct of thieves and cutpurses, and when James I ascended the throne, it was found that the fear of death was quite insufficient to check that mutual hatred which urged the Scotch and English to use the knife (*p*) against each other. Years rolled on; and, although in the days of Cromwell, a slight relaxation of licentiousness took place, it was but to dam up, for a moment, the tide of drunkenness and debauchery which defaced the reign of Charles. The rapier flourished, with the abuse of the bottle. Soon after this the offence of maiming decreased amongst the higher ranks, owing, without question to the gradual disuse of

(*p*) A short dagger which they wore. The phrase, " at daggers drawn," was familiar to those times.

swords, but, most of all, to the dawn of education. It was reserved for the robber, and a few victims to unbridled passion, to commit those excesses which, formerly, had scarcely any bounds In 1783 such cruelties were perpetrated on the highway, that the recorder was directed to make a special report to the king of those convicts who had plundered, under such circumstances of aggravation. The report was made, and five individuals quickly selected for execution; and the practice of treating offenders in that manner prevailed for some time It became necessary, however, to increase the vigilance of the police; and when the war broke out in 1793, robberies immediately declined. They were still more diminished during the long Bonapartean war; and it was not until the peace of 1814, that the calendar of the Old Bailey again presented a formidable catalogue of footpads and street-robbers. However, there was an interval of rest from war in 1802, and, upon reference to the tables, it will be discovered that the list was more than doubled immediately. This afforded a colour for the preamble to Lord Ellenborough's act, which stated, that "divers cruel and barbarous outrages had been wickedly and wantonly committed, either with an intent to murder, or to rob, or to maim," &c ; so that, notwithstanding the executions of 1783, and the following years (and they were severe enough), the offence of cruel robbery ceased only upon the sound of the trumpet, and revived again upon the approach of peace. Then, secondly, with respect to those persons who have been guilty of these sad offences through impulses of passion, they will be found in the pages of our calendars from time to time, sometimes in fewer, sometimes greater numbers, according to the prevalence of the temptations which have overcome them. Intemperance, revenge, want of self-command, passions of all kinds, have always maintained a succession of victims, and it is only through the progress of education that we shall be able hereafter to trace the decline of sudden violence. We invite attention to the following tables, reserving a very few observations for the close of the subject at the end of these written testimonies

---

I.—A Table of Executions in London and Middlesex, from 1731 to 1755, for Shooting and Stabbing.

Year	Ex.	Offence and Place.
1731—1749	Nil.	
1750	1	Shooting at an informer, whilst standing at his door, through malice.
1755	1	Shooting at a man on the York coach-box, who was defending the coach.—Total, 2. (q)

(q) From a MS.

II.—Table of Convictions and Executions in London and Middlesex, from 1756 to 1832, for Shooting, Stabbing, &c.

Year	Con.	Ex	Offence, &c.
1758	1	1	Shooting, with intent to rob on the highway.
1763	1	1	The like offence. (*r*)
1765	2	2	Coventry Act Slitting a gentleman's nose in the Strand, who had seized a boy in the act of picking his pocket.
1768	8	8	Coalheavers at Shadwell, shooting at Mr. Green, who had resisted their combination to raise the price of wages.
1770	1	1	Shooting at the executor of the prisoner's brother (malice)
1771	1	1	Shooting—malice—because the prosecutor had informed against the prisoner for poaching.
1773	2	1	1 Shooting at a person in the highway, with intent to rob.
			1 Shooting at a watchman in the street. Executed.
1774	1	0	Shooting at a magistrate in a passion, who had committed his servant. He was, probably, reprieved on the ground of insanity.
1775	1	0	Shooting at a patrol in the street, who was about to apprehend him.
1777	1	0	Shooting a man in his own house, under an idea that he had harboured the prisoner's wife.
1778 (*s*)	3	3	1 Shooting at a watchman, who was about to apprehend the prisoner in the act of burglary.
			1 A transport, shooting at the boatswain of a convict-ship, in an attempt to escape.
			1 Shooting at a woman in a fit of jealousy.
1782 (*t*)	2	2	1 Shooting—intent to rob in the street.
			1 Shooting—attempt to escape out of Newgate.
1783 (*t*)	1	1	Revenge — for preventing a robbery—Holborn.
1786	1	0	An Excise officer, shooting a porter in the street, whom he stopped with some brandy.

(*r*) A man was acquitted this year for cutting his wife's throat, because the maiming did not come within the Coventry Act.

(*s*) A man was convicted on the Coventry Act, but the judges decided in his favour for want of a sufficient lying in wait.

(*t*) These cases seem to be omitted in the Parliamentary Return.

Year	Con.	Ex.	Offence, &c.
1790	2	2	Shooting at a Custom-house boat.
1795	1	0	Shooting at a man in a dwelling-house (sudden impulse).
1797	2	2	Shooting at a corporal, out of revenge, because he was seeking for deserters.
1799	2	2	Shooting at Bow-street officers on Hounslow Heath—intent to rob.
1800	1	1	Shooting at a watchman, who disturbed prisoner in the act of burglary.
1802	1	0	Shooting at a man in his own house, intent to rob.
1803	1	0	Shooting at a man in the street, because he had refused to introduce the prisoner to a lady, for whom the latter had conceived a regard.
1804 (u)	4	0	2 Stabbing constables in the street 1 Stabbing a woman with an iron crow-bar Prisoner was endeavouring to escape, after having gone into a house to commit felony 1 Stabbing an officer, who had apprehended the prisoner stealing coals
1805	3	2	2 Stabbing a watchman in the street.—Burglary. 1 executed. 1 Stabbing a person in the street, who attempted to secure the prisoner. Executed (x)
1807 (y)	1	0	Shooting at a lady in Fleet-street (impulse).
1808	3	1	1 Stabbing a constable in the street in a riot. 1 Stabbing a woman in the street, because she refused to live with him. 1 Stabbing a servant, prisoner being disturbed in robbing a house. Executed.
1809 (z)	1	0	Stabbing a man in a public-house in a fit of drunkenness.

(u) Observe, that Lord Ellenborough's Act had now come into operation.

(x) This is the same person who was convicted of stabbing the woman in 1804. He made several blows at different people.

(y) Six persons *acquitted* for stabbing in this year.

(z) Acquitted this year — shooting, three, stabbing, four.

Year	Con.	Ex.	Offence, &c.
1810 (a)	3	1	1 Shooting at a woman in a house in a fit or bad temper.
			1 Attempting to shoot at a man in his own house, with intent to rob. Executed
			1 A girl of 14, attempting to poison her mistress out of revenge.
1811 (b)	4	2	2 Spaniards, stabbing a man coming from a public-house through a fancied affront. Executed.
			1 A Lascar seaman, who stabbed two men, the first for trying to secure him, in order that he might be sent back to his own country, the second, the person who was sent to apprehend him.
			1 A Portuguese, cutting a man in the street through a supposed affront.
1812 (c)	1	1	Shooting at a neighbour in the highway (malice, and lying in wait). (d)
1813 (e)	0	0	
1814 (f)	4	0	1 Stabbing a schoolmaster (sudden attack).
			1 Stabbing a shipmate in a quarrel, by a foreigner
			1 Stabbing a patrol with a hatchet (drunkenness)
			1 Stabbing a publican (passion)
1815 (g)	2	1	1 Stabbing his fellow-journeyman (sudden attack).
			1 Eliza Fenning, for administering poison. Executed.
1816 (h)	0	0	
1817 (i)	1	0	Cutting a woman-servant with a knife, who had disturbed the prisoner, in his attempt to rob the house.

(a) Six *acquitted* for stabbing.

(b) Two, stabbing ; one, attempting to shoot, acquitted.

(c) Acquitted, shooting 1, stabbing 3, and 1 no bill — 4.

(d) This was Bowler. His insanity was so certain, that, at the *present day*, no government could consent to ratify such an execution.

(e) Acquitted, attempting to shoot, 1 , stabbing, 3.

(f) Acquitted, shooting, 2 , stabbing, 7.

(g) Acquitted, shooting, 1 , attempt to shoot, 1 ; stabbing, 3.

(h) Acquitted, shooting, 1 , and 1, no bill — 2. Stabbing, 3, and 1 insane, 4.

(i) Acquitted, stabbing 4 , and 1, no bill.

Year	Con.	Ex.	Offence, &c.
1818 (*k*)	0	0	
1819 (*k*)	2	1	1 Stent, for stabbing his wife, upon a suspicion of her adultery. Reprieved
			1 Shooting a man on the highway, intent to rob Executed.
1820 (*k*)	2	1	1 A lad of 18, who stabbed a man for laughing, because he fell over a barrow Reprieved.
			1 Stabbing a watchman, intent to commit burglary Executed.
1821 (*l*)	2	1	1 Stabbing a person through jealousy. Executed.
			1 Stabbing a person, with intent to rob him
1822 (*m*)	1	0	Stabbing a man with a pitchfork, on account of his interfering between the prisoner and a woman, whom the latter kept.
1823 (*n*)	5	2	1 Stabbing (jealousy).
			1 Cutting a young woman with a hatchet (evidently deranged)
			1 Stabbing a man when asleep (revenge). Executed
			1 Stabbing his wife (jealousy, and constant disagreement) Executed.
			1 Stabbing a man, with whom he had a dispute about some property.
1824 (*o*)	5	2	3 Shooting on the highway, intent to rob. Two executed
			1 Shooting at General Burton (jealousy)
			1 Stabbing a watchman Attempting to escape, having committed burglary.
1825 (*p*)	2	0	1 A lad of 17, for stabbing a constable (passion)
			1 Stabbing a man with whom he had been fighting.
1826 (*q*)	0	0	
1827 (*r*)	1	0	Stabbing his wife in a passion.

(*k*) I have not been able to find any return of acquittals for these years.

(*l*) Acquitted, for the three offences of shooting, stabbing, and administering poison, 11. The Parliamentary Return for this year appears to be incorrect.

(*m*) Acquitted, 7 ; and 1, no bill.   (*n*) Acquitted, 6.

(*o*) Acquitted, 3.   (*p*) Acquitted, 5.

(*q*) Acquitted, 8 ; and no bill, 2 — 10.

(*r*) Acquitted, 6, and no bill, 1 — 6.

Year	Con.	Ex.		Offence, &c.
1828 (s)	5	2	1	Shooting (passion).
			1	Higgins, the fishmonger, for stabbing the street inspector (malice and drunkenness) Executed.
			1	Stabbing a man (sudden passion).
			1	Abbott, cutting his wife's throat (jealousy). Executed.
			1	Stabbing a man (jealousy).
1829 (t)	2	2 (u)	1	Shooting at a woman (jealousy). Executed.
			1	Attempting to strangle an infant. Executed.
1830 (x)	4	0	1	Stabbing his landlord in a passion, because he interfered between the prisoner and his wife.
			2	Stabbing a person with an umbrella, who was watching them when about to commit a robbery.
			1	Stabbing his wife (passion)
1831	6	0	1	Stabbing a policeman (revenge)
			1	Stabbing a policeman, about to apprehend a woman (passion).
			1	Stabbing a man for interfering in a quarrel (passion).
			1	A woman stabbing another woman in a passion (intoxication).
			1	Stabbing his wife (jealousy).
			1	A Portuguese stabbing a man in a quarrel.
1832	4	0	2	Intent to rob.
(to Sept. inclusive)			1	Striking his master with a piece of wood, in consequence of a dispute about wages. (revenge).
			1	Striking a man with a hammer in a quarrel.

Summary of the Motives, as in the case of Murder, ante. p 120.

Attempt to escape	.	.	4	Passion and quarrel	. 28
—— at infanticide			1	Revenge	. 1
Drunkenness		.	3	Riot	. . . 1
Impulse (sudden)	.	.	4	Robbery and burglary	. 27
Jealousy		.	11	Smuggling	. . . 1
Malice	.	.	20		

(s) Acquitted, 11, and no bill, 1 — 12.
(t) Acquitted, 6, and no bill, 1 — 7.
(u) The offence of attempting to strangle here, makes a fourth crime, under Lord Lausdowne's Act, and must, accordingly, be added to the list.   (x) Acquitted, 7, and no bill, 2 — 9.

II.—Table of Convictions and Executions on the Circuits, for
maliciously Shooting, Stabbing, &c

HOME, 1755—1817.

	Con.	Ex.
Shooting	25	10(y)
Stabbing, from 1804	19	8

WESTERN, 1770—1818

	Con.	Ex.
Shooting	27	5
Stabbing	0	0

OXFORD, 1799—1819. Lent Assizes.

	Con.	Ex.
Shooting and Stabbing . .	16 (z)	0

NORFOLK, 1768—1818.

	Con.	Left for Ex.
Shooting	17 (a)	4
Stabbing, from 1804 . . .	4	2

MIDLAND, 1805—1817, inclusive

	Con.	Ex.
Shooting	20 (b)	1
Stabbing	8	0
Administering poison, with intent to murder	1	1

NORTHERN, (c) 1804—1817.

	Con.	Ex.
Shooting	2	1 (d)
Stabbing	4	2 (d)
Administering poison, with intent to murder	1	0

DURHAM, 1755—1819. Lent Assizes

	Con.	Ex.
Shooting (e)	1	1
Cutting and maiming in 1814 . .	1	0

LANCASTER, 1798—1819 Lent Assizes.

	Con.	Ex.
Shooting, stabbing, &c. . . .	10	2

(y) Of which seven convictions took place in the year 1817.
(z) Very few of these were executed, but I have not been able to
procure accurate returns.
(a) Six of these in 1805 for shooting at one person.
(b) Ten of these in 1817.
(c) Westmoreland, Northumberland, Cumberland, York.
(d) The acquittals very numerous.   (e) Several acquittals.

III.—Table of Persons convicted, executed, acquitted, &c. for
Shooting, Stabbing, and administering Poison, in England and
Wales, from 1821—1830, without London and Middlesex

Year.	Con	Ex.	Acq no Bill, &c	Year.	Con.	Ex.	Acq. no Bill,&c.
1821	12	3	48	1826	14	1	33
1822	33	9	41	1827	35	5 (*f*)	47
1823	14	5	49	1828	20	5	52
1824	21	3	50	1829	65	10	50
1825	17	1	40	1830	28	1	52

We will add a few words to these tables. In considering
whether the capital punishment should be remitted for these offences, it is gratifying to observe, that the same difficulty does
not present itself, which induced us to hesitate in cases of
murder. The law of Moses permitted a compensation, or rather
a retaliation, for wounds It was the eye for the eye, the tooth
for the tooth, the wound for the wound. (*g*) We are, therefore,
referred to the original principle upon which English criminal
jurisprudence is supposed to proceed, namely, the *prevention of
crime.* And here we are met by a strange inconsistency, for an
attentive notice of the various cases will shew, that executions
have, in most instances, proceeded from the nature of the wounds,
and not from an independent consideration of the offence If a
man have been *grievously* hurt, the sentence of death has commonly
been carried into effect. This is *vengeance* upon the criminal.
If the mischief have been trifling, the prerogative of mercy has
been usually exercised, and thus the true principle has been entirely lost sight of, through the operation of an inconsistent selection of objects for punishment. Humanity shudders at the
infliction of grievous wounds, and therefore the Privy Council
have allowed the law to be enforced; but the real point is, whether
the executions have been productive of more command of temper,
and a greater dread of using the knife or the gun. Unless this
end shall have been accomplished, it appears useless to suffer our
feelings to interfere, by endeavouring to distinguish between severe and moderate injuries.

Now it may be fairly collected from the tables, that whenever
there has been a sufficient exciting cause, there has been a criminal of the class under discussion. We have already suggested
this, and need not dwell upon it The Spaniards who suffered
in 1811, for cutting one of our own countrymen, were not meritorious victims, so as to prevent the Lascar and the Portuguese
from committing similar outrages in the same year. Their ex-

(*f*) By another return, 6.
(*g*) Exod. xxi. 24, 25.

amples did not satisfy the principle of prevention Revenge, malice, passion, intemperance, will yield to education, but not to the scaffold. When a man raises his weapon to hurt his neighbour, the fear of death is never present with him, consequently a capital penalty in his case is inefficient, but the exercise of the moral energies will become so habitual through the means of education, that a man will rarely ever be betrayed into such a frame of mind, as to induce even the *temptation* of assaulting another. But, lastly, it seems that the crime of stabbing has not declined If the reader will consult the list of acquittals, he will find that the judge is for ever leaning to the side of mercy, that the jury are quite prepared to second his wishes; that, in many cases, the offence has not been proved, because, had death ensued, it would not have been murder, and, on the whole, that the number of cases in which there are verdicts of not guilty, are in the proportion of, at least, three to one (*h*) For these reasons, and under these circumstances, it is certainly desirable that the extreme punishment should be abolished It has been created during the rage of crime, but it has not answered its purpose It has afforded another instance of the futility of opposing violence by vindictive enactments, but it has failed in its object of raising the fear of death, because the principles of human nature are at variance with its ordinances.

Rape, &c.

1. Rape
2. Carnal Knowledge of Female Children under ten years of age
3 Administering Poison with intent to procure Miscarriage, the woman being quick with child.

These are the offences which more particularly regard females The two first have been the subjects of capital punishment for a long period, but the latter was one of the felonies created by Lord Ellenborough's Act, and continued by the late statute, 9 Geo 4 which consolidated the law of injuries relating to the person.

It is said, that rape was punished capitally amongst the ancient Goths, but however this may be, it is certain, that the Saxons were content for many years to visit it by pecuniary compensations, according to the condition of the party violated A widow, for instance, was to be indemnified by the payment of twice the amount of her *mundbyrd*, or estimated value of her protection under the laws of the realm. (*a*)   A virgin's honour was to be re-

---

(*h*) In London and Middlesex, and on the circuits, the proportion has been still greater.

(*a*) For, the disturbance of a widow was punished by fines accord-

deemed by a fine equal to the price of a freeman's head (b)   If, however, she were a slave, 50s were paid to the owner, whether her father or master, and if the owner pleased, the ravisher was compelled to buy her for his wife (c)   There was a difference if the person violated were with child. (d)   If the act were done by a *slave*, mutilation was the punishment, and the same penalty awaited persons of every degree who should compel a maiden of tender years. (e)   Then, with respect to married women, the fine for rape fluctuated according to their condition.   The forcing of a ceorl's wife was to be visited by a payment of 5s to the husband, and a fine of 60s (f)   If the ravished party were of an illustrious family, the offender was compelled to redeem his fault by the price of his life, (g) and it will be remembered, that a slave was to endure mutilation   And lastly, if a nun were the object of this violent lust, the criminal was declared unworthy of Christian burial, unless he should pay as high a redemption as in cases of murder. (h)   Thus matters continued until the reign of the Conqueror, if we except that the various pecuniary compensations were ratified from time to time by succeeding Saxon kings (i)— But let us just observe here, that many of our histories and Cyclopædias speak of a capital punishment for rape in the time of Athelstan, and they affirm, that the offence was capital till the Norman invader ruled here.   That the consequence of not paying the *were*, was death, we can readily allow, and in this sense we must understand the position laid down; but with respect to the statement concerning Athelstan, whoever will take the trouble to read through the laws of that monarch will find that no such severity was introduced by him. (k)   The system, in fact, was one of compensation for injuries, " which is the true reason that pecuniary punishments were so frequent, and corporal and capital punishments so uncommon, in those ages " (l)

Copying the example of the Saxon discipline in the case of slaves, William I. ordained castration as the penalty of an accomplished rape.   He punished the attempt by fine, and the con-

---

to the rank of the party.   Four ranks are enumerated (Turner's Anglo-Saxons, iii. 72.)   Mundbyrd signifies *patrocinium* (Spelman's Glossary).   Wilkins, Leg. Anglo-Saxon. p 7, pl. 75.   Turner. ii. 495.
  (b) Wilkins, p 6, pl 73.   (c) Id. p. 7, pl. 81.
  (d) Id. pl. 83.
  (e) That is, immature—non tempestiva.   Wilkins, Leges Ælfredi, p. 40, pl 25.   (f) Id. p 37. pl. 10.
  (g) Id. ibid. pl 11.   (h) Id. p. 73. pl. 4.
  (i) See Wilkins, p. 123, and p. 142.   Leges Cnuti, pl. 49 & 52.
  (k) Neither in his Laws, nor in the Judicia Civitatis Lundoniæ.   See Wilkins, pp. 54-72.   Reeves, ii. 38, 125
  (l) Henry's Great Britain, 8vo. iii. 421.

summation by mutilation. (*m*)   And now the tide of barbarous justice was fast setting in, of that retribution which consigned one man to the fire, another to the rack, another to emasculation, a fourth to the boiling cauldron

In the time of Bracton, they proceeded to put out the eye which beheld lustfully, as well as to destroy the offending members; but it may be added, that the severity of the infliction depended much upon the character and the will of the woman. (*n*)   For in early times, if she consented to marry her ravisher, the demands of the law were satisfied.   And it was customary for such a result to take place, the union being quite optional on the woman's part. (*o*) Edward the First, the English Justinian, produced an entire revolution with respect to the incidents of this crime   His ordinance concerning it led to the abolition of the old laws and usages upon the subject.   His plan was to try a very mitigated penalty, and he awarded two years' imprisonment, together with fine at his discretion, against all ravishers of women and children. (*p*)

However, as there was now no longer any money payment for the injury, the experiment did not answer, for fine and ransom to the Crown had not the same effect as a pecuniary compensation to the aggrieved woman.   Accordingly, the mischief increased, as it is said, (*q*) nay more, the lenity was productive of most terrible consequences, (*r*) and the legislature, not having a notion of raising the moral energies of the people, had immediate recourse to the pains of felony, (*s*) and we have remained in the same condition ever since.   For as soon as the art of reading became sufficiently known to bring offenders within the benefit of clergy, a statute of Queen Elizabeth was made, excluding (amongst many others,) all felonious ravishers from the privilege   And a similar denunciation took place against those who should abuse any woman-child under the age of ten years (*t*)   Thus, for five centuries, we have virtually had a capital punishment for rape, by reason of the ignorance of early times, and the penalty has been direct for nearly three hundred years.

Results.—Now, with respect to the consequences of this severe penal infliction, it will appear from the number of acquittals, both at the Old Bailey and on the Circuits, that juries have been most unwilling to convict, and instead of protecting the injured honour of a woman, the feeling has been, for the most part, to save the

---

(*m*) Wilkins, p. 222, pl. 19.   See id. p. 242.

(*n*) Reeves, ii. 38.

(*o*) Glanvill, lib. 14. c. 6.   See also Fleta, lib. 1. c. 33.   The Mirror, cap. 2. § 21.

(*p*) Reeves, ii. 125.   Russell, ed. 1819, p. 800.   East, 434.

(*q*) Russell, p. 801.   (*r*) Ibid.

(*s*) Reeves, ii. 211.   About ten years after the passing of the former act.   (*t*) Reeves, v. 118.

criminal. The truth is, that the offence has been pretty generally visited by execution, especially in the cases of violating infants, but neither with regard to grown persons nor to children has the mischief diminished in the least. Human nature has remained the same, its depravities have continued to break forth, sometimes in a greater, sometimes a less degree, but so far from being affected by capital punishment, it will be found, that in 1816, and 1824, there were the fewest committals for rape after a most striking and unprecedented number of acquittals Lord Hale has said, that rape is a most detestable offence, but that it is an accusation easily to be made, and hard to be proved, and harder to be defended by the party accused, though never so innocent (*u*) The truth of this observation has been so sincerely felt, that the number of bills for rape ignored throughout the country, together with the catalogue of acquittals, is prodigious. And it is not pleasing to reflect, that many cases of capital conviction have taken place upon the most fallacious testimony. There is another reason also for the extremely small list of convictions for the greater offence It is most familiar to lawyers, who are compelled in the discharge of their duty, to see that the injury to the woman has been consummated, or at all events, that the most pregnant evidence is laid before the jury to that effect. This difficulty, although it may have enhanced the page of acquittals, cannot apply to the bills which have been returned, ignoramus We have referred to the books where the necessary information upon this point may be found (*x*)

It is not our intention to enlarge upon this subject here, but let us reverse the picture for a moment, and see how juries have dealt with indictments for assaults with intent to ravish The reader will find a table in the note, (*y*) and his conclusion must

---

(*u*) Historia Placitorum Coronæ, p. 635

(*x*) Wilkins, Leges Anglo-Sax. p. 222, pl. 19. Si compresserit. Russell on Crimes, ed. 1819, p. 803-807 Moody and Malkin's Reports, vol. ii. p. 123, in the note. Russell's Case. East's Pleas of the Crown, p. 436-441.

(*y*) Rape — Seven Years — England and Wales

Convicted, 51—Executed, 19—Acquitted, &c 264—Total charged, 315.

Assaults, with intent to Ravish.—Same period.

	Con.	Acq		Total charged.
1824	43	26	(Acq. 12, No bill, 14)	69
1825	42	23	(Acq 17, No bill, 6)	65
1826	83	34	(Acq. 16, No bill, 18)	117
1827	64	47	(Acq. 27, No bill, 20)	111
1828	78	50	(Acq. 31, No bill, 19)	128
1829	69	39	(Acq. 25, No bill, 14)	108
1830	41	46	(Acq. 28, No bill, 18)	87

So that, as the capital convictions decrease, and the executions become

be self-evident, when he reflects that, as the catalogue of malicious shootings and stabbings swells the list of intended murders, so these lustful attacks augment the calendar of rapes, as far as the intent can be considered ; and, consequently, as far as the *capital punishment applies*

Instances of the practical mischief of such a penalty in cases of rape will be given hereafter, and we will, therefore, conclude by observing, that since the days of the Saxons, indecent outrages have been increasing, and that the merit of our ancestors consisted not so much in their rules of pecuniary compensation, as in "their high estimation and rigorous exaction, even among the servile, of female virtue " (z)

I.—Table of Convictions and Executions in London for Rape, &c. from 1699 to 1755.

Those marked thus* are cases of abuse of female children under 10.

Year.	Con.	Ex. (a)
1706	1*	1*
1709	1	0
1721	1*	1*
Total	3	2

II.—Table of Executions for London and Middlesex, from 1731 to 1755. (M.S.)

Those with this mark † are cases of children.

Year.	Ex.	Year.	Ex.	Year.	Ex.
1733	1	1739	2	1744	1†
1735	4	1740	1(b)	1748	1
				Total	10

---

fewer, the crime itself (as in 1830) declines. This is owing to *education.* Observe the small proportion which the acquittals bear to the convictions in the cases of the minor offence.

(z) Turner's Anglo-Saxon Hist. iii. 75

(a) There were other convictions at the Old Bailey for Middlesex, and *many acquittals.*—See Trials (1718) ii. pp. 274, 276. Trials (1742) i. pp. 14, 24, 97, 198, 308, 310, 34 , 369 , vol. ii. pp. 202, 296, 299, 303, 318 , vol. iii. pp. 40, 51, 66, 71, 95, 196, 234. Many of these cases, we must regret to say, were rapes upon infants, and the acquittals were as three, if not four to one, of the *capital* offence.

(b) The woman died in this case, but the jury brought in a verdict of natural death.

III. Table of Convictions and Executions from 1756 to 1830.

Year	Con.	Ex.	Year	Con.	Ex.
1762	3	0	1801	1	1
1766	1	1	1808	1	0
1767	1 spec. verd		1809	2	2
1768	1	0	1810	1	0
1769	2	1	1815	1	1
1773	1	1	1816	1	0
1777	1	1	1817	1	1
1778	1	1	1821	1	0
1779	1	1	1822	1	0
1780	1	0	1825	1	1
1793	1	0	1826	1	1
1794	1	1	1827	1	0
1796	2	2(d)	1829	2	0
1797	1	1	1830	0	0
1798	1	1			

Committals and Acquittals for Rape, in London and Middlesex, from 1805 to 1817.

Year	Con.	Acq.	Year	Con.	Acq.
1805	5	5	1812	6	6
1806	5	5	1813	4	4
1807	4	4	1814	2	2
1808	4	3	1815	7	6
1809	6	4	1816	2	1
1810	5	4	1817	5	4
1811	5	4			

The same, from 1821 to 1830.

Year	Con.	Acq.	Year	Con.	Acq.
1821	4	3	1826	4	3
1822	5	4	1827	5	4
1823	6	6	1828	3	3
1824	2	2	1829	9	7
1825	7	6	1830	10	10

IV.—Table of Convictions and Executions on the Circuits.

		Con.	Ex.
Home	1689—1718	7	3
	1755—1817	43	25
	Total	50	28
Western	1770—1818	29	20
Oxford	1799—1819 (Lent)	6 (e)	0

(d) Here the Parl. Return gives only one ; but two persons, named Davenport and Scott, were certainly executed in this year.

(e) No return of specific executions during the *whole* time

		Con.	Ex.
Midland	1805—1817	5	0
Norfolk	1768—1818 (Lent)	17	11
Lancaster	1798—1819 (Do.)	5	2
Durham	1755—1819 (Do)	1	0(g)
Northern	1804—1817	8	6

V.—Table of Committals, &c. in England and Wales, from 1821 to 1830.

Year	Com.	Con.	Ex.	Acq.	No Bills.
1821	39	6	3	33	[acq. 16—no b. 17]
1822	49	10	6	39	[acq 14—no b. 25]
1823	48	11	8	37	[acq 22—no b 15]
1824	46	9	3	37	[acq. 16—no b 21]
1825	43	6	3	37	[acq 20—no b. 17]
1826	29	4	2	25	[acq. 14—no b. 11]
1827	48	11	2	37	[acq. 20—no b 17]
1828	41	5	3	36	[acq. 23—no b. 13]
1829	54	7	3	47	[acq 30—no b. 17]
1830	54	9	3	45	[acq 27—no b. 18]

Sodomy and Bestiality.

From the consideration of rapes upon infants, cruelties at which every man of moral energy must shudder, we descend by an easy transition to the lowest and deepest shades   Justly, indeed, have writers shewn their hatred of the most abominable propensities of nature, but whilst they have declared their resolution to make the least possible mention of those deeds, it has been found impossible to avoid such explanations as the subject itself demands. We shall follow their example of brevity, but must record fearlessly our opinion upon the expediency of punishing with death the crime ' *inter Christianos non nominandum* '(k)

The punishment of death has been, however, awarded against it for many generations.

So strong indeed was the vengeance which men entertained against the criminals, that the measure of punishment was the chief thing thought of. The old Goths either burnt or buried alive the victims, and these tokens of vengeance continued for many centuries (*l*) But there was an interval, for although

---

(*f*) The grand jury ignored the bills for rapes on several occasions.

(*k*) So called, because at the coming of Christ the Pagans were unusually given up to such practices, and the apostles strongly commended their converts not *even to mention* those as well as other indecencies.

(*l*) Blackstone, iv. 216.

Alfred included the crime of bestiality amongst his class of capital offences,(m) it seems that in the reign of Edgar, both that and sodomy were visited by the ecclesiastical discipline of fasting, and abstinence from the Lord's supper (n) However, matters did not long continue thus. In the reign of William I., it is probable that castration was the penalty, and very soon afterwards, we are assured, that the old custom of burning and burying were the law of the land in this respect.(o) But when Richard I. came to the throne, the punishments were again altered, and it was the rule to hang a man and drown a woman (p)

Notwithstanding this, it is said that the Lombards introduced the vice into England in Edward the Third's time.(q) Probably they revived it here, and it is likely that it continued more or less until the days of Henry VIII, when an act passed, making it felony without benefit of clergy, and although the repealing act of Queen Mary interrupted the course of punishment for a moment, the fifth of Elizabeth re-enacted the statute of Henry entirely and absolutely.(r) Women then suffered by the rope as well as men, and the law on the subject has remained the same to this present day, the consolidating act of Lord Lansdowne (s) merely declaring that the two offences under consideration shall be punished with death.

Two reasons will perhaps be offered in vindication of the extreme infliction in this case First, the prevention of the crime Secondly, the Divine command Blackstone puts it thus —— " This the voice of nature and of reason, and the express law of God, determined to be capital " (d) We will say a few words upon the point in this place, because, although we shall return to other offences in a future chapter, it is by no means our wish to mention this uninviting topic any more. Now as to the voice

---

(m) Wilkins, Leg. Angl Sax. p 31, pl. 31.

(n) Id. p. 90, pl. 16 Hayward writes thus —— " But afterwards it was esteemed fit, that this general excommunication should be repealed. The pretence was, for that the prohibiting, yea, the public naming of that vice, might inflame the hearts of ungracious persons with desire unto it. But wise men conjectured, that after this severe restraint of marriage in the clergy, it did grow so frequent and familiar among them, that they would not give way to so general a punishment.—Lives of the Norman Kings. p. 295.

(o) Russell, ed. 1819. p 814, note, citing Britton, who states the punishment to be burning, and Fleta and the Mirror, calling it burying alive. Reeves, ii. 252.   (p) 3 Inst. 58.

(q) Coke's Reports, xii. 37. Blackstone, iv. 215. Colquhoun on the Police, p. 46

(r) Reeves, iv. 317. Id. v. 125. Russell, ut ante, p. 815. n. (b).

(s) Which repealed that of Henry VIII.

(d) Commentaries, vol. iv. p. 215.

of nature, that is the voice of vengeance, and therefore cannot be
listened to   Such a voice would often condemn a man to die for
a deed of which he might be entirely innocent. Such a voice
would outstrip the just indignation which every man must feel
against the crime. The voice of reason is entitled to more consideration   But inasmuch as the diligent reader of the tables
which we have subjoined will find that the punishment of death
gives no test whatever of the prevalence of the crime, as the
number of acquittals for the greater offence will be found infinitely beyond those for the lesser, and as the executions themselves will appear to have been sufficiently rigorous, a reasonable
man will pause before he gives his sanction to the continuance
of the capital penalty. The truth is, that notwithstanding the
most inexorable strokes of justice, the horrid propensity has
multiplied amongst us lately. And yet, while we cannot but
allow this, we are enabled to admit, on the other hand, that if a
man be not indicted capitally, juries will do their duty, and will
consign an offender to the oblivion which he deserves. Thus the
expediency of punishing the crime capitally, is nullified by the
results of severity, on the one hand, and of the mitigated proceedings on the other (e) Still there remains the consideration
of the Divine command. And there is no doubt but that, in the
sight of God, it is a most grievous and awful sin, and that His
holy eyes must turn away from such a violation of His own image
with disgust. There is not any question, also, but that He ordered the immediate execution of the Sodomite, or unnatural
person, (f) but, in the very same chapter, there is an equal denunciation against adultery, cursing of father and mother, sooth-
saying, incantations, and diviners. Will it be urged, that adultery
and abuse of parents should be forthwith punished with death?
The reason fails at once, and it is not necessary to dwell upon

---

(e) See also Colquhoun, p. 46. " It has been doubted, however,"
says the learned writer, whether the severity of the punishment of a
crime so unnatural as even to appear incredible, does not defeat the
object of destroying it, by rendering it difficult to convict an offender."

(f) See Leviticus, ch xx. v. 13, and 15, 16, not to mention his destruction of Sodom and Gomorrah. It seems that no fair argument
can be drawn from 1 Kings, ch. xxii. v. 4, 6, (Vulgate, 3 Kings) where
it is said, that Jehoshaphat took out of the land the remnant of the So-
domites. For first, the theocratical government had ceased, although
the Jews were still the favourite nation of God, and, therefore, the king
of Judah acted according to his discretion, as we do at this day. And,
secondly, the Hebrew word בער may well signify, to clear quite away,
to banish   As in a law mentioned by Wilkins, " Si alienigeni coitus
suos dirigere nolint e regione cum possessionibus et peccatis suis exter-
minentur." p. 142, pl. 52. Moreover, if our translators had thought
that בער inflicted a capital punishment, they would have said *consumed,
burnt with fire*, because the word has both these meanings.

the subject. But the truth is, that the Israelites lived under the immediate government of God, as their *King.* In the sight of such a monarch there could be no perversion of justice, no distorting of evidence, no doubt as to guilt or innocence. The same Being ruled over the Jews, whose searching Spirit compelled Achan to give up the scarlet garment and the two hundred shekels of silver. The cloudy pillar was with the people; the presence of their God was manifested, the ark of the covenant, with the ceremonies, dwelt in the midst of them—every possible revelation was afforded that they lived under a theocracy. And when at length they asked another King, the Most High Ruler was displeased with their ingratitude. Can we draw a comparison between the *judicial evidence* of those times and our own? The conclusion (I firmly believe) is, that we have have no right to put any man to death, for any crime whatever, unless in the *immediate* defence of ourselves, our properties, our internal peace as a nation, and our country at large.

Education, *moral* and *political*, will lessen this offspring of indecency. (g) It will lead to the multiplication of capital, with comfort and *economy*, it will endear the ties of legitimate and *prudent* marriages, and, above all, will ensure that command of temper, which, while it controls natural, will also restrain unlawful lusts. The baser herd, if any there shall be, will then take refuge in a corner Beset by the more stinging pains of *moral outlawry*, they will tremble at the very light of heaven; and, as their ranks thin through disease and death, few—none, perhaps, will succeed them, for the glory of universal intelligence will shine, and men at large will have LEARNT THE RESPECT DUE to their natures.

I —Table of Convictions and Executions, in London, for Sodomy, from 1699 to 1755.—(Parl Papers, 1819, viii. p. 146)

Year.	Con.	Ex.
1725-6	2 (h)	2
1727-8	1	1
1729-30	1	1
Totals . . .	4	4

(g) We meet with cases of sodomy chiefly in towns, of beastiality in the country (as the returns will prove), but let us always add, that neither offence is at present by any means predominant, when we consider the dense mass of population.

(h) It appears, however, that there were two other convictions, and another execution in this year. In fact, there was a gang of these bad persons, and the witness against them, an accomplice, deposed to the

II.—Table of Convictions and Executions for Sodomy and Bestiality, from 1756 to 1830, for London and Middlesex.—(Parl. Papers, 1819, viii p 154.)

Years.	Con.	Ex.	Years.	Con.	Ex.
1757	1	0	1808 .	1	0
1761 ...	1	0	1809 ...	1	1
1770	1	1	1810	2	2
1772 ..	1 (*i*)	0	1814 . .	1	1
1776 .	. 2	2	1815 ...	1	1
1796 '	. 1	1	1816	2	2
1797 ..	1	0	1819 (*l*) .	1	1
1803 .	1	1	1820 ...	1	1
1804 ..	1	0	1822 ..	3	3
1806 (*k*) .	1	1	1828 . .	2	0
			Totals . .	26	18

Assaults with Intent to commit, &c.—7 Years. London and Middlesex.

Years.	Con.	Acq	No bill.	Years.	Con	Acq.	No bill.
1824	6	2	2	1828	14	4	10
1825	14	3	2	1829	6	4	6
1826	3	4	1	1830	19	10	13
1827	9	9	3				

singular fact, that he had been abominably connected with three of them, and they were all executed. There were several acquittals, and many cases of misdemeanour, but for the honour of human nature, the crimes of this kind from 1699 to 1755, have no mentionable proportion to those of rape, although we do not propose, of course, to justify the latter offence.

Note.—The capital convictions in London *and Middlesex* from 1731 to 1756 were very rare indeed, *if any*, and there were not many cases for the attempt.

(*i*) This case is not in the Parliamentary Report. The man was not executed.

(*k*) In 1805, Acq. &c.	1	In 1821, Acq &c.	2
1806, —	2	1823, —	5
1807, —	2	1825, —	2
1809, —	1	1826, —	1
1810, —	2	1827, —	2
1812, No bill, &c.	2	1828, No bill,	1
1815, Acq &c.	2	1830, Acq &c.	3

I have not the return of acquittals for 1818, 19, 20.   Total, 7 Years, 16

(*l*) These years, 1819 and 20, are from a MS.

Assaults with Intent, &c — 7 Years.— England and Wales, 1821 to 1830

Years.	Com.	Conv.	Acq.	No bill	Years.	Com.	Conv.	Acq.	No bill.
1821	16	7	3	6	1826	35	20	11	4
1822	33	23	5	5	1827	45	23	13	9
1823	44	27	7	10	1828	60	27	10	23
1824	27	15	4	8	1829	35	14	8	13
1825	40	25	10	5	1830	62	28	17	17

III.— Convictions and Executions, for similar Offences, on the Circuits.

	Years.	Con.	Ex.
Home	1689—1718—*nil*		
,,	1755—1817	15	13
Western . . .	1770—1818 , ...	7	4
Oxford . .	1799—1819, Lent Assizes	3	No return of ex
Midland .	1805—1817	3	0
Norfolk . . .	1768—1818	4	3
Durham . .	1755—1819, Lent Assizes—*nil*		
Lancaster . .	1798, Lent—1819		
,,		1805	5	6
,,		1810 . 1	1
Northern . .	1804—1817	1	0

IV.— Committals, Convictions, Executions, Acquittals, &c. in England and Wales, from 1821 to 1830.

Years.	Committed.	Conv.	Exec.	Acquit.	No bill.
1821 12		1	0	3	8
1822 . . 13		4	4	5	4
1823 18		3	3	6	9
1824 13		1	1	9	3
1825 9		2	2	4	3
1826 . . 4		1	1	3	0
1827 . . 11		1	1	7	6
1828 . 12		2	0	3	7
1829 10		1	1	6	3
1830 . . 20		5	4	8	7

SECTION IV.

Of Capital Punishments in England for offences against Property.

WE have gone through the offences against the government, those against religion and those which concern the persons of individuals, and have now arrived, fourthly, and lastly, at the crimes which affect property

If a person deprive another of his money, or goods, by putting him in fear, this is *Robbery* If a house be broken open for this purpose, or fraudulently entered, *in the night, whether any thing be taken or not*, it is *Burglary* If the breaking take place in the day-time, and there be an *accompanying theft*, this is *House-breaking.* If the robbery, or attack, be made upon the high seas, it becomes the offence of *Piracy*, and there is the *Plunder of a Wreck.* All these are capital crimes, and relate to some act of *stealing*, or an *intent* to commit depredations

The following are malicious injuries to property.

Arson, i e. the burning of houses, and other buildings, (*a*) and *Burning*, of any stack of corn, grain, pulse, straw, hay, or wood, (*b*) and of ships. (*c*) *Riotous demolishing of property*, (*d*) and *endeavouring to cause a shipwreck, damaging a shipwrecked vessel*, or *hindering a shipwrecked person in the act of saving his life.* These also are punishable with death (*e*)

We must beg the attention of the reader while we advert to each of these crimes, assuring him, at the same time, that we will not dwell a moment longer upon any one of them than the subject may reasonably demand. First, then, of

Robbery.

We shall begin with the history, and then proceed to the results of the punishment for this crime.

The most common robberies have been on the highway, and in houses "Highway robbery was, from the earliest times, a sort of national crime," says Hallam "Capital punishments, though very frequent, made little impression on a bold and licentious crew, who had, at least, the sympathy of those who had nothing to lose on their side, and flattering prospects of impunity." (*f*) Men inherited the principles of the ancient Germans, amongst whom robbery was a laudable enterprise, if committed without the territories of the state to which the plunderers belonged. (*g*) And from these loose notions of property we can easily trace the bold recklessness which distinguished the Falstaff, and the outlaw of Sherwood Forest. Our ancestors, always saving of human life, decreed that robbery should be punished by a penalty of 6 shillings, and rapine (*h*) by the restoration of the booty, and a

(*a*) Mentioned in the second section of 7 & 8 Geo. 4. c. 30.
(*b*) See the 17th section   (*c*) Sect. 9.
(*d*) Sect. 8.   (*e*) See Ch. 2. Sect. 1. supra.
(*f*) Middle Ages, ii. 376, 377.
(*g*) Henry's Great Britain, i 208, ii. 291.
(*h*) Wilkins, p. 3. pl. 19.
(*i*) Wilkins, Leg. Ang. Sax. p. 17, pl. 10 Leges Inæ, and see id. pl. 12.

fine of 60s (*i*) And there again was the restriction above alluded to, '*provided the deed were committed within the bounds of our kingdom,*' (*k*) otherwise it was no offence If the convicted person were the leader of a band exceeding thirty-five men, he was compelled to pay his *were*, or the price of his life (*l*) The same system, again, was pursued in the days of Ethelred and Canute, only that the *were* was required, instead of the simple restitution and fine (*m*) When William the Norman came to the throne, it is well known that he mixed his own customs with the Saxon laws, as well as that he abolished capital penalties throughout England The punishment of robbers, therefore, continued the same But Henry I took away the weregild from theft and robbery (*n*) In his day outrages and plunder had greatly increased, and it was not surprising that he should fall into the plausible error, that death would arrest the number of depredators A man named Dunne was a cause of particular annoyance He flourished in some ' mighty woods,' near the junction of the Watling and Ickening ways, and the monarch, hearing of his exploits, ordered the forest to be cleared away, and founded a borough there. *Dunstable* was soon a safe and populous place, famous for its fairs and market, its palace, and priory. (*o*)

We have now done with the history of the punishment for robbery It was made capital, we find, in the reign of the first Henry, and it remains the same at this day. However, a man might take advantage of the trial by duel , and there was the appeal of the *crimen roberiæ*, which compelled the accused to venture the combat, or suffer the legal purgation. (*p*) And, if the robber were taken on the hue and cry, it seems that he could not avail himself of the duel (*q*) Upon the discontinuance of these tests the offence was deemed felony, and for many years criminals, being unable to read, were hanged. But, at length, learning revived, and thieves began to " bear themselves bold of their clergy," so that the legislature interfered, and debarred them of that privilege, first, in respect of *highway* robberies, and afterwards, generally, whether in the road, in a house, or elsewhere. (*r*) And, lastly, the consolidating act, passed in the last

---

(*k*) Ibid.   (*l*) Wilkins, p. 17, pl. 15

(*m*) Id p. 118, and p. 143, pl. 60, Leg. Cnuti. See also Henry, ii. 289-292.

(*n*) Latrocinium Wilkins, p. 304 and 242, [Roberia]. Reeves, i. 193. The punishment was hanging, but in Chester they used the custom of beheading for some time afterwards. Colquhoun, p. 52. " No money should save thieves from hanging," said Henry I.—Hayward, p. 284

(*o*) Hayward's Norman Kings, p. 282.

(*p*) Reeves, i. 199.   (*q*) Ibid.

(*r*) Reeves, iv 316, 470, 478, and see p. 538. Russell, ed. 1819, p. 987

reign, makes robbery, by name, a capital offence   It may just be added, that the assault, with intent to rob, incurs a mitigated penalty, although it was once understood, that " if a man comes to rob me, and I am stronger than he, and overcome him, yet is he guilty of felony."   This opinion prevailed for some time, and only yielded in the reign of Edward IV. (s)   Thus, we have briefly shewn that robbery has been punished with death in this country from the early part of the thirteenth century, excepting only two short intervals when the benefit of clergy interfered.   The first of these was very partial, and lasted for a few years in the reigns of Henry VII and Henry VIII when robbers read for their lives; after which clergy was taken away from highwaymen   The second continued till 3 and 4 William and Mary, when all robbers were deprived of their reading privileges   But we will forthwith proceed to examine the results of the punishment, and see how it happened that neither this nor any other severity operated upon the principles which govern the customs (t) and causes of plunder.

Results —If Buonaparte called us, with more truth than people are willing to allow, a nation of shopkeepers, we might well be christened, in early times, a nation of robbers   Not that this remark applies to the days of the Saxons, to those wise eras when a man was bound, like the sow-gelder in Don Quixote, to wind his horn for a signal of his approach, when a host was responsible for the conduct of his visiter, and when he who stole was made to yield a goodly recompence to the plundered   In those days a person might go in safety from one end of Britain to the other, for there was, in fact, a greater unity of interest and privileges amongst our countrymen   If a theft were committed, a kinsman would strive to raise the weregild, and the offender dared not trespass a second time upon the bounty of his relations, or, perhaps, he would have to undergo the purgation of the legal ordeal, and no one would bribe the priest a second time in his behalf   Or he might find compurgators to answer for his behaviour, and these would hardly screen him from a second charge.   Life was not so much the precious toy, as the well-being of a man in society was valuable to him   But when the Norman invasion swallowed up the credulous, brave, and much calumniated English, a system of criminal jurisprudence was introduced, from which we have never recovered   The Conqueror, indeed, abolished capital punishment, but he laid waste the coun-

---

(s) Reeves, iii. 413.
(t) Such as cruelty, violence, on the one hand, — mercy, forbearing conduct on the other.

try from the Ouse to the Trent, from the Trent to the Humber. He multiplied and heightened the temptation to rob by impoverishing his subjects; and the disrespect which his successors manifested towards capital, augmented the distress and the highwaymen Rufus, indeed, was so inconsistent, as to declare to the Jews, that if they would fight against the Christians, and overcome, he would be one of their sect. (*u*) Henry I brought in the death-sentence for robbery. At this time, so far from being in a peaceful condition, the country was full of marauders. The example of their chiefs had vitiated the principles of the people, and the infliction of death only served to make them more daring The rapacity of the sovereigns, the lawless incursions of the barons, the griping avarice of the clergy, were circumstances which aggravated the evil. Whole villages were plundered, and a guilty participation in these wrongs was clearly traced to the royal household (*x*) In fact, the league and covenant of plunderers was established, and it has never been dissolved Dunne ravaged Bedfordshire (*y*), Robin Hood rallied his merry men in Sherwood Forest (*z*), Sir Gosselin Denville, with his band of outlaws, settled in the North (*a*) About this time also, the pope having sent over two cardinals to mediate a peace between Edward II. and the Scots, Sir Gilbert de Middleton and Sir Walter de Selby surprised and robbed them But this was too great an exploit, and, accordingly, they were seized and executed (*b*) Just before this, however, in the reign of Edward the First, it had become necessary to provide against the murderers, incendiaries, robbers, and thieves, which infested the country; and certain officers, called judges of traile-baston, (*c*) were sent into various parts of the kingdom, and they are said to have executed their commissions with much spirit (*d*) Yet it may be observed, that the demand for such a severe inquisition arose out of the Scottish war, (*e*) which bred many dissolute and mischievous spirits; and we have seen, that the next reign afforded ample instances of unsubdued freebooters. And it is not unworthy of remark, that a most formidable army of robbers, which ravaged France in the reign of Edward III. were disbanded soldiers. (*f*) The truth is, that the conduct of the monarchs was the most ob-

---

(*u*) Stow's Chronicles, p. 129. (*x*) Hume, ii. 227, 228.
(*y*) Temp. Henry I. (*z*) Temp Richard I.
(*a*) Temp. Edward II. Lives of Highwaymen, p. 15. Life of Edward II. by E. F. p. 43. (*b*) Ibid.
(*c*) Traybaston — Trahe baculum.
(*d*) Henry's Great Britain, iv. 372.
(*e*) Spelman's Glossary in Voc. Trailebaston.
(*f*) Barnes's Edward III. p. 611.

vious harbinger of thieves   In fact, "the Crown carried on the war against capital with an industry that could not be exceeded by that of the nobles, or the people."(g)   Depopulated villages, ruined trade, uncultivated fields, were amongst the sad incidents of that period. If there were any drawback upon the invasions of the sovereign and the clergy, it was accomplished by merchants, who, in their turn, fortified their commercial guilds with most anti-economical monopolies.   Thus the rich formed one class, the poor another   The freebooter flourished; and it is not a little curious to observe, that these independent plunderers were amongst the first to disencumber themselves from the trammels of priestcraft.   They thought it an excellent hit if a monk passed by their track   But we must hasten   Are not our earliest recollections imbued with the fat knight?   How can we forget the man of Gad's Hill, the executioner of the executioner, him to whom it was once said, "Make thy body less, and thy grace more," but who had the wit to answer— "Do not grieve at this, Master Shallow, I shall be sent for in private to him; he must seem thus to the world."   Falstaff died about the 1st or 2d year of Henry V. broken-hearted, because he was reprieved for transportation, after a capital conviction at Maidstone Assizes.

The wars of York and Lancaster were not calculated to restore domestic peace, and we must not start, therefore, to hear that 72,000 persons died on the scaffold in the reign of Henry VIII, of whom many were robbers (h)   Indeed Sir John Fortescue, in Henry VI.'s reign, made it a boast, that more Englishmen were hanged for robbery in one year than French in seven.   And the Chief-Justice also observed, that "if an Englishman be poor, and see another having riches, which may be taken from him by might, he will not spare so to do"(i)   The suppression of the monasteries, the inefficient poor-law which succeeded, the interference with the wages of labour; the rigid ordinances against paupers, the self-willed absolutism in matters of religion—were combinations of blunders which could not fail to perpetuate the race of robbers in the days of good Queen Bess, and the unpromising Stuarts   But it could lead to no practical result if I were to go into the history of thieving in these times; and the time would fail me to tell of the famous Captain Hind, of Claude Du Val, of Colonel Jack, Thomas Savage, the GOLDEN FARMER, (k) Nicholas

(g) Rights of Industry, sect. 1, p. 81.
(h) "As to housebreakers, and robbers on the highway, no body thought of saving them from the gallows, and yet the number of robberies did not decrease "—Letters on Capital Punishments, p. 13, 1770.
(i) Hallam's Middle Ages, ii. 377
(k) Whence Golden Farmer Hill in the Western Road, just beyond Bagshot.

Horner, and many other such worthies.(*l*) It seems, however, that in 1649 a price was set upon highwaymen's heads, like the wolves' in King Edgar's days; for there were two orders of Parliament first, to give 10*l.* to every one who should bring in a highwayman; and, secondly, to give reprieves to persons guilty of robberies, if they should discover any of their accomplices. (*m*) And now, if the reader please, we will advance to the year 1689, from whence we have a flow of regular tables, which will enable us to demonstrate, with greater accuracy, the hopelessness of persevering in the use of the rope for this offence A particular mark has been made to distinguish the years of war from those of peace, because our ancestors had an idea (and a very just notion it was) that disbanded soldiers most frequently became audacious robbers Depraved by licentious conquest, they have with difficulty been made subject to the more careful arts of peace

---

Tables of Convictions and Executions for Robbery.

HOME CIRCUIT

Years of War.	Con.	Ex.	Years of Peace	Con.	Ex.
1689—1697, Highway	77	41	1698—1702, Highway	50	35
„ Elsewhere	6	4	„ Elsewhere	13	3
	83	45		63	38
1703—1713, Highway	41	21			
„ Elsewhere	20	7	1714—1718 (altogether)	38	26
	61	28			
Total 8 Years . . 83	45		Total 5 Years 63	38	
„ 11 „ . . 61	28		„ 5 „ . . 38	26	
„ 19 „ . . . 144	73		„ 10 „ . . . 101	64	

(*l*) See the Lives of Highwaymen, and Celebrated Trials, 1825, ii. p 114

(*m*) Miscellaneous Sheets in British Museum, March 2, to Nov. 26, 1649, p 89, and see also, as to outrages by soldiers, pp. 60, 73 ; p. 91.

LONDON.

Years of War.	Con.	Ex.	Years of Peace.	Con.	Ex.
1703—1713	9	3	1699—1702	2	1
11 Years	9	3	3 Years	2	1
			1714—1738 (n).....	49	30
1739—1748 (o). ...	39	18	15 Years . .	49	30
10 Years (p)..	39	18	1749—1755	16	12
			7 Years . ..	16	12
Total 21 Years ..	48	21	Total 25 Years .	67	43

Executions only—London and Middlesex.

Years of War	Ex.	Years of Peace.	Ex.
1739—1748 (q) ...	108	1731—1738, 8 Years ..	134
		1748—1755, 8 Years .	140
Total 10 Years ...	108	Total 16 Years .	274

When William III. came to the crown, a little in advance of that system of public credit which has so long retarded the progress of civilization, Old Mobb, a most industrious labourer in his vocation, was within a few months of his final exit Old Mobb was he who robbed Judge Jefferies, as he was going to his country seat. The hero of the Western Assizes had recourse to morality, and talked about soul and body; but it was in the wrong place, for the highwayman answered by shewing the weapon with which he had shot two of his lordship's servants, and so took fifty-six guineas without more trouble. (r) Mobb perished in 1690, being convicted upon thirty-two indictments out of thirty-six! He was succeeded, however, by Whitney and other famous roadsters,

---

(n) Excepting a Spanish war which began in 1718 and ended in 1719

(o) It should be considered, that war with France was not declared till 1743 , with Spain it began in 1739.

(p) And note, that of these there were seventeen convicted and thirteen executed in one year (1743-4).

(q) From 1739 to 1743, we were at peace with France.

(r) Lives of Highwaymen, p. 153.

some of gentle blood, others mere sons of idleness, but chiefly
" miserable, hardened wretches," as the poor ordinary used to
call them when all his means of exhausting their impenitence had
been eked out. Robbing the mail was now becoming very usual .
in fact it signified little to the freebooter where his plunder lay,
provided he had a good horse. And about this time, also, Turnham
Green, Hounslow Heath, and Bagshot, began to acquire that ce-
lebrity for which they were so long afterwards distinguished " I
hope," says a writer of these times, " the honest part of the soldiery will forgive me, if I think we have many incorporated in
their companies, as fit for the triple tree as any that have graced
that structure for a great while "(s) And he then goes on to say,
that idleness is the mother of mischief This circumstance,
combined with the consequences of a disbanded soldiery, cannot
be too much considered in legislating upon the offence of robbery.
It is not necessary for us to dwell upon these reigns It may be
observed, however, that executions for robbery were most frequent, (t) that it was not uncommon to charge a man with eight
or ten indictments, that it was quite customary to hang daring
thieves in chains; and mercy was so little thought of, that the
slightest aggravating fact was sufficient to ensure the warrant for
execution, even when it had been intended to grant a reprieve (u)
At length, in 1730, *in the midst of the peace*, matters assumed a
very threatening aspect. " Thieves and robbers were now become
more desperate and savage than ever they had appeared since
mankind was civilized. In the exercise of their rapine, they
wounded, maimed, and even murdered the unhappy sufferers
through a wantonness of barbarity." (x)

The periodicals of those days also propagated the alarm.
Gangs of rogues used to rush into houses masked, and there they
would commit great outrages, so that there was a reign of terror
" Notwithstanding the number of criminals condemned at the
Old Bailey," said Mr Urban, " street robbers and house-breakers
abound, and are very numerous." (y) This was immediately
after the hanging of several robbers at Tyburn, attended by a
guard of fifty soldiers Smollett was not far from the mark
when he attributed this state of things to " degeneracy, corruption, and the want of police, in the internal part of the king-

---

(s) Street Robberies considered, p. 51, in " The Practice of Robbers "
(t) See " Hanging not Punishment Enough," 1701.
(u) See Complete Collection of Trials, 4 Vols 1721. Select Trials,
4 Vols. 1742. Remarkable Trials, 1765, vol. 1. The Newgate Calendar. Lives of Highwaymen.
(x) Smollett's Continuation, ii. p. 494
(y) Gent. Mag. 1735, p. 162, and see p. 106. Hanway's Defects
of Police, p. 219.

dom " (z) Accordingly, the evil went on.   In 1737, Turpin, the
famous man of that name, committed a robbery *per diem*, and
terrified the citizens of London exceedingly by saying, that he
wanted to kill two men, and then he should not mind being
taken ; and very soon afterwards there was another congregation
of the most formidable gangs   In 1751, it was acknowledged
that travelling on the highways was very hazardous, and that it
was almost unsafe to walk the streets ; and, even at that day,
people were not wanting, who said, that it was " surely a vain
attempt to put a stop to such crimes by the halter ;" and, arguing
with much sense, they admitted their ignorance of the true cause
of the distemper. (a)   Think of our persevering obstinacy in
1832 !

The Seven Years' War, which began in 1756, diverted the
public attention from the causes of the late increase of robbers,
because the evil was never felt so much during the campaigns
with France   But the country had no sooner returned to peace,
than the mischief broke forth more strongly than ever, and with
it the most earnest inquiries into its origin   Hanway, who wrote
about this time, declared that he had lived under the most despotic
governments of Europe and Asia, yet he was free from violence
and the dread of robbery " Here," says he, " I am not so happy ·
the caution with which it is necessary to live, is the heaviest tax
I ever paid in any country (b)   I cannot return to my home, not
even in my chariot, without danger of a pistol being clapped to
my breast "(c)

Convictions and Executions for Robbery, in London and
Middlesex, 1756—1830

Years of War.	Con.	Ex.		War.		Peace.		
1756—1762....	41	33	7 yrs.	41	33			
Years of Peace.								
1763—1776...	309	126				14 yrs	309	126
Years of war								
1777—1782(d)	155	67	6 yrs .	155	67			
Years of Peace.								
1783—1792.	356	146				10 yrs.	356	146
Years of War								
1793—1801. .	138	30	9 yrs .	138	30			

Forward 22 yrs 334 130   24 yrs. 665 272

(z) Continuation of Hume, ii 494.
(a) Fielding, also, the celebrated novelist, published his " Enquiry
into the cause of the late Increase of Robbers" in 1751.
(b) Defects of Police, p. 224   (c) Ibid.
(d) In the year of the riots there were Con. 44. Ex. 34.

Years of War	Con. Ex.	War.	Peace.
Brought over.... 22 yrs. 334 130			24 yrs 665 272

Year of Peace.

| 1802...... | 22 | 0 | 1 yr . 22 0 |

Years of War.

| 1803—1814 .144 14 | 12 yrs. 144 14 | | |

Years of Peace. (c)

| 1815 Sept. 1832,438 58 | | | 18 yrs .438 58 |

Totals 34 yrs. 478 144   41 yrs. 1125 330

Convictions and Executions on the Circuits.

			Con. Ex.		
Home	.1755—1817	.	Highway .920 252	} 958	270
"			Elsewhere . 38 18		
Western	1770—1818........		Highway ..482 113	} 498	117
"			Elsewhere 16 4		
Oxford	. 1799—Lent, 1819	..	Robbery ..104 0		
Midland	.1805—1817 .	.	Highway . 72 3	} 77	3
"			Do house . 5 0		
Norfolk	. 1768—1818	......	Robbery . 203 76		
Lancaster	1798—Lent, 1819	..	Robbery . 96 33		
Durham	..1755—Lent, 1819	.	Robbery . 19 3		
Northern	. 1804—1817 .	... .	Robbery 39 8		

England and Wales—Ten Years of Peace—1821—1830

Year.	Com.	Con.	Acq.	No bill, &c	Ex.
1821	311	160	105	46	22
1822	278	141	96	41	15
1823	201	113	64	24	5
1824 .	258	124	108	26	6
1825 .	189	93	78	18	6
1826 ..	306	144	129	33	15
1827 ..	384	204	115	65	17
1828 .	314	155	128	31	5
1829	299	147	113	39	12
1830 .	301	166	102	33	5

But the war broke out again in 1777, and in 1779 the charges of robbery had diminished more than one half This last struggle, however, was but of short duration, and there followed a peace of ten years, which formed a remarkable era in the annals of open violence The pacification, in fact, had scarcely begun, when the

(e) Excepting the 100 days, and the American war.

capital convictions at the Old Bailey, for robbery, went up to 60 in one year; 43 more followed in the next year (1784); 41 in 1785, 46 in 1786, 38 in 1787; 26 in 1788; 40 in 1789, 15 only in 1790, 35 in 1791, and 33 in 1792, the last year of the peace. But war had no sooner been proclaimed again, than the convictions declined again once more to one half; and, before the century had closed, the proportion was still less. Not that the executions decreased when the war of 1783 ceased Quite sufficient was the measure of capital punishment at that time to deter even a demon, if death could have had any weight in the balance. It was in 1782,-when the new decrees of inexorable justice were first enforced—it was in the year before the peace when the list at the Old Bailey stood thus.—Con. 37, ex. 21— The Recorder of London was directed to report, almost instanter, such cases of plunder as were connected with cruelty, with an intimation that no mercy would be extended, upon any solicitation whatever He was not backward in doing so; but in the very next year the convictions amounted to sixty. The people came up, as the author's late esteemed friend, Mr Shelton, once said, *like cattle*, and the speaker was a moderate and wise man. However, the judge who pronounced sentence was not wanting on his part. He spared neither invective nor exhortation, he shook his head with the signal of dreadful certainty, and spoke of a speedy execution (*f*) The clergyman co-operated, he strove to commit his unhappy flock to a late repentance; he lamented over their obduracies, and wondered at their indifference; but, alas! it was a time of peace, and fresh sheep were on their way to the slaughter. But did the cruelty diminish? Let us appeal to the records of the times. the search may be painful, but the result will satisfy the honest inquirer that repeated cases of barbarity followed these executions The rigour of the law might have had other results. it might have excited a still greater ingenuity on the part of counsel for prisoners; it probably enhanced the number of acquittals—it certainly increased the recommendations to mercy by the juries, appeals which were but little regarded The judges, however, on their circuits, and the Privy Council, in cases from the Old Bailey, have acted ever since upon the principle of discriminating between mere cases of robbery, and such as are accompanied by cruelty, with what success the very frequent instances of severe outrage too strongly testify But now the public mind was aroused. The press was beginning to expand its giant strength, the people at length revolted against the idea of cutting off so many human beings annually. Fielding, the great novelist, had written " An Inquiry into the Causes of

---

(*f*) The severity of the law had like to have added murder to robbery in almost every case.

the late Increase of Robbers;" Hanway's " Defects of Police"
was before the public, " Thoughts on Capital Punishment, in a
Series of Letters," had been brought out in 1770 ; every month
witnessed some observation, by the periodical press, upon the
uselesness of spilling blood. Boswell complained to the moralist with whom he conversed, that he had one morning been a
spectator of the execution of fifteen men before Newgate. The
point began to undergo discussion. the policy of allowing blood-
money or rewards for taking highwaymen, began to be suspected.
But still nothing was done. We are now speaking of the years
of peace between 1783 and 1792, and executions were never
more unsparingly decreed than during that period At length
some " benefactors of their species" bethought themselves of an
improvement in the system of police They were fully borne out
in their position by the public voice. (g) In vain did the citizens
of London remonstrate against the proposed bill In vain did
they petition about " the wisdom of their ancestors the regular
administration of justice—the entire subversion of the chartered
rights of the greatest city in the world !"(i) In 1792, the bill
passed for constituting official magistrates in Westminster, South-
wark, and other places, and in the same year war was declared
against the French Republic That which is called a curious
coincidence followed Here was, on the one hand, a new police
act • on the other, a declaration of war The public supposed
that the chief object of the bill was to prevent robberies, burglaries, and other atrocious offences.(i) The truth was, that no such
provisions were contained in it, but it facilitated in some degree
the access which was wanted to active and diligent justices in all
parts of the metropolis, and taking that into consideration, together with the war against France, we find as a fact that in 1793,
immediately afterwards, the convictions at the Old Bailey, for
this offence, *went back from* 33 *to* 18 , *and the executions from* 11
to 4 From this depreciation they never recovered till the peace
of 1814, if we except 1802, when they rose to 28 (double of the
preceding year), and that was the year after the peace of Amiens.
No sooner, however, had the Buonapartean war ceased, than the
numbers again advanced ; and in 1816 and 1817, the convictions
had accumulated to 48 and 47. But the schoolmaster was now

(g) See Gent. Mag. 1785, p. 951 A Plan of Police, &c. Lond.
1786.

(h) Petition against the Police Bill. Gent. Mag. 1785, p. 569.
In fact the wisdom of our ancestors, the Anglo-Saxons, was of a very
superior kind. See also Parl. History, vol. xxix p. 1178. Gent. Mag
1785, p 962.

(i) Colquhoun on the Police, p. 509.

firm at his post, the police underwent vast changes; (*k*) and, in 1821, the offence of robbery again declined in London and Middlesex, notwithstanding—first, *the continuance of peace*, secondly, *the increase of population;* and, thirdly, *the clemency of the times*

Table of Convictions and Executions in London and Middlesex, from 1815 to 1830 —(Sixteen years' Peace.)

	Acq. and no Bill, &c.			Con.	Ex.	Total.
1815	30	and	11	15	1	56
1816	35	and	13	48	1	96
1817	37	and	8	47	4	92
1818	—	and	—	28	2	—
1819	—	and	—	31	4	—
1820	—	and	—	35	··	—
1821	29	and	5	31	10	65
1822	34	and	12	18	3	64
1823	12	and	1	13	1	26
1824	14	and	3	10	2	27
1825	22	and	6	12	—	40
1826	51	and	17	36	7	104
1827	27	and	8	39	4	74
1828	46	and	7	23	3	76
1829(*l*)	25	and	11	18	5	54
1830	17	and	3	9	1	29
			Total ...	413	58	

N.B.—In order to prevent mistakes or errors in judgment, we have subjoined an account of the offences which were visited by execution in 1820 and 1821, when the executions increased so much.—

1820	3	Robbing in the Harrow Road.
	1	Opening of the Regent's Canal
	5	Common robberies
	2	*Abominable* extortion
Total	11.	
1821	1	Woman—robbing in a house.
	1	Extortion *abominable*
	8	Common robberies
Total	10.	

(*k*) See Minutes of Evidence before a Select Committee of the House of Commons, 1816 Strong Admonitions, London, 1812. Ann. Register, 1817, p. 356.

(*l*) New Police at Michaelmas, 1829 — note the difference in 1830.

After these severities, it is neccessary just to mention, that the streets still continued to be in a most unsafe condition, and that juries were so alarmed as to acquit or find no bill against more than one half of the persons charged in the next year, 1822

With all these facts before us, it is not surprising that we should require the abolition of the capital punishment for robbery The high roads are comparatively safe, because they are guarded by armed patrols, the streets are equally tranquil, because of an efficient police, and the same preventive force restrains the crime of robbery in dwelling-houses. There is one other mode of plunder, which has occasionally been resorted to by men of desperate character, and it is that of making abominable threats It took its rise about the year 1770, and, though few have been base enough to adopt it, execution has usually followed It does not seem desirable to continue the extreme penalty of robbery in the case of crime which has but few names in its catalogue, which, if it increase at all, does so in the face of an uncompromising rigour, and which, if it do not, owes its rarity to the honour of human nature, rather than the fear of death

Should robbery again advance. by reason of the distresses of the labouring class, let us raise the standard of moral economy against it, instead of invoking vengeance on the criminals and aggravating their sorrows by useless deeds of excessive justice. Let us teach around us the glorious results of the multiplication of property and capital, and the strict demands of prudence; for thus shall each of us lend his aid in hastening the day when a man shall walk from John o' Groat's to Mount Edgecumb, in perfect harmlessness, himself also a peaceful passenger.

2. *Burglary and Housebreaking*

Burglary and housebreaking, the one a felonious violation of a dwelling-house by night *with intent* to commit a felony, the other a breaking *and* stealing during those hours when there is sufficient light to see a man's face, have nearly gone hand in hand with robbery, the first, perhaps, being rather the elder brother Whilst some plunder afar off throughout the country, says Spelman, these (the burglars) more forward, attack boroughs, break into villages and houses, and make spoil (*k*) Burglary was the hamsoken of the Saxons, and for some time was punishable by a fine. For if any one overstepped a boundary, or broke into an enclosure, he was to forfeit in the first case four, in the latter six shillings (*l*) But this impunity was not of very long duration, for Canute placed housebreaking amongst his five inexpiable

(*k*) Glossary, p. 93.
(*l*) Wilkins, Leges Ang Sax p. 4, pl 28, 30.

crimes (*m*) In the reign of William the Norman, as capital punishment was abrogated, the burglar of course was not executed,
but in the reign of Henry I the offence in question again became
an object of rigour,(*n*) although the criminal might still redeem
himself by the payment of his weregild. In Fleta's time death
was once more the penalty, and it has continued the same ever
since. The nature of the offence, however, underwent alteration
at different periods of our history, and it was not always punishable by hanging Britton, an old writer, in the reign of Edw I.
calls burgessours, or burglars, persons who feloniously in time
of peace break churches or the mansion-houses of others, or the
walls or gates of cities or boroughs, except infants under the
age of discretion, and poor people, who, through hunger, enter
the house of another for food, and take under the value of 12*d* (*o*)
And if these persons were taken in the fact, it seems to have
been customary, in the time of Edward II, to behead them.(*p*)
The crime was now of very extensive definition (*q*) But in the
next reign (Edward III.) the same distinction prevailed between
robbery and burglary, which is the law of the land at the present
day For if a man committed ever so much violence on another
in the highway, and did not take any thing, it was not a capital
felony; whereas, if a thief broke into a house by night, and yet
took nothing, he was liable to be hanged (*r*) The only difference
was this in Edward the Third's day it was enough if a person
broke the house, although he might not intend to steal, whereas
the latter ingredient is absolutely necessary to constitute burglary
at present (*s*)

When Edward VI came to the crown, clergy was taken away
from housebreakers either by day or night,(*t*) and this gives us
occasion to remark, that in the fourth year of his reign, and not
before, the judges held solemnly, that burglary could only be
committed in the night (*u*) Consequently, it is clear, that prior
to this decision, felonious breakings, in either case, came under
the denomination of burglaries, and when that distinction was
laid down, it is also plain that the two crimes were separated,
although, in both cases, it was necessary that some person should
be within the house at the time of committing the felony And
here we leave *burglary*, whose capital punishment we have distinctly traced to the time of Edward VI, only observing that
Mr Peel's Act renewed the extreme penalty.

(*m*) Id. p. 143, pl. 61
(*n*) See Wilkins, p. 242, pl. 10, and 244, pl. 13, 246, pl 22.
Russell, ed. 1819, p. 900, note. Coutumes Anglo-Normandes, par
M. Houard, ii. 238.   (*o*) Reeves, ii. 274
(*p*) Id 352.   (*q*) Id. 351
(*r*) Id iii. 123.   (*s*) Id. iv. 472.
(*t*) Id. p 472, and v. 118, Eliz.   (*u*) Id. p. 473.

A few words more will conclude our detail of the punishment for housebreaking. It happened in the reign of Queen Elizabeth, that several robberies were perpetrated in the houses of poor persons who were gone out to their labour, by breaking the door and taking whatever could be found The legislature of the day considered that this mode of depredation had arisen from an idea that it was not so penal to rob in this manner as if any person had been within the houses Accordingly, without considering how infinitely greater the temptation was, they made it equally penal to break a house in the day-time, no person being therein, as to commit burglary, or force the door by day with people at hand, provided the property stolen amounted to five shillings (r) And this, excepting the estimate of the thing taken, is now the law of the land, for the words of the consolidating statute are —" If any person shall break and enter any dwelling-house, and steal therein any chattel, money, or valuable security to any value whatever—every such offender, being convicted thereof, shall suffer death as a felon."(z) The amount is, consequently, *now* immaterial,(a) and thus we have shewn that housebreaking, accompanied by theft to the value of 12*d*, has been a capital felony from very early times; and that, since the days of Elizabeth, it has been quite as penal to rob a house when the inmates have been absent, as when present.

Results — There is good reason to believe that the mischief of housebreaking has proceeded in a pretty steady rate since the Conquest, as well as that it was not so common in the times of our ancestors, the Saxons. We feel, however, that to go through the stages again, as we did in the case of robbery, would only fatigue the reader unnecessarily (b)

(r) Reeves, v. 119 Russell, 971.
Whence it was that juries, who often thought that the criminal might stand a chance of being hanged, resorted to their favourite practice of lessening the amount of the things stolen. Prosecutors were quite ready to combine with them, and hence the verdict " Guilty, 4*s.* 10*d* " which was not capital. Sometimes they have said, " Not guilty of housebreaking, but guilty of stealing in the dwelling house to the amount of 40*s.*"
(z) 7 & 8 Geo. 4 c. 29, § 12.
(a) If the least thing of the least value be taken, it is now capital.
(b) If he would like to read of the famous Jack Sheppard, of Judge Harrow, the Flying Highwayman, and other such remarkable burglars— Blake, otherwise Blue Skin, &c., together with the gradual advance of the science of housebreaking, from the simple easy practice of standing one upon the other's shoulders two or three deep, to the very perfection of picklock-key machinery — the Newgate Calendar, and the Select Trials from 1689 to 1764, will furnish sufficient materials. See also Remarkable Trials, 2 Vols. and Celebrated Trials, Lond. 1825.

Convictions and Executions for Burglary and Housebreaking.
HOME CIRCUIT.

Years of War.	Con.	Ex.	Years.	Total. War.		Years.	Peace.	
1689—1697, Burg.	101	55	8	101	55			
Housebr.	24	15		24	15			
Years of Peace								
1698—1702, Burg	59	35				5	59	35
Housebr.	27	18					27	18
Years of War								
1703—1713, Burg	69	42	11	69	42			
Housebr.	24	12		24	12			
Years of Peace.								
1714—1718, Burg.	73	56				5	73	56
Housebr.	3	3					3	3
			19	218	124	10	142	112

LONDON ONLY, WITHOUT MIDDLESEX

Years of Peace.	Con.	Ex	Years.	Total. War.		Years.	Peace.	
1699—1702, Burg	17	9				3	17	9
Houseb	1	1					1	1
Years of War.								
1703—1713, Burg.	28	15	11	28	15			
Housebr.	6	1		6	1			
Years of Peace.(c)								
1714—1738, Burg.	49	28				15	49	28
Housebr	10	5					10	5
Years of War (d)								
1739—1748, Burg.	8	4	10	8	4			
Housebr	0	0		0	0			
Years of Peace.								
1749—1755, Burg.	11	6				7	11	6
Housebr.	0	0					0	0
			21	42	20	25	88	49

(c) Except a Spanish war of a year and a half in 1718.
(d) War with Spain, 1739 , war declared with France, 1743.

Executions only.—*(MS.)*

LONDON AND MIDDLESEX

			War.	Total. Years.	Peace.
Years of Peace					
1731—1738, Burg.	29			8	29
Housebr.	17				17
Years of War.		Years.			
1739—1748, Burg.	33	10	33		
Housebr.	10		10		
Years of Peace.				Years.	
1749—1755, Burg.	32			8	32
Housebr.	5				5
		10	43	16	83

Convictions and Executions, for Burglary and Housebreaking, in London and Middlesex, from 1756 to 1832.*(c)*

	Con.	Ex.	War Years.			Peace Total. Years		
Years of War								
1756—1762, Burg.	14	6	7	14	6			
Housebr	1	0		1				
Years of Peace						Years		
1763—1776, Burg	230	111				24	230	111
Housebr	8	3					8	3
Years of War			Years.					
1777—1782, Burg.	95	55	6	95	55			
Housebr	9	3		9	3			
Years of Peace						Years		
1783—1792, Burg	254	141				10	254	141
Housebr	36	15					36	15
Years of War.			Years					
1793—1801, Burg	142	22	9	142	22			
Housebr.	27	2		27	2			
Years of Peace.						Year		
1802 ——, Burg	14	1				1	14	1
Housebr	2	0					2	0
Years of War.			Years					
1803—1814, Burg	190	23	12	190	23			
Housebr.	56	0		56	0			

(e) See Parl. Papers, 1819, viii.

	War		*Peace.*
Years of Peace.	*Years*		
1815—1832, Sept B 494 52	(*f*)18	494	52
H.(*g*)450 20		450	20

Total .... 34 years B 441 106	41	992	305
H 93 6		488	38

Convictions and Executions on the Circuits

				Con.	Ex
Home,	1755—1817	....	Burg	782	238
			Housebr	316	40
Western,	1770—1818	....	Burg.	705	131
			Housebr	303	20
Oxford	1799—1819, Lent,		Burg.	389	0
			Housebr.	͏66	0
Midland	1804—1817	....	Burg.	184	13
			Housebr.	58	1
Norfolk	1768—1818	....	Burg	364	99
			Housebr	105	8
Lancaster	1798—1819, Lent,		Burg	142	30
			Housebr.	2	1
Durham	1755—1819, Lent,		Burg	18	2
			Housebr.	9	0
Northern	1804—1817	...	Burg	79	7
			Housebr.	12	0

England and Wales, from 1821 till 1830 —(Ten Years of Peace)

Year.	Committed		Con.	Acq.	No Bill, &c.	Ex
1821	Burg	467	294	121	52	29
	Housebr	210	167	31	12	5
1822	Burg	496	322	84	90	23
	Housebr.	142	102	25	15	1
1823	Burg	402	261	99	42	11
	Housebr.	170	124	26	20	1
1824	Burg.	460	302	88	70	13
	Housebr.	176	128	33	15	0
1825	Burg.	428	276	101	51	12
	Housebr	150	112	27	11	0

(*f*) Excepting the 100 days, and the American war

(*g*) In 1828 the act passed which made housebreaking capital, although the articles stolen were of the smallest value, and no less than sixteen of these executions took place in 1828, 1829, and 1830. There was only one convict hanged in 1832, for housebreaking.

Year.	Committed.		Con.	Acq	No Bill, &c.	Ex.
1826	Burg.	476	309	115	52	10
	Housebr.	168	125	27	16	0
1827	Burg.	572	368	136	68	10
	Housebr.	300	240	44	16	0
1828	Burg	249	171	45	33	3
	Housebr	491	350	102	39	11
1829	Burg.	171	108	35	28	4
	Housebr.	181	561	167	53	10
1830	Burg.	155	104	30	21	2
	Housebr.	718	527	136	55	6

Convictions and Executions in London and Middlesex, for Burglary and Housebreaking, from 1815 till 1830.

Year.		Acq. and no Bill			Con.	Ex.	Total.
1815	Burg.	15	and	2	40	1	57
	Housebr.	4	and	1	3	0	8
1816	Burg	30	and	5	52	2	87
	Housebr	2	and	0	14	0	16
1817	Burg.	31	and	9	44	3	91
	Housebr.	4	and	0	20	0	24
1818	Burg	0	and	0	25	3	0
	Housebr	0	and	0	15	0	0
1819	Burg.	0	and	0	29	1	0
	Housebr.	0	and	0	22	0	0
1820	Burg	0	and	0	26	5	0
	Housebr	0	and	0	20	2	0
1821	Burg	18	and	3	33	5	54
	Housebr	2	and	1	12	0	15
1822	Burg	25	and	6	38	12	69
	Housebr.	6	and	0	6	1	12
1823	Bur	22	and	3	33	5	58
	Housebr	3	and	0	12	0	15
1824	Burg.	23	and	4	31	3	58
	Housebr	5	and	1	10	0	16
1825	Burg.	22	and	3	40	6	65
	Housebr	8	and	0	15	0	23
1826	Burg.	24	and	5	37	1	66
	Housebr	8	and	0	20	0	28
1827	Burg	21	and	4	33	2	58
	Housebr.	5	and	2	28	1	35
1828	Burg	4	and	2	14	1	20
	Housebr	34	and	9	59	8	102
1829(h)	Burg.	3	and	0	7	2	10
	Housebr.	37	and	9	40	6	86
1830	Burg.	6	and	1	4	0	11
	Housebr,	34	and	9	47	2	90

(h) New Police

However, there were times when greater alarm prevailed upon the subject than at others, and it seems that in 1783, or thereabouts, the public attention was fully aroused to the numerous cases of skilful burglaries. If Mr. Hanway declared that he could not ride out in his chariot without fear of being pistoled, it was equally just, that those who formed designs upon others had now matured their art, and that housebreaking had become a science. Upon the discussion of the bill for imprisoning persons found in possession of pick-lock keys, or other such implements, it was said that villains had invented instruments for their purposes which no ordinary fastenings could resist. A pamphlet was soon after published upon the subject,(h) but notwithstanding all the cautions which could be devised, not excepting a machine for the prevention of housebreaking, its decline was only contemporaneous with the war of 1792, and the New Police Act. For the system had been too well arranged to yield suddenly, although in some years as many as four-fifths of the convicted burglars were executed. So that if the rope could have done any thing, here was, at all events, a fair trial. But the fact was, that the matter went forward upon principle, the thieves planned their burglaries, and *made their contracts with the receivers on the evening before the plunder* (i) If the police, or the care of the family to be robbed were too vigilant, the business dropped; but the old gentlemen with their crutches and dark lanthorns were rather objects of ridicule, than useful terror. So that nine times out of ten, the deed was successfully accomplished

The same important difference between the years of war and peace may, accordingly, be adverted to with propriety in the present instance. For no sooner had the peace of Amiens terminated, than the housebreakings again most materially diminished, and no sooner had we returned to peace in 1814, than the very next year exhibited a catalogue of forty convictions for burglary at the Old Bailey, instead of the usual average of twenty, or at most thirty, and in 1816, the number was fifty-two. And in the country, the convictions mounted up at once to 216, being (with one exception) beyond *a hundred more* than in preceding years. Housebreaking in the day-time also, was greatly aggravated both in town and country. Then, with respect to the effect of increased executions, it is to be especially remarked, that we have no occasion here to give an explanatory note, as we did in the matter of robbery, because the inefficacy of severe punishment stands manifest, without such an explanation.

(h) Outlines of a ready Plan for protecting London and its environs from the Depredations of Housebreakers, Street, and Highway Robbers. Lond. Richardson, 8vo. 1s.

(i) Colquhoun, p. 103.

First, in respect of the offence itself, which decreased considerably in the years 1818, 1819, and 1820, in London and Middlesex, notwithstanding the most signal clemency of the sovereign. Secondly, if we look to the effect of executions in the years of peace between 1783 and 1792, for although 29 were put to death out of 37 in one year, 26 of 42 in another, 27 out of 38 in a third, the mischief did not materially abate till the war, and then the catalogue declined at once. Thirdly, in 1822, after the clemency we have spoken of, burglaries again advanced, and execution was done upon 12. But instead of a marked decrease, the lists of 1823 and 1824 shewed a very slight reduction, and in 1825 the convictions were more numerous than ever. On the other hand, juries (as the case is always,) increased their acquittals And the same remark respecting acquittals and the ignoring of bills will apply to the returns of England and Wales in 1821 and 1822, when the executions in the country were much augmented. Again, housebreaking, which has always been treated with far greater lenity than burglary, did not advance either in England at large, or in London, in consequence of that mildness The tables will shew this, and the result, to a dispassionate person, will be very satisfactory

Now, it is always desirable to arrive at the truth, and it really seems that an *occasional* decrease of the offence after numerous executions (which sometimes, though for the sake of humanity rarely happen,) proves only this. There is a certain class of acts which the Judges and Privy Council deem aggravated, and which, accordingly, they visit with execution Burglary increases in one year, and diminishes in another, from a variety of circumstances, as war, peace, distress, and other incidents Among the capital convicts in a high year is to be found a larger number of cases which come within the above rule. In another year probably the aggravated cases are fewer This seems to be a fair solution of the question, and a reasonable test to abide by.

A great falling off of the convictions for burglaries, and a vast increase of those for house-breaking, will be found in the year 1828, and afterwards. The reasons for this change are attributable to Mr Peel's new Act.

1. Many buildings within the curtilage of the dwelling-house, to break which was burglary, before the new Act, were placed within the protection of an entirely new provision, and the capital offence in respect of such buildings was abolished.

2 It no longer became necessary that house-breaking, as distinguished from burglary, should be proved to have been done in the day time, consequently, if any doubt existed as to the proof of burglary, the indictment would be drawn for breaking the house.

3. This circumstance accounts for the increase of convictions for house-breaking.

4. The convictions for house-breaking have also been increased, because it is sufficient now to prove a larceny of the smallest value

5 The new police have certainly succeeded in thwarting many intended schemes of plunder in London, and, accordingly, the aggregate convictions for burglary and house-breaking in 1829 and 1830, when impartially considered, will appear to have been comparatively lower than in former years.

Piracy.

We shall be very short upon pirates, because it is to be feared that many years must elapse before the country will be sufficiently enlightened to deal leniently with these freebooters of the ocean. They have so long been called the enemies of mankind, that any plea on their behalf would seem to be unavailing   Yet as far as capital punishment concerns their deeds, no other than Pope, the poet, has furnished an argument against it—

> " When savage pirates seek through seas unknown
> The lives of others, vent'rous of their own."

This recklessness, this mighty hazard of life, renders the penalty of death absolutely abortive, and then you must recall the principle of vengeance, which all thinking men recoil from with disgust Like the armed smuggler, the pirate will have his illicit traffic, and *if no mercy be shewn him, he will mount his death's head, battle-axe, and hour-glass* To extinguish piracy, there must be a great harmony amongst nations on the one hand, or a vast increase of general integrity on the other.   The golden day will arrive when these advantages will be secured to us, perhaps, indeed they may rise contemporaneously, but until then, it is in vain to menace the buccaneer and the corsair, for while he has the means of getting his rough livelihood, he will flourish, in spite of death and hangings at the yard-arm

When the old buccaneer gang ce   rob the Spaniards, it was not because of the executions wh   had been done upon their confederates, but because the West Indian prizes grew scarce, *through the caution of their owners.*   When the Eastern piracies succeeded, the booties which went so often to Madagascar, were the first stirring causes which worked upon the pirates; *the deaths and tortures to come had no place in their thoughts, or if ever they did rise to view, it was only to be despised with scorn* (*b*)   And in addition to these fostering excitements, our own privateering excursions were not exactly calculated to diminish the predatory bands of discharged or disloyal seamen by the force of moral example.(*c*)

(*b*) See Piracy destroyed, Lond 1701.

(*c*) When Alexander reproached the pirate for his calling, he said, in answer, that it was because he had but a single vessel. " Had I a

I

There are usually two ways of dealing with these plunderers
The first is by a summary execution, and this is a very common
practice amongst foreign nations　The second, and that which
we adopt, is to secure persons, thus seized in the act of depredation, and bring them to trial at the nearest court within our jurisdiction　The first course is the most justifiable, if the pirates be
engaged in an active and murderous warfare, because it then becomes a measure of self-defence to destroy them, and this is, perhaps, the one of the very few cases in which capital punishment
can be defended　If rioters assail a city, and burn every house
within their reach, if disaffected persons plunder the shopkeeper
and ravage with an universal violence, if the public peace be en-
dangered by a mischievous and destroying rabble; here, instead of
the present forbearing spirit of the military, should be the very
scene of capital punishment　The lives and capital of the quiet
portion of the community ought not to be at the mercy of a ruin-
ing populace, and the general welfare of the community ought not
to be compromised by the tardy muttering of the riot act　Here,
almost in the only case when a stern hand should be raised, there
is too often a mawkish, a hypocritical clemency, and the large
majority of the just suffer for the unrestrained ferocity of the
cruel　It is so with regard to piracy, or rather, it should be
so, but on the very instant when self-defence ceases to come in
question, capital execution should be blotted out　Therefore, we
conclude, that the cold calculating sentence of the judge, by which
he condemns the freebooter to die,—three, perhaps, six months
after his offence, ought to be abrogated.　The public voice comes
round to the side of mercy, and exclaims against the shedding of
blood under the cold pretence of satisfying offended justice.

Piracy was originally cognisable by the civil law, and was tried
before the admiral, his lieutenant, or commissary　But according
to that code, no judgment of death could be given without confession, and, therefore, the torture was allowed　However, it obtained but little in our happy country, for the Duke of Exeter
was the first who caused the engine of barbarity to be brought to
the Tower in the reign of Henry VI, and so soon as the reign of
Charles I the judges decided against its being inflicted upon
Felton (*d*)　Nevertheless, it may be observed here, that when the
torture was abolished, the custom of convicting upon circumstantial evidence gained more ground, so that although we got rid of
the rack, we departed from the wisdom of our ancestors, who inflicted a smaller pecuniary fine when the party was not taken with
the *mainour*.　By this indulgence towards the testimony of colla-

---

fleet," observed the corsair, "I should have been a mighty conqueror"

(*d*) See Reeves, IV 302. East, P. C. p 796. Russell, ed. 1819. p. 135

teral circumstances, we have been plunged into mazes which have too frequently ended in the destruction of innocence. It may truly be added, (and we do not mean to speak harshly,) that the admission of such evidence upon trials *touching life or death*, is as great a curse as the country knows   It encourages the romantic follies of the imagination, it vitiates the practice of the public press, (an invaluable engine of good,) it misleads the judgment, by laying a stress upon imaginary trifles, finally, it endangers the liberty and life of the subject.   But let us return,—begging pardon for this digression   In the reign of Henry VIII. an act was passed, ordaining, that all offences done upon the sea, &c where the admiral pretends to have jurisdiction, should be determined in " such county as should be limited by the king's commission," as if the offences had been committed on land   Piracy was made capital, but not a felony   Then, by a statute of William the Third, piracies committed under colour of any commission from any foreign prince or state, or pretence of authority from any person whatsoever, were declared to be capital   And this last class of crimes were pronounced to be *felonies*.   Lastly, the 18 Geo 2. enacted, that piracy committed under an enemy's commission should be visited by capital punishment, and the parties convicted were to be dealt with in the same manner as other pirates, felons, and robbers —The following acts are also declared by various statutes to be punishable as piracies

1 The forcibly entering of merchant ships, and destroying of goods. (*e*)

2. The trading with pirates, fitting them out, supplying them with stores, or consulting with them in any way. (*f*)

3. The illegal ransoming of neutral ships which have been made prize (*g*)

But proceedings on these last mentioned acts are of very rare occurrence

These laws have remained in force ever since, and the judges who at present try pirates at the Old Bailey derive their commissions from the statute of 28 Henry VIII.

With regard to the results of the punishment for piracy, we hope it will be sufficient to refer to the books in the note, (*h*) for we are anxious to maintain our promise of brevity upon this sub-

---

*(e) 8 G 1. c. 24 , 2 G 2. c. 28.   These offences are in effect treasons, as well as those mentioned in the statute of William, and they are made triable as piracies.   All treasons, it will be remembered, are felonies.   By the ancient common law, piracy by a subject was considered to be a species of treason , by an alien it was deemed to be felony only   (*f*) 8 G. 1 c. 24.

(*g*) 52 G 2 c. 25.   See East, P. C. 801, where it is questioned whether the act be in force or not ?

(*h*) Complete Collection of Trials, 1718, vol. 2, p. 1, &c., p. 172,

ject   We might enter into a history of the restless buccaneerings
which have often made the ocean a scene of alarm and turbulence,
but it would detain the reader if we were to do so, without rendering any benefit to the great cause   It is sufficient for us to have
negatived the principle of prevention as applicable to the penalty
of death.

Plunder of Wrecks

There is not a civilized individual in the kingdom who does
not feel the utmost abhorrence of the lawless plunder which takes
from a shipwrecked sufferer the last remnant of his broken fortunes   But the ignorant, stupid, unenlightened persons, who take
goods under such circumstances, are by no means aware of their
degradation in the scale of human society   The able and sensible
Judge Hale was not capable of throwing off the superstitions of
his day respecting witchcraft, and how can we then expect that
the inhabitants of our coasts will suddenly give up their lucrative
practice of wrecking?   A very little learning, however, will in-
form us, that the lord high admiral, and the lord of the manor
were, in old days, by far the most extensive wreckers, and the
poor people, who have followed their example, have only not
abandoned their vocations, for want of the education which would
teach them how ill, how inhumanly, how imprudently they act.—
Blackstone mentions that the Visigoths inflicted severe punishment upon robbers of this class, and the ancient Neapolitan institutions were equally rigid, whilst other nations, on the contrary,
have permitted the plunder of wrecks with impunity, those especially in the neighbourhood of the Baltic Sea   In early times our
own people were very much in the dark upon this subject, for the
law was, that when a wreck happened, the goods passed out of
the original owner, and vested in the king.   But by degrees more
humanity prevailed, and in the reign of Edward III. the property
in the wrecked vessel was ordained to be delivered to the merchants, provided that they would pay a reasonable reward to the
salvors   However, the practice of robbing the unfortunate mariners still prevailed, so that it was determined by the legislature to
afford a more active assistance.   Accordingly, acts were passed
in the reign of Queen Anne, and George the First, by which the
principal officers of towns near the sea were enjoined under a
penalty, to interfere on behalf of the wreck; and many have been
the battles which these officers, with their bands of men, have

---

twenty four hanged at execution dock, 1700, p 317, vol. iv. pp 207,
312-322. Johnson's Lives of Highwaymen, Pirates, &c. passim. Piracy Destroyed. Lond. 1701. Trials (British Museum) under the head
of *Tryals* of Pirates. Russell on Crimes, ed. 1826, p. 100. Last,
P. C. p 792. Rees's Cyclopædia, tit. *Piracy.*

waged against the illiterate plunderers   Moreover, all persons
secreting goods were to forfeit treble their value, and so far it was
well.   But not satisfied with this restraining ordinance, the legislature, in the 26th of George the Second, was induced to go further, and yielding to the impulse of feeling, they enacted a capital
punishment.   This heavy dispensation has continued ever since,
and has been incorporated into Mr Peel's late Acts, which consolidated the offences relating to larceny and malicious mischief. (*i*)

The results of the act in question have not been pregnant with
executions.   There have, in fact, been very few capital convictions, for a general idea of right prevailed amongst the poorer
classes for many years, and they almost always contrived to
escape detection   They thought they had as much right to take
the goods when the ship was stranded, as to catch a hare, or other
wild animal, which we know to be a common notion amongst our
labourers, and how could it be otherwise, when the chief persons
of the land had been accustomed for so many centuries to claim
the booty, and when again the law recognised so feebly the right
of property in shipwrecks, that it was necessary to pass the statutes of George the First and George the Second, in order to avoid
the technical difficulty?   There was an execution at Lancaster in
1767. and one, I believe, at Hereford in 1775, for plundering a
wreck in Glamorganshire   The offender in the last case was a
considerable farmer   There may be more, (*k*) but after a diligent
search, the author has not been able to find half a dozen convictions, and as the crime was once extremely common, (*l*) its diminution must be attributed to the advance of moral feelings, and
not to the influence of capital executions, which have never happened   This sanguinary ordinance, therefore, it may justly be
concluded, should be blotted out of our statute book

Rioters

In a former section we treated of the mischiefs of rioting as far
as they had reference to the violation of the public peace   We
spoke of the offence as an evil affecting the government   In the

---

(*i*) See, upon this subject, Encyclopædia Britannica, tit. Wreck
Russell, ed 1826, p 194.   East, P. C 606.   The Pernicious Practice
of Wrecking, Lond 1767

(*k*) In 1817 a person was convicted at Durham, but reprieved, and
in 1822 there is a return of one conviction for England and Wales, and
another in 1823, but no execution followed.   In 1809 there was an acquittal on the home circuit, and one was acquitted at Durham in 1817

(*l*) "One word more, brethren," said the parson, who observed his
congregation on the alert, a wreck having been announced — "One
word more," — and he opened the door of his pulpit.   "Let's all
start fair."

present place we propose to deal with the subject of popular tumults with relation to its effects upon private property, for Mr Peel's consolidating act has declared, that the demolishing, pulling down, or destroying any church, chapel, *house, stable, coach-house, out-house, warehouse, office, shop, mill, malt-house, hop-oast, barn,* or *granary,* or any *machinery* used in any manufacture or mine, shall be punished with death

And the *beginning* to demolish, &c is equally penal

The mechanics who have lately assembled in the north, for the purpose of manifesting their sense of the improvements which are required in our constitution and government, would have smiled, if this sentence of the 7 and 8 Geo 4 had been read over to them. Mourning over their misguided brethren of Bristol and Nottingham, they would have clapped their hands close to their sides, and said—" We want to destroy no property   We know well enough that the demolition of every house will be felt in the end as a subtraction of so much capital from the general stock which is to help to maintain our families   We know also, that the same law we have heard read, was made on purpose for the labouring class, and many of them have perished under it   But now we are fully well aware that we can meet and remonstrate against corruption, without injuring the hair's breadth of a piece of mortar, and we know, lastly, that the multiplication of capital will go hand in hand with the decline of our burthens"   Education will thus make the statute a dead letter, unless our legislators should do themselves an honour by erasing it before the spread of moral economy.   Not that the maintenance of so severe an enactment has the most distant effect of repressing or preventing riots   Far from it   We are about to shew this in conjunction with the history of the punishment.

Convictions and Executions for demolishing houses, &c in London, from 1714 [when the act passed] to 1755

Year	Con.	Ex	Remarks
1715-16	6	5	For demolishing the Mug-house in Salisbury Court, Fleet-street The cry was, " High Church and Ormond" " No Hanoverians " A man was also tried and acquitted for the murder of Daniel Vaughan, in the same transaction. His name was Read

Executions in London and Middlesex, from 1731 to 1755 (M.S)

Year	Ex	Remarks.
1749	1	*Penlez,* for beginning to pull down Peter Wood's house, in the Strand. *Wilson* was convicted, but reprieved

Convictions and Executions in London and Middlesex, from 1756 to 1830

Year	Con	Ex	Year	Con.	Ex.	Year	Con.	Ex.
1780	33	18	1794	4	1	1795	1	1

Remarks.—The riots of 1780 need not be particularly detailed. They are familiar to every one; but the poor people who suffered were to a great extent *ignorant of having committed any crime* Those of 1794 were directed against the *recruiting houses*, and the conviction in 1795 was for the same cause

Since 1795 there have been other riots, (as is well known,) that of Spa Fields notoriety, for example; but it should be remembered, that if a robbery be committed, the parties are indicted for the stealing, and not for the riot, and thus it was that Cashm in suffered for his share in that transaction.

Convictions and Executions upon the Circuits.

	Year	Con	Ex	
Home	1689—1718	0	0	
	1755—1817	5	1	Three for pulling down mills in 1772; 2 for demolishing houses in 1796, and one executed.
Western	1770—1818	4	2	1 Somerset, 1780, executed 3 Hampshire, 1796, 1 executed.
Oxford	1799—1819 (Lent)	0		
Norfolk	1768—1818	0	0	
Lancaster	1798—1819 (Lent)	0		
Durham	1755—1819 (Lent)	0		
Midland	1805—1817	0	0	
Northern	1804—1817	0	0	Two acquitted in 1805, and three no prosecution Two acquitted in 1815

England and Wales, from 1821 to 1830.

(Under the head " Riot and Felony.")

Year	Con	Ex	
1821	2	1	But these persons were convicted of *remaining one hour after proclamation*, and these cases have been already noticed, (ante.)
1826	48	0	The Blackburn Riots
1828	2	0	

Besides these convictions, there have been the results of *Special Commissions*, which have been issued from time to time, against the Luddites, for example, against the Birmingham rioters, in 1791, and the Southern agitators in 1830 and 1831

It is not to be supposed, that because the statute against demolishing houses was passed so late as in the reign of Geo I, there had, therefore been no riotous assemblages amongst the people   On the contrary, from time immemorial, occasional outbursts of public feeling have manifested themselves, and the only difference between the past and present times is, that in former days this general exhibition of the nation's wishes was accompanied by force, whereas now we are gradually advancing to a more peaceful though not less striking demonstration of our desires The monarchs of old were accustomed to designate any sudden gathering which seemed displeasing to them, by a term no less formidable than treason, so that in the time of Edward III it was counted a triumph for liberty, that "riding armed" should no longer be deemed treason, unless it were accompanied by such circumstances as made it a levying of war. (a)   But in the reign of Edward VI the meeting together of twelve persons or more was again made high treason under certain circumstances, (b) and it was not until the death of Queen Elizabeth that the offence again partook of a milder character   Even in subsequent times, the judges assisted in keeping up the tone of severity against rioters, by countenancing those constructive treasons which are so objectionable, and which Luders discusses so ably in his tracts They held that the design of pulling down *all* meeting-houses, and *all* bawdy-houses, and so on, was a levying of war within the 25th of Ed. 3., so that the London apprentices could not rise in those times with entire impunity.   But sundry acts of violence which were committed upon the happening of the Hanover succession, induced more resolute and definitive measures   And, accordingly, the statute of George the First imposed the penalty of death upon any person who should assemble to the disturbance of the public peace, and demolish, or begin to demolish, (amongst other things) any house, barn, stable, or outhouse.   The 9 Geo. 3 extended this provision to the destruction of mills, and a subsequent act of the same reign included buildings or engines used in trade or manufactories   The consolidating act of the 7 and 8 Geo 4, then continued the offences just mentioned in the list of capital crimes, and thus we are situated at the present day with respect to riots accompanied by the destruction of property, or attempts to effect such mischiefs

With regard to the results of the punishment, the records of our own times are sufficient to satisfy us upon this point   But we have already made all the observations which this part of the subject seems to demand, in a prior page, and will refer the reader there. merely observing, that when the rioter is punished capitally for pulling down a house, he is ostensibly so treated for the benefit

(a) Reeves, ii. 454.   (b) Id. iv. 475, and see p. 487.

of others, and not *selected* as a monument of vengeance This is
the true principle The very fact of a *selection* is odious, and cannot
be supported upon any reasonable ground of justice or humanity
When you *select* a criminal for execution, you visit his iniquities
upon his own head, for all are equally guilty, and as executions
for rioting are always odious, excuses will ever be suggested for
the man when he comes to suffer " Semel insanivimus omnes "
And besides this, upon the very next exciting opportunity, the
unheeding mob will rise again, (as they have universally acted,)
thereby annihilating the force of example, and the imaginary principle of prevention Let us trust in God, that we may never
more hear about the giving of directions to the sheriff for the *pre-
paration of a scaffold to execute five persons* (c)

Malicious Injuries to Shipwrecks, and Mariners

1 Exhibiting false signals
2 Destroying a shipwrecked vessel or cargo, or doing any
thing tending to occasion the loss of a ship
3 Impeding a person endeavouring to save himself from shipwreck.

From the wilful demolition of buildings there is an easy transition to the subject of malicious injuries And indeed, in many
cases, the offence which we have been describing is quite   wilful
as those of which we are now about to treat, although it   true
that upon most occasions the turbulent rioting is the chief object
in view The one class of crimes embraces a general, the other
a particular mischief

The capital felonies which are now under consideration, were
created by the 26th of George II The words of the present
act may, perhaps, be rather fuller, but in the main the same
offences are pointed at It is obvious that we shall not detain
the reader respecting these inhospitable evils, for the observations
which were made upon the plunder of wrecks, apply for the
most part to these deeds also It is evident that such actions
can only be adopted for plunder, or, possibly for smuggling
purposes; and as to the destruction of the wreck or cargo, it
might be practicable sometimes to convict an offender of this
latter charge, when it might not be so easy to bring home to him
the fact of larceny But the convictions upon this subject are
very few in number, perhaps not a dozen altogether, so that a decrease of crime in this respect cannot be attributed to a fear of

---

(c) See, upon this subject of rioting, Sir William Jones's Inquiry
into the Legal mode of Suppressing Riots, Lond 1782 An Address
to the Common People on Riots, by Luke Booker, LL D. , and Watt's
Bibl. Britannica, tit. Riots. Encyclopædia Brit. tit Riots. Russell
on Crimes, ed. 1826, p 247. Archbold's Peel's Acts, 1. p 210
Trials, 1721, vol. iv. pp 1-38, &c &c.

the scaffold, nor would it be more philosophical to assert that the apprehension of death has deterred people from doing acts which at a very late period were really a disgrace to the inhabitants of the coast. (d) We beg to refer the reader to the observations at the end of "Plunder of Wrecks," which sufficiently explain our ideas on this point, and we will pass on to the important and formidable offence of arson

Arson and Burning.

Arson, strictly speaking, is the burning of buildings, as churches, dwellings, &c. (e) Burning is the destruction of other property than houses But we shall apply the term arson indiscriminately to both in the course of the following pages It is held, and not without justice, to be a most fearful and criminal act The evils which it occasions are so considerable, and the wealth extinguished by it is so great, that it may be said to injure the public welfare as much as any offence punishable with death in this country The question is, how to prevent the commission of so ruinous a crime; for, at certain intervals, it breaks forth with a most overwhelming triumph, sweeping away houses, cattle, ricks, sometimes the lives of citizens, in its unnatural career Alas! if the poor misguided, illiterate, neglected creatures, who are chiefly the authors of this havoc, could but know the extent of misery they hurl upon themselves and their children by this wanton extinction of serviceable capital, (f) they would use more constitutional means of advancing their depressed pittance of wages They would take heed, not to mob-orators and writers as ignorant and more profligate than themselves, but to that still small voice of education now stealing through the land, and which ere long will prostrate those heavy burthens and evils (g) whence their poverty accrues

Our ancestors treated incendiaries with severity. They made indeed, a distinction, as we do, between burning houses and ricks, and the destroying of trees in a wood, or standing crops of corn. They admitted a compensation in the latter case, together

---

(d) See the Gentleman's Magazine for 1808, pp. 29, 122, 197. East. P.C. p 1100. Russell on Crimes, ed 1826, p 513.

(e) Although it was said originally to have been the burning of corn or houses in times of peace, (Reeves, ii 274, 351). But the technical definition has been narrowed since See East, P.C. p 1012, and other writers on the Criminal Law.

(f) "In simple theft the thing stolen only changes its master, but still remains in esse for the benefit of the public, whereas by burning, the very substance is absolutely destroyed."—Encyclopædia Brit. tit Arson.

(g) High rents, tithes, other imposts, but, above all, *bad domestic economy.*

with a *wite* to the crown, (h) we transport for seven years, in the former, they put the criminal to the fire or water ordeal, (i) we punish with death.   If the party thus compelled to undergo the legal purgation were convicted, (k) it was left to the chief magistrate of the district to punish capitally, or not, at his discretion (l)   Athelstan enacted, that the incendiary should be put to death if he could not deny the fact with which he was charged   If he would deny, he was put to the triple ordeal, and if then convicted, he was to find *borh* (bail or sureties,) (m) or lose his life. (n)   Canute enumerated burning among his five inexpiable crimes. (o)   In the reign of the Conqueror, the capital punishment was discontinued, but it soon revived again, and by our ancient common law, the course was to prosecute an appeal of arson in the same way as murder or robbery. (p)   If the party were taken in the fact, or if there were a very vehement suspicion against him, he was to purge himself *per legem apparentem*, (q) otherwise he might wage his duel   Then, upon being vanquished, he had judgment to be hanged, for this was probably the earliest punishment.   However, the law of retaliation obtained shortly afterwards, since we find, that offenders of this class were to be burnt, that they might "suffer in the same manner in which they had offended." (r)   This was in the reign of Edward I   In the next reign, burners were described to be those who set on fire a city, town, house, *man*, beast, or other chattel, feloniously, in time of peace, for hatred or revenge.   And those who *threatened* to burn seem to have been concluded under the same penalty (s)   The next account we have of the law respecting incendiaries is, that they were at one time deemed traitors.   But this was only under the following circumstances.   Letters had been sent containing demands of money, accompanied by threats that if the order were not complied with, the person's house should be burnt   This offence was declared to be high treason (t)   It did not, however, long maintain that character, for the statute of Edward

---

(h) Wilkins, p 21, pl. 43.   Leges Inæ, id. p 37, pl. 12   Leges Ælfredi

(i) Id. p. 26, pl. 77.   Leges Inæ.   The accused might take his choice

(k) "Si impurus sit."   See Turner's Anglo-Saxons, ii. p 508

(l) As note (c).

(m) See Turner, ii. 499.

(n) Wilkins, p. 57, pl. 6.   Leges Æthelstani.

(o) Wilkins, Leges Cnuti, pl. 61.

(p) Reeves, i. 199. citing Glanvil.

(q) That is, to find compurgators.

(r) Reeves, ii. 274. citing Fleta.

(s) Id. ii 351. citing the Mirror.

(t) Reeves iii. p. 285.

VI (*u*) again reduced all treasons within the limits of 25 Ed. 3
Further, in the latter end of Henry the Eighth's reign, it was made
felony to burn any frame of timber belonging to a house, (*x*) and
by another statute passed rather earlier, clergy was taken away
from arson An act of Edward VI., however, caused a temporary
restoration of this benefit; but in the next reign, that of Philip
and Mary, accessaries were deprived of clergy, and it was held,
that principals, by implication, were also excluded The offence
of arson seems now to have been narrowed in respect of its original signification, and to have applied to churches, houses, and
other buildings only. For we find an act of Elizabeth, (*y*) which
made it felony without clergy to burn any barn, or stack of corn
or grain, in the northern counties, and another of Charles II., by
which the burning of ricks, stacks, out-houses, and kilns, in the
night time, was created a felony A like punishment was awarded
in the same reign against persons who should burn ships to the
prejudice of the owners, freighters, or under-writers (*z*) The
offender might elect, however, in the case of burning ricks, to be
transported for seven years Next came the Black Act, (*a*) making it capital to set fire to any house, barn, or out-house, or to
any hovel, cock, mow, or stack of corn, straw, hay, or wood, to
rescue any person in custody for such crimes, or by gift or promise to procure the commission of them Matters now continued
stationary till the reign of George II , when it was determined to
extend the capital punishment to the burning of coal-mines, as
well as threatening by anonymous or fictitious letters to burn
houses, barns, and other property ; (*b*) and in the ninth year of
the next reign, mills were included among the subjects of arson. (*c*) Then followed acts taking away clergy from the setting
on fire ships of war, arsenals, and timber in the dock-yards, (*d*)
also, works and ships, &c in the port of London, (*e*) ships generally, (*f*) houses, barns, &c , with intent to defraud or injure, (*g*)
and buildings or engines used in trades and manufactories, with
a like intent (*h*) And lastly came the consolidating statute, 7 and
8 Geo 4. c. 30, which repealed several of the statutes just mentioned, and prescribed the capital penalty against arson for the

---

(*u*) 1 Ed. vi.

(*x*) Reeves iv. 290   (*y*) 43 El. c 13.

(*z*) And similar acts were passed in the reigns of Queen Anne and
George I.

(*a*) 9 Geo. I. c. 22. repealed.

(*b*) 10 Geo 2. c. 32. repealed.   (*c*) 9 Geo. 3. c. 29. repealed.

(*d*) 12 Geo. 3. c. 24. s 1. Burning ships, stores of powder, &c is
also death by the articles of the Navy. 22 Geo. 2. c 33, art 25.

(*e*) 39 Geo. 3. c. 69. s 104 (local act)

(*f*) 33 Geo 3 c. 67. repealed.   (*g*) 43 Geo. 3. c.58. repealed,

(*h*) 52 Geo. 3. c. 3. repealed

most part, as it exists at this day. The following descriptions of
property are within the protection of the second section :—

Churches, chapels, (including dissenting meetings) houses, sta-
bles, coach-houses, out-houses, ware-houses, offices, shops, mills,
malt-houses, hop-oasts, barns, granaries, buildings or erections
used in carrying on any trade or manufacture.

The fourth section, mines of coal or cannel coal.—The ninth
section, ships.—The seventeenth section, stacks of corn, grain,
pulse, straw, hay, wood

Results.—Readers of history will probably allow, without much
difficulty, that, in spite of the severest penalties, incendiaries have
come forth, from time to time, to blast the fruits of the earth,
and the labours of man, with their unpardonable deeds It
seems, therefore, sufficient to point to the experience of later
times in our own country, rather than enter into a laboured and
useless detail of former acts of violence

Not to mention the great national calamities, (as the Fire of
London) which have been attributed, perhaps erroneously, to
wilfulness, it is well known, that the middle of the reign of
George I. the years between 1760 (*h*) and 1770, and the memorable times of 1829, 1830, and 1831, have been especially distinguished for the crime of arson. And it may be added to this
statement, that the perpetrators of these mischiefs have escaped
more uniformly than any other class of offenders. (*l*) The chief
inducements which have led to the incendiarisms in question,
have been, for the most part, the high price of corn, the low rate
of wages, and, (which is by far the most uncommon) the temptation to defraud insurance offices, by destroying premises pro-
tected by policies.

Now in 1753, when a considerable aggregate of malicious fires
was recorded, it was well known that no mercy would be shewn,
on any consideration, to a convicted incendiary, and yet the devastation of property was as vast as it was daring. Capital punishment could not restrain the excesses, and the test, therefore, of
severity failed, decidedly, in its application. The same observation attaches to the years 1760—1770 . then (as, indeed, at present)
the heaviest punishment for arson was nearly certain But let us
have recourse to another test with respect to these incendiaries,
namely, the price of wheat. In 1753, the value of a quarter of
wheat in Windsor market was 2*l.* 4*s* 8*d.* which was *higher than*

(*k*) Especially 1762; but scarcely one of the tremendous acts of incendiarism was traced home to the offender.

In 1768 a man was hanged for robbing General Conway's house, and
setting fire to his library.

(*l*) The year 1753 was also famous for fires of this description.

it had been for twelve years before, and from 1763 to 1770, the price continued to be fearfully dear. It is true, that after 1770 the market did not decline; but this fact will not aid the advocates for continuing the capital penalty. For the events and dates alluded to prove that the original excitement arose from the high state of the wheat market and the history of those days shews us, that the burnings continued, with unabated animosity, in the midst of strict searches, examinations, convictions, and executions, so that, when at length the conflagrations began to cease a little, it was clear, that the ignorant populace had abstained from their havoc, rather from a failure in their experiment than an apprehension of its consequences. The recent disasters of 1829 and 1830 will place this matter in a still clearer light. In the former of these years, a low rate of wages, by comparison unprecedented, had exasperated the agricultural population They, accordingly, determined upon avenging their supposed wrongs, and commenced a destruction of corn and machinery, with which every reader is most familiar Of course, it was expected, that persons convicted of arson at this period should be inexorably punished, and the judges, consequently were found ready to sign the fatal sentences Yet, out of thirty-seven charges in 1829, eight only were substantiated, and of forty-five charges in 1830, there were no more than fifteen convictions Of these convicts, only three were actually put to death in 1829, and six in 1830, and, even in some of these very cases, the guilt of the offenders was believed by juries upon that most unsatisfactory testimony, circumstantial evidence. Amidst such a reluctance on the part of juries to pronounce a criminating verdict, and such difficulties of proof, it was not very probable that the crime itself, which arose out of starvation and oppression, should be materially lessened. Accordingly, we find that the mischief went on entirely irrespective of capital punishment In some countries, fires broke out immediately after the most solemn parade of execution; and, in Cambridgeshire, where two unfortunate men were hung upon a second conviction, (the first being technically deficient) the work of the incendiary proceeded almost as soon as the scaffold was removed Now, notwithstanding the violent invectives, which unthinking and hasty persons are accustomed to pour forth against criminals of this order, it seems impossible that the halter can be much longer tolerated in this country as a mode of checking arson *Even if every man convicted of the offence were put to death,* (a measure, which being founded on certainty, seems by far more reasonable than the constant interpositions of mercy) you could not diminish, materially, a disposition to do wrong, which is unaffected by the fear of death Much less can such a result be accomplished under the present vacillating administration of the penal law The happy change which has lately taken place in the career of incendiarism, might be more properly attributed to the pledges which were held out to the peasantry during the troubles, than to any severity of punishment. But, in truth, a careful consideration of historical events, respecting these popular outrages, will lead us to the conclusion, that they are like a fever, which must arrive at its crisis ere it declines. In 1830, as on former occasions, both at home and abroad, there was an outbreak of frenzy, which raged fiercely, till it had exhausted itself by its own violence; and again, as on former emergencies, some poor obscure persons were the objects of condign penalty, whilst their inflammatory seducers escaped unhurt. The subject may be regarded in different aspects, but in whatever view it may be so contemplated, neither the fear of execution, nor the examples of sufferers, will be found to have any place in the origin, advance, or decline of the evils under consideration. Education, political and moral, will alone operate to check these senseless ravages of property. The people will soon be taught that their true interest lies in the unlimited multiplication, not in the diminution, of capital. And they will rapidly learn, also, that if prosperity be delayed through an unwholesome state of their laws, there is, in lieu of insane and wanton devastation, a legitimate mode of attaining to that healthy course of government, which will ensure their well-being, without adding to their burdens.

We will add only a few words on the subject of prosecutions by the insurance offices. It might be imagined, that because there have not been many cases at the Old Bailey upon this grave charge, the offence itself is of rare occurrence, and hence it might be argued, that the capital punishment has operated efficiently in producing a useful terror. But, perhaps, no charges are made with greater caution than those accusations of arson at the suit of fire-offices. The managers are justly apprehensive of alarming the public, and they are, besides this, but indifferently regarded by juries, who have, for many years, exercised a systematic tenderness with regard to human life (m)

The truth is, that there is a considerable number of cases pregnant with suspicion; and it is said, that about one-sixth of the fires in London arise from wilful causes, and of these last, an infinite majority proceed from a direct design to defraud the insurance offices; so that, far from death being an active agent in the prevention of crime, the results of the capital penalty for arson prove the direct contrary. And it will be remarked, that incendiaries of this description have seldom met with a commutation of their doom. From whence we collect, that a repeal of the severest penalty in this respect would be productive of a

(m) If the insurance-office succeed in convicting, they, of course pay nothing for the damage which has happened.

greater display of justice—a larger number of convictions And this is *the fact*, for the opinions of thinking men concur in the idea, that, under a more mild administration of the laws, offenders, who now escape the consequences of their fraudulent burnings, would be prosecuted almost in every instance, and, for the most part, convicted

Convictions and Executions for Arson in London, from 1699 to 1755.

Year.	Con	Ex	Offence.
1736	1	1	For setting fire to the Bell Inn in Warwick-
	Total 1		lane.

Executions in London and Middlesex, from 1731 to 1755.

1736	1	1	As above

Convictions and Executions in London and Middlesex, from 1756 to 1831

Year	Con.	Ex.	Offence, &c.
1780	1	0	Special—and judges in his favour Tenant in possession, under an agreement for a lease for three years, from a person who held under a building lease
1785	1	0	A boy of 17, for setting fire to Parsloe's Subscription House in St. James'-street His servant It was doubtful whether the lad was not insane
1787	1	1	A girl of 19, for setting fire to her master's barns, it seemed from a sudden impulse
1788	1	1	Intent to defraud insurance-office
1790	2	2	The famous incendiaries, Jobbins and Lowe, who set fire to Mr. Gilding's house, in Aldersgate-street, for the purpose of plunder The address of the recorder is worth looking at. (*Gent. Mag* vol 60, p 1141)
1791	1	1	A pot-boy, for burning the Wreatsheaf in Red Lion-street, *probably for the purpose of plunder.*
1794	1	0	Setting fire to a house, with intent to defraud the insurance-office.
1803	1	0	A woman, for burning a house in Edmund's court, Russell-street—almost insane
1807	1	0	Died in gaol —Setting fire to a house, with intent to defraud the London Assurance Office.
1809	1	0	Setting a house on fire at Stanmore. The prisoner was a very poor man, and the cause did not appear

1811	1	1	Setting fire to his lodging, obviously with intent to defraud the Phœnix Fire Company
1814	1	1	Sturman, for burning his house, in order to defraud the Globe Insurance
1822	1	0	A woman, for setting fire to her master's house.
1824	1	0	Setting fire to his dwelling-house, with intent to defraud the Sun Fire Office.
1826	1	1	White, the bookseller, in Holborn, for burning his house, to defraud the British Fire Insurance
1829	1	1	Setting fire to the floor-cloth manufactory at Chelsea, by a discharged servant—malice.

In 1832, Smithers, of Oxford-street, was convicted of *murder*, by setting fire to his house, and thereby causing the death of some of the inmates. His object appears to have been to defraud the insurance-office

---

Acquittals, &c. at the Old Bailey, from 1805 to 1830

Year.	Acq.	No Bill, &c.	Year.	Acq.	No Bill, &c.
1805	0	2	1818 & 1820	0	No Return
1806	0	0	1821	0	0
1807	1	0	1822	0	0
1808	0	0	1823	1	1
1809	0	0	1824	4	1
1810	1	0	1825	0	0
1811 & 1812	0	0	1826	0	0
1813	2	1	1827	0	0
1814 & 1815	0	0	1828	1	1
1816	0	1	1829	1	0
1817	0	0	1830	0	1

Convictions and Executions on the Circuits for Arson

	Years.	Con.	Ex.
Home ...	1689—1718	2	1
"	1755—1817	24	11
	Total	26	12
Western .	1770—1818 . ..	19	12
Oxford ...	1799—Lent, 1819,	7	
Norfolk ...	1768—1818 ..	14	8
Midland .	1805—1817	8	1
Lancaster ..	1798—Lent. 1819,	6	5
Durham ...	1755—Lent, 1819,	0	0
Northern .	1804—1817	2	0

Acquittals, No Bill, &c. on the Circuits, for Arson

	Years.	Acq	No Bill.
Northern	1804 — 1817	13	2 — Total, 15
Home	1805 — 1817	8	8 — Total, 16.
Western	1805 — 1817	18	14 — Total, 30
Oxford (no return for 1805)	1806 — 1817	16	4 — Total, 20.
Midland	1805 — 1817	6	3 — Total, 9.
Norfolk	1805 — 1817	6	15 — Total, 2,.
Lancaster	1805 — 1817	11	0 — Total, 11.
Durham	1805 — 1817	1	0 — Total, 1

Convictions and Executions for Arson, together with the Acquittals, &c for Ten Years, from 1821 to 1830, in England and Wales

Year.	Con.	Acq.	No Bill, &c.	Total	Ex.
1821	5	8	13	26	0
1822	17	22	8	47	6
1823	6	11	11	28	0
1824	6	14	8	28	1
1825	7	8	7	22	1
1826	3	8	6	17	1
1827	3	6	5	14	0
1828	2	4	8	14	0
1829	8	15	14	37	3
1830	15	15	15	45	6

And the following are the Convictions and Executions, from 1805 to 1818, for England and Wales

Year	Con.	Ex	Year	Con.	Ex
1805	3	2	1813	6	3
1806	1	0	1814	6	3
1807	0	0	1815	4	1
1808	2	1	1816	8	2
1809	1	0	1817	11	8
1810	1	0	1818	7	3
1811	2	1			
1812	6	5		58	29

Forgery

The subject of forgery has been postponed until the close of this part of our undertaking, under an idea that a general commutation of punishment would have been effected by the new act in respect to that offence. But, notwithstanding the reasonable, and, indeed, unanswerable suggestions of the Lord Chancellor, wills, and powers of attorney to transfer stock, or receive dividends, at the Bank, India House, and South-sea House, have been made exceptions, in the clause which repeals the capital penalty. With respect to wills, they were originally omitted in the famous

clause which Sir James Mackintosh carried against Sir Robert
Peel then secretary of state, and which was subsequently re-
jected by the House of Lords   Sir James declared, that the re-
taining of the punishment *in the case of wills* was entirely contrary to his own opinion, and that he had only consented through
deference to others.

Then, secondly, the powers of attorney were excepted at the
express request of the Bank , and it is impossible not to perceive,
that the conduct of Fauntleroy has had great weight in alarming
many persons for the security of their funded property.   Fauntl-
leroy, however, it should always be remembered, committed his
iniquities with the capital penalty hanging over his head.   Now
the cases, both of wills and powers, seem to have proceeded
chiefly on the ground of the serious mischief which the forgers of
these instruments inflict on the community.   The greater the injury, the more inexorable the sentence   Such is the opinion of
those who advocate the continuation of death in matters of forgery.   But this is, in effect, taking vengeance on the criminal, not
upon the crime, and such a course is hostile to the known principles of our criminal jurisprudence   It will be answered immediately, that by severity, it is intended to deter others ; but
this is only the old, inefficacious plea of ignorance, because prevention, in this, as well as other cases, is in no wise accomplished
by the formidable threatenings of the law

It is very singular, (and, indeed, incidents of the kind have
happened before, as if to forward the cause of humanity) that
several instances of forged wills have occurred within a very
recent period.   Here is an increase of the crime, not only of the
particular cast which the statutes so uniformly denounce, but in
respect of which, also, the last penalty of the law (but for the bill
before the House) would, in all probability have been carried into
execution.   When the principle of prevention is urged for the
purpose of counteracting a mitigated punishment, it is desirable
that a circumstance like this should not escape attention.

———

The following tables will, perhaps, throw some light upon the
subject.

I.—Executions in London and Middlesex for forging Wills and
Powers of Attorney on the Bank, East India, and South Sea
Companies, from 1731 to 1763, inclusive.

		Ex.
1742	(Will)	3
1757	(Power of Attorney, South Sea Company)	1
1762	(Will)	3
1763	(Power of Attorney, South Sea Company)	1
	Total	8

II.—Convictions and Executions for the same offences in London
and Middlesex, from 1764 to 1831

Year		Con.	Ex.	Year		Con.	Ex.
1766	(Power of Attorney	1	1	1799	(Will)	1	1
	to defraud the Bank)			1800	(Power of At. Bank)	1	1
1771	(Will)	2	2	1802	(Ditto)	1	1
1773	(Will)	1	1	1804	(Ditto, *Ann Hurle*)	1	1
1778	(Power of At. Bank)	1	1	1806	(Will)	2	2
1783	(Will)	1	1	1807	(Will)	1	1
1785	(Will)	1	1	1812	(Will)	1	1
1786	(Will)	1	1	1816	(Power of At. Bank)	1	1
1787	(Will)	2	2	1817	(Ditto)	1	1
——	(Power of At. Bank)	1	1	1822	(Ditto)	1	1
1793	(Will)	1	0	1824	(Ditto)	1	1
1794	(Will)	1	1	1829	(Will)	1	0
1796	(Will)	1	0	1832	Sept. inclusive (Do.)	5	0
——	(Power of At. Bank)	1	1				

Now, after reading these tables, and considering at the same
time the singular fact before adverted to, (that is to say, the forgery of wills) it is difficult to conclude, that the punishment of
death has been efficient. From time to time there have been persons adventurous enough to brave the severest threatenings of
the law, and now, when the legislature has abolished the ancient
rigorous enactments in a majority of instances, it has happened,
that the most inexpiable form of the crime, the making of false
wills, is on the increase. This fact is worth more than the theo-
retical reasonings of a century.

But we must add some few further proofs in contravention of
the exceptions latterly introduced in the new repealing Act.
First, it is to be observed, that the forging of actual *transfers* of
stock receipts, of accountable receipts, dividend warrants, and
other instruments connected with the Bank, has been necessarily
left out of our calculations, because these offences are no longer
capital. The cases of illegal transfers were by no means uncommon Then, again, there were many occasions upon which the
criminal never appeared at the bar of justice The counterfeiting
of powers of attorney is an act which belongs in a great measure
to persons in a higher condition than ordinary offenders, and very
many of these, rather than be exposed to the disgrace of conviction, and the certainty of execution, have determined on being
their own destroyers

Again, seamen's wills form no part of our catalogue But no
one who reads the Old Bailey records can do otherwise than
bear testimony to the numerous frauds upon the Navy Office, by
means of these false instruments, as well as by forged letters of
attorney, to receive the wages or prize-money due to sailors.
And it was customary to punish those who were found guilty of

these acts with a formidable perseverance, so that blood may be
justly affirmed to have flowed very freely for these forgeries.
Yet victims were always ready for the sacrifice, and it was not
till the decline of war, and consequently the cessation of profits,
that the calendar of prisoners decreased in this respect

Let us hope, then, that the excepted forgeries will soon be reduced to the mild measure of those whose doom has been already
mitigated   The Bank may indeed feel aggrieved by the recollection of the rogueries of Fauntleroy, but they may rest assured,
that if ever again a like needy banker should become desperate
through distress, he will embark in the same career of perilous
adventure, unless withheld by moral feelings, or checked by an
almost superhuman vigilance.   On such an emergency, neither
the apprehension of disgrace, nor the fear of the scaffold, will be
present to his mind   To dwell, therefore, upon Fauntleroy's mis-
deeds as a ground for perpetuating the capital punishment in
cases of forged powers, would be in truth to entertain sentiments
of resentment against the criminal, and this is contrary to the principles of our law.   Be it said once more, and once for all, that
the restoration of the offender, and not his ruin, much less his
death, ought to be the chief aim of correction

APPENDIX.

No. I.

High Treason — relating to the Coin

[The author hesitated for some time before he decided to pub-
lish the history and results of the capital punishment for coining
and stealing in a dwelling-house The reason of this doubt naturally sprang from the repeal of those severe penalties. The
author considers, however, that he will be justified in giving the
original matter in the form of an appendix, because it is possible
that some persons may not be entirely satisfied with the remission
of the capital pains which has taken place; and it is moreover
desirable that the community at large should be made acquainted
with the entire failure of severity. Under these impressions, the
subjects of *Coining, Stealing in a Dwelling-house, Horse, Sheep,
and Cattle stealing*, have been included in the following pages.

The author has suppressed that which he has written upon forgery, because it seems quite impossible to return to the capital
punishment for that offence. Indeed, the crimes excepted out of
the late act will, probably, be very soon included in a new statute
of repeal.]

ORIGINALLY, no offence against the public standard money was
capital, for in the early times of society, the value of an incorrupt
coinage could not be appreciated, as it afterwards came to be in
the days of extended commercial intercourse. But, as Rapin
observes, " the consequences [of coining] made the penalty very
great."(a) Probably, the first threat of severity against the fabri-
cators of false money took place in the reign of Athelstan. when
the right hand of the offender was adjudged to amputation, and
afterwards to be fixed to the workshop from whence the false ma-
terial had sprung; but the accused might purge himself by the

(a) History of England, fol. i. 160. The authority to regulate the
coin amongst the Anglo Saxons seems to have resided in the Wittenage-
mote. Henry's Great Britain, ii. 258.

fiery ordeal. (*b*)   Next, in the reign of Ethelred, a capital penalty
was denounced against such criminals, but the king might pardon
them, that is, according to the custom of the times, he might
commute the punishment for a weregild, or fine. (*c*)   As the
trade of the country advanced, a more jealous attention was paid
to this subject, and whilst the government regarded the coiner as
an agent of mischief, it was awakened also to the evils which re-
sulted from the exportation of good money, and the importation
of bad (*d*)   It is true that this illicit traffic did not induce the
pains and penalties of a traitor, but the way was now prepared
for those severe enactments, which, till very lately, have been the
law of the land in respect of coining   The consolidating statute of
25 Edward III. declared the following treasons — counterfeiting
the king's money — importing false money similar to the money of
England (*e*)   But the counterfeiting of foreign coin *current* here
was found to be obnoxious, and that offence was, accordingly,
made treason, (*f*) and so, soon afterwards, was the importation
of such money. (*g*)   Fraud, however, was again at work; and
persons contrived to make money by *clipping, washing, rounding,*
or *filing* the coin.   These offences were speedily declared treasonable, whether committed upon British or Foreign coin, provided it were current here (*h*)   It seems, that as long as a chance
of lucre remained, the offenders were adroit in evading the law,
for in less than twenty years after the passing of the last statute, we
have the extensive words following: *by any art, ways, or means
whatsoever*   These words were applied to the impairing, dimi-
nishing, falsifying, scaling, or lightening the said coin, and all
these deeds were adjudged treasons. (*i*)

Marking the edges of coin had not yet been anticipated by the
law, and, further, parties bent upon fraud had devised a mode of
gilding or silvering coin, or blanks, or gilding silver blanks, and
thus created a branch of very profitable commerce   In the reign
of William III all these discoveries were declared to be treason-

---

(*b*) Leges Anglo Saxonicæ, by David Wilkins.   Leges Athelstan*,
141, p. 59   Nemo monetam cudat extra portam.   Ibid.   Henry's Great
Britain, ii. 299

(*c*) Leges Anglo Saxonicæ, by David Wilkins. Liber Constitutionum,
temp. Æthelredi, p. 118,   "Monetam, qui in ligno operantur, vel ali-
cubi aliter."   Ibid.

(*d*) See Reeves, ii. 228, and his Chart of Criminal Law.   4 Hen. 4.
c 18. [repealed.]

(*e*) See Reeves, iii. 117.

(*f*) 1 Mar. s. 2, c. 6, and to forge foreign coin *not* current was declared to be misprision of treason by 14 Eliz. c. 3, and see also 37 Geo.
3. c. 126, 43 Geo. 3 c. 139, s. 3.

(*g*) 1 and 2 Ph. & M c. 11.

(*h*) 3 Hen. 5. s. 2. c. 6, 5 Eliz. c. 11. s. 2.   (*i*) 18 Eliz. c. 1.

able; (*k*) and by a subsequent act, (*l*) the making of shillings or sixpences to resemble guineas or half guineas, as well as the making of halfpence or farthings to resemble shillings or sixpences, were subjected to the like penalty. And by 56 Geo. 3. c. 68. s. 17. the new silver coinage was expressly placed within the protection of all prior existing statutes

We have now spoken of coining, and the importation of false money,—it was reserved for the reign of William III. to extend the offence of treason to the possession of tools used in the fabrication of the standard The making or mending of any coining instrument was then pronounced treason; (*m*) and it is curious enough to observe, that the crime itself must have been carried on to some extent in spite of the sanguinary code, or there would have been no occasion for this statute against the machinery. Conveying away of the Mint tools, receiving, or hiding them, were also made treasonable by the same act (*n*) Then, with regard to the uttering of counterfeit money, that also might amount to treason, as if one forged the money, and another by previous agreement, sent it, here was an aider and abettor, and, consequently, a principal traitor (*o*) But on a general principle that offence amounts only to felony or misdemeanour. These appear to be all the treasons upon this subject, but as the capital felonies relating to the coin have not been many, it may not be amiss to mention them also very briefly in this place, because we shall then have before us all the offences punishable with death under that head at one view.

We have said that the government was displeased with the exports and imports of bad money. In the reign of Edward I the *statute de monetá* punished the importation of clipped or counterfeit money, *for the third time*, with death and forfeiture, and the importation of certain coins, called *pollards* and *crockards*, was likewise declared under the same monarch to be capital. (*p*) The people who were usually employed in this traffic could rarely, if ever, read, and therefore their lives, not being redeemable by the benefit of clergy, were absolutely at the king's disposal. Various other statutes were made upon this subject of exportation and importation. (*q*) Then, again, it was made felony to make, buy, or import, *gelly halfpence, suskins,* and *dodkins,* (*r*) to multiply gold or silver, or use the craft of multiplication, (*s*) and at

---

(*k*) 8 & 9 Gul. 3. c. 26 , 7 Ann, c. 25.
(*l*) 15 G. 2. c. 28. s 1.   (*m*) 8 & 9 Gul. 3. c. 26. s. 1.
(*n*) Sect. 2.
(*o*) Russell on Crimes, ed. 1819, 1. p 107. See Colquhoun on the Police, pp. 192-195.
(*p*) Reeves, 11. 228, and his Chart of Criminal Law.
(*q*) See the Chart.   (*r*) Reeves, 111. 261.
(*s*) Reeves, 111. 238.

a subsequent period, when new severities were devised against coining, the blanching of copper for sale, with some other kindred offences, was declared capital (*t*) And so, indeed, afterwards, was the counterfeiting of the copper coinage, (*u*) but since the benefit of clergy had become considerably relaxed in the reign of George III. (when this latter offence was made felonious) so as to include all offenders, whether they could read or not, it had no harsh operation as a punishment of death It was, moreover, made felony to put off any counterfeit milled money at a lower rate than its denomination imported. (*x*) This was in the reign of William III and the same protection was afterwards extended to copper money, (*y*) but the enlargement of the rule concerning clergy took away from these statutes also the painful effects which would have followed them in the olden time

However, the *uttering* of false *gold and silver* coin was a capital offence after a prior conviction; (*z*) and the *third* offence of uttering gold Louis d'ors, and silver dollars, was declared equally penal by an act of George III. (*a*)

Results. — Probably, if ever there were an instance of an absolute failure on the part of the legislature to check crime by means of severity, the case of coining, with its kindred offences, may be presented as the example. Such had been the prevalency of this misconduct, that Ethelred thought himself under an obligation to restrain its career. The right hand of the offender was cut off, and fixed with nails to the door of his house, (*b*) and his life, as we have seen, was at the king's disposal But those who dealt fraudulently in coin soon discovered, that by concealment, and fearlessness of consequences, they might amass a considerable fortune. Accordingly, the very persons who were intrusted with the making of the standard, both debased the money, and diminished its weight. Henry I. then added the penalty of castration to the Saxon punishment, but the '*evil continued to increase.*' (*c*) At length he caused forty-six out of fifty persons to undergo the punishment, and it is supposed that he forthwith issued a new coinage, (*d*) thus, in a great measure, *preventing* the

---

(*t*) Russell, ed. 1819, i. 98.

(*u*) Id 79.

(*y*) Id. 112.

(*a*) Id. 118, 119.

(*c*) Id. 520.

(*x*) Russell, ut supra, 109.

(*z*) Id. 113.

(*b*) Lingard's England, i. 529.

(*d*) Id. 520. See also Hayward's Lives of the Norman Kings, p. 280. Edgar had previously pursued the same steps. His coin " had become so diminished in weight by the fraud of clipping, that the actual value was very inferior to the nominal , he therefore had new coins made all over England." Turner's History of the Anglo-Saxons, ii. 270.

evil which he had so unmercifully visited. Nevertheless, the penalty which the Norman monarch had introduced was, doubtless, worse than death, so that, admitting this stroke of vengeance to have deterred criminals, no argument can be established from thence in favour of the rope (*e*) It will be recollected, that the fraud just mentioned was the act of the moneyers themselves; and some years. probably, elapsed, before the counterfeiting of coin by *strangers* became a subject of attention. However, it is quite clear that the severity of Henry left no very lasting remembrance, and that it operated the less as an example, because the next monarch, Stephen, was himself accessary to the debasing of the coin of the realm. (*f*) And in imitation of his faithlessness, every lord of a castle, having assumed both a civil and criminal jurisdiction, began to coin money in his own name. (*g*)

One of the most meritorious acts of Henry the Second's government was to restore the impaired money to its former weight and fineness, (*h*) but it appears from Glanvil, that false coining was by no means suppressed in this reign, (*i*) and it is further observable, that the punishment had now been confined to drawing on a hurdle and hanging, as it was until the late act. And, indeed, so far from suppressing the mischief, future monarchs rather advantaged themselves of the breach of the laws, than enforced their severities, so that we must postpone the further illustration of our position until after the reign of the Edwards. For whilst the Jews were clipping on all sides, so much so as to diminish the trade and honour of the country as a commercial nation, Edward I. was buying in bad money at a rate below its value, in order to gain by the traffic, and he is said to have fined some persons who ventured to disturb his iniquitous monopoly (*k*) The parliament, however, were not so negligent; and we have seen, that the importation of base coin was prohibited in 27th Edward I. and that coining was enumerated amongst the treasons of the famous statute, 25th Edward III. Still it would be unfair to argue against the efficacy of capital punishment, when the sovereign was holding forth an example so degrading. Executions, moreover, in the time of the third Edward were very rare. (*l*) But, after the act of treasons, we may form our conclusions with as much con-

---

(*e*) And we could not, in these days, have recourse to a punishment against nature. Barbara Spencer, who was executed for coining in 1721, declared that she was not "*covetous of life*, but could not bear the thoughts of burning." Admitting that this savage punishment would prevent the crime, (which we cannot concede,) it is clear, that we could not at this day return to the burning of women.

(*f*) Lyttelton's Henry II. i. p. 382.
(*g*) Ibid. Hallam's Middle Ages, i. 162, note §.
(*h*) Littleton, ii. 79.   (*i*) See id. iii. 218.
(*k*) Hallam, ii. 518, note †.   (*l*) Barnes's Edward III. p. 467.

hdence as during the reign of Henry I., and thus we find that, notwithstanding the doubts which were entertained whether the offence were not traitorous, people went on clipping, washing, and impairing the money, until it was declared by an act of Henry V. absolute treason to treat the coin in that manner. (m) Then came the provisions in the reign of Elizabeth One of the statutes declared, that since the repealing act of Queen Mary, which had abolished that of Henry V. the practice of clipping had been more boldly continued. This, however, does not furnish an argument in favour of capital punishment, because it appears that at the time of this increase of offences, there was no punishment at all for the evil complained of; and the observation that it had of late advanced, tacitly acknowledged that it had previously existed, although in a minor degree

We must now request the reader's attention to the important discussion which took place in William III.'s reign, upon a proposition to establish an entirely new coinage. It had, indeed, been a complaint in the time of the Commonwealth, that the statutes relating to the coin had not been sufficiently enforced, (n) and in the time of Charles II there was some legislation upon the subject, (o) but in the reign of William, the greatest commercial men bent their minds undividedly to the question of which we are speaking. An adulterated coinage, a declining trade, a scantiness of treasure, were the vexations under which the nation laboured at this crisis. The statutes of Edward III and Elizabeth were still in force. But what were the opinions of those who carefully studied the subject at that period? Not merely that it was impracticable to restrain crimes by penalties alone, but that even capital punishment was not to be adopted, and to this last suggestion the exceptions are very rare.

"It looks but like beating the air," says one writer, "to endeavour the prevention of clipping, &c, or otherwise debasing the coin of this kingdom, till the same be all new minted, and made of less intrinsic value; which being done, it will appear very easy; for the temptation (i. e. interest or gain), which is the cause, being thereby taken away, the effect will naturally cease."(p) This writer, whilst he wished it be made capital to export more than 10*l* of the coin without license, proposed fine and banishment only for counterfeiting and debasing it. (q) He ends the tract with these words, in Italics.—"Thus all temptation (which is profit) being taken away, the effect will cease."(r)

(m) Reeves, iii 261.
(n) See Whitelock's Memorials, p; 395.
(o) See Reeves' Chart of the Criminal Law.
(p) Tracts in the British Museum, entitled Banks—Coin—Insurance, vol. x No. 34.   (q) Ibid.   (r) Ibid.

Another, who spoke of the deficiency of the coin as being notorious, proposed its restitution, but accompanied by protecting penalties short of death (s) A third, while he allows that it should be high treason to coin any bullion, admits plainly that " counterfeiting of money is very much practised, to the great abuse of his majesty and subjects, for want of a method to prevent and discover the persons offending therein "(t) He, however, never ventured to propose, that the possessing of coining tools should be treasonable, according to the late law. A fourth speaks of the coins as " being abominably adulterated, diminished, and debased ;" and attributes the evil mainly to the " villany and guilty practices of goldsmiths, bankers, refiners, and money-brokers, &c , who have been gainers, encouragers, receivers, and purveyors, to this abominable crime "(u) And when he says, in a future page, that the crime of *counterfeiting* money being punishable with death, is " likely to have fewer offenders,"(x) his assertion does not seem to be quite in keeping with what he had previously advanced. For after his denunciation of the goldsmiths and others, as above, he adds, that they all are, consequently, " sharers in the guilt of so much blood as the severity of our law hath drawn down to punish it," i e the crime of coining (y) And thus, in deprecating the sad consequences of this connivance by monied men, he is found to confirm the important fact advanced by contemporary writers, that, so long as temptation existed, it was impossible to restrain the offence.

The country had thus the severe statutes of Edward III., of Elizabeth, and of William, before their eyes. Here were statutes sufficient, at all events, to occasion a serious thought before they should be violated, if indeed thoughts of the future be ever present with unfortunate criminals But it is a surprising fact, that whilst the Parliament thus sanctioned the most extreme punishment for debasing their new coinage, no fewer than *seven men* and *one woman* had been put to death at Tyburn at the same time, not more than a year, or two years at the farthest, before the passing of the new act. (z) And did the fresh indignation of the law control the mischief? So far from that result, we find amongst the records of that date frequent executions of persons for the offences of counterfeiting, clipping, and coining. It is not necessary to multiply facts . the annals of the age are sufficient to prove the absolute inefficiency of the capital law, if a search be

---

(s) Id. No. 19.
(t) Id. No. 36, p. 3, and see id. Nos. 19-40 inclusive.
(u) A Discourse of Money, London, 1696, pp. 75, 77.
(x) Id. 190.   (y) Id. 77.
(z) Remarkable Trials, 1718, i. 57.

made with due diligence. (*a*)   The executions referred to, it should moreover be noticed, took place, for the most part, soon after the passing of the new measure; and there followed a constant succession of others, even unto the period of our times.   And the offence increased, because profit could be derived from it, and because the generality of the people saw no evil in it.   It was like the taking of game, which the populace at large look upon as no wrong.   When Barbara Spencer came to die, in 1721, for coining, she declared, that she had learnt her art of a man and woman who had made their fortunes by the trade, and had retired.   She would not discover them, for, she said, it would be a pity to ruin those who had given over the practice, *when hundreds lived secure in London who still continued it.* (*b*)   The testimony of a convicted felon is worth nothing in the eye of the law; but here is a practical condemnation of legal bloodshed, at the foot of the gallows, made disinterestedly, and without entreaty.   And thus, as we proceed in the last century, we find the same careful concealment working successfully for years in the pursuit of illegal gain (*c*)   Now and then a criminal is entrapped, discovered, and executed, but others succeed to his exertions, perhaps to his materials, and the great game of profit is carried on in defiance of death and punishment. (*d*)   Nor did the severity of the law diminish with the wane of this century.   The following tables will prove this fact, as well as the truth of the inflexibility of prior executions.

I.—Table of Capital Convictions and Executions for Coining, in London, from 1699 to 1756, and in London and Middlesex, from 1756 to 1800.

Years.	Con.	Ex.	Years.	Con.	Ex.
1699—1700	4	0	1708-9	0	0
1700-1	1	0	1709-10—1719-20	*nil*	
1702-3	0	0	1720-1	1	1
1704-5	1	1	1721-2—1736-7	*nil*	
1705-6	0	0	1737-8	1	1
1706-7	0	0	1738-9—1747-8	*nil*	
1707-8	0	0	1748-9	3	0

(*a*) See id. p. 201.   Two hung for coining immediately after the new act.   See also pp. 188, 202, 228, 293, vol. ii p. 15, &c.   See also Russell on Crimes, ed. 1819, vol. i. pp. 71-127.   Leach's Crown Cases, and East's Pleas of the Crown, vol. i. chap. iv.

(*b*) Newgate Calendar, i 35.

(*c*) See Gentleman's Magazine, 1776, p. 92.

(*d*) See Select Trials, Lond. 1764 — 4 volumes, with an index at the beginning of each volume.

Years.	Con	Ex.	Years.	Con	Ex.
1749-50—1757	*nil*		1781	2	1
1758	2	2	1782............	4	4
1759—1765........	*nil*		1783.	2	1
1766,............	1	1	1784............	0	0
1767.............	1	1	1785............	0	0
1768............	0	0	1786...	2	2
1769.	0	0	1787..	1	1
1770,...........	0	0	1788........	6	3
1771.	1	1	1789	5	5
1772.	3	2	1790........	6	4
1773......	2	1	1791.	0	0
1774.............	2	1	1792-1795 .. .	*nil*	
1775............	5	5	1796............	2	0
17 6............,10	10	7	1797.	2	2
1777.........	1	1	1798.	5	2
1778........	1	0	1799...........	0	0
1779.............	4	3	1800......	2	0
1780.............	3	3			
			Totals... .	86	56

On the Home Circuit there were :

Years.	Con.	Ex.
From 1692 to 1718.......... .	34	16
1755 to 1784........	6	3
1785 to 1804..	14	10
Totals.	54	29

Some tables of the other circuits, not, however, very perfect, will be found in the Parliamentary Returns referred to.

II.—Table of Executions for Coining in London and Middlesex from 1731 to 1750 (e)

1731....0		1739....1	
1732....0		1740....0	
1733....2		1741....0	
1734....3		1742....0	
1735....0		1743....3 (f)	
1736....0			
1737....0			[been hung.
1738....3	1 Committed suicide in Newgate, who would have		

(e) This Table differs from the preceding, because it contains the executions in *Middlesex* as well as London.

(f) It was made high treason in the preceding year to wash shillings, half-pence, or farthings, so as to resemble the gold coin of the realm. But in less than six months afterwards, four persons were capitally convicted of the offence.

1744 0	1748.....0
1745....0	1749....3
1746....1	1750....1
1747....0	

Total 16

III.—Table of the Executions for Coining in London and Middlesex from 1749 to 1764 (g)

† Years of war — the rest were years of peace.

1749....3	1758 †..3 (h)
1750....1	1759 †. 0
1751.. .0	1760 †..0
1752....0	1761 †..0
1753....0	1762 †. 0
1754....0	1763....0
1755,...0	
1756 †..0	Total 7
1757 † 0	

IV.—Table of Capital Convictions and Executions for Coining in London and Middlesex from 1761 to 1800, both inclusive, specifying the nature and number of the offences. (i)

The years marked thus * do not agree with the Official Report returned by the Clerk of Arraigns. The reason is simply this — the Return comprises the actual executions *in each year*. The above Table gives the executions which followed the offences, although such executions might not have taken place until the ensuing year. For instance, convicts at the December sessions are usually executed in January or February. The differences will be reconciled by adopting this suggestion. Those marked thus † are years of war.

	Conv.		Ex.
1764...	0	....	0
1765....	0	....	0
1766....	1	Diminishing.....	1
1767....	1	Filing and diminishing	1
1768....	0	....	0
1769....	0	....	0
1770....	0	....	0
1771....	1	Shillings and six-pences. . ..	1

(g) From an Official Return printed by order of the House of Commons
(h) One of these was a *joint* offence.
(i) This Table differs from Table I., because it not only shews the Convictions and Executions in Middlesex as well as London, but also distinguishes the offences more particularly, and shows whether they are joint or several.

	Con.		Ex.
1772	3	(2) Guineas	2
1773	2	(1) Guineas, (1) having engines for milling money in possession	1
* 1774	(*l*) 2	Shillings and sixpences	1
* 1775	†. 5	(2)—(2)—1 having a mould for milling................. ..	4
* 1776	.. 10	....	7
1777	†..1	Colouring metal to resemble half-crowns and shillings	1
1778	†. 1	Having a punch	1
1779	†..4	(2) Shillings, (2) sixpences....	3
1780	†..4	(2) Shils & sixps. (1) half-crs. shils & sixps. (1) col. metal ..	2
1781	†..2	(1) Shils (1) half crowns	1
* 1782	†..3	(1) Having a mould, (2) silver	3
* 1783	3	(1) Having a mould (1) shils .	2
1784	..0	....	0
1785	0	. ...	0
1786	2	(1) Halfpence—benefit of clergy having been before allowed — (1) shillings [a woman.]	2
1787	1	Colouring sixpences	1
* 1788	6	(2) Shillings—(2)—(2).	5
* 1789	5	(2)—1 Shils.—(2) half-crowns.	5
1790	6	(1) Colouring—died in Newgate. (2) Shils (3) sixpences..	4
1791	0	....	0
1792	0	....	0
1793	†..0	....	0
1794	†. 0	....	0
1795	†..0	....	0
1796	†..2	Shillings and sixpences	0
1797	† (2)	Colouring blanks for half-crs. shils and sixps	2
1798	†(*m*)5	(1) Half crs. shils. & sixpences. (4) Women colouring metal to resemble silver.....	2 1 woman
1799	†..0	....	0
1800	†..2	(1) Having a cutting engine, (1) col. base coin to resemble silver.	0

Total 74   53

(*l*) 1774. In this year, a man named Thomas Ives was executed The Official Return is *nil*.

(*m*) 1798. In this year, a man and *a woman* were executed. The Official Report returns but one person.

Note.—Several persons were acquitted for coining, between the years 1791 and 1797.—And observe, that the parenthesis ( ) denotes a joint offence. (*n*)

We will now pause for a moment The executions for coining during the years comprehended in the last table, bear a proportion to the convictions of *three-fourths*, within a fraction. We have, therefore, made good our assertion, that as the century declined, mercy made no advances in respect of coiners. The same proposition will be found applicable to convictions in the country (*o*)

But it will be said at once, that the rigour of punishment diminished the offence, or, at all events, stemmed its increase, and reference will be confidently made to those years in which neither conviction nor execution happened Now, although recourse might be had to a variety of arguments and proofs, all tending to shew the futility of such a conclusion, it will be better to advert immediately to the state of things in 1800, concerning the money of the realm It might be said, that the art of coining successfully was at one time in few hands; that several persons made their fortunes by the trade, and retired from any further realization of its dangerous profits, that the extreme difficulty of detecting offenders, has fully proved the security and secrecy of the crime; that the newspapers have often teemed with cautions against *gangs* of coiners, when a severe example has just been made, or, perhaps, impended, at the particular time, in a word, that the advance or diminution of the evil may be said to depend more upon the chances or casual incidents of profit, than upon any circumstances of conviction or certainty of execution And attention might again be invited to the observations which were offered prior to the insertion of the above tables But the condition of the metropolis in the latter period of the last, and early years of the present century, (with all the death-inflicting statutes at command, and the full tide of execution in practice,) sufficiently demonstrates, that the plan of restraining the issue of counterfeit money by stern penal laws was a failure. We proceed to prove the fact. At, or nearly about this time, there were in Lon-

---

(*n*) The Official Tables may be found as follows
I.—London and Middlesex, 1749—1818. Parl. Papers, 1819, vol. xvii. p. 297.
II.—London, 1699—1756, and London and Middlesex, 1756—1804. Parl. Papers, 1819, vol. viii. p. 146, being in the Appendix to the Report from the Select Committee on the Criminal Laws
(*o*) The author began the task of collecting the Convictions on the Circuits, but he found that great uncertainty met him at every step, and he consequently desisted. This observation applies to the last century, as we have regular Returns from the Clerks of Assize during the greater number of years since 1800.

don and the country 54 coiners, and 56 large dealers, besides 10 die-sinkers, whose names, characters, and pursuits were perfectly well known (p) Scarcely a waggon or coach departed from the metropolis which did not carry boxes and parcels of base coin to the camps, sea-ports, and manufacturing towns. (q) Indeed, the vast increase and extensive circulation of counterfeit money, particularly of late years, was too obvious not to have attracted the notice of all ranks. (r) The great dealers were in the habit of executing orders for the town and country with the same regularity as manufacturers in fair branches of trade. (s) There stood upon the register of the solicitor to the mint, within seven years, then last past, no fewer than 650 names. " And yet," continues Colquhoun, " the evil is not diminished." (t) The truth was, that the whole kingdom groaned under the calamities of a spurious coinage The merchant and the tradesman were never secure from anticipations of probable loss, and as this injury was often realized, commercial men were exposed to an inconvenience of no trifling consideration. One of the chief London coiners acknowledged to Mr Colquhoun, that he had coined to the extent of two hundred thousand pounds in counterfeit half-crowns, and other base silver money, in less than seven years, (u) and this, says the author whose work we are quoting, is the less surprising, because two persons can finish to the amount of from £200 to £300 per week (x) This latter observation brings us to the question of profit, for unless there were some pecuniary advantage, there would be no coining, and whilst there exists any such gain, we argue, that *capital punishment* affords no protection Now, in the first place, an admirable and masterly imitation of a guinea was made, bearing the date of 1793, whose intrinsic value was not above eight shillings (y) There was not, however, a very great number of these, but the profit was obviously considerable. Then followed the base silver Now the ordinary counterfeit shilling was worth from two to four pence, and it passed in general through several hands before it came to the public customer. There was, of course, a gain upon each change of the ownership, till the fabricated commodity was transferred from the common utterer to the public. It is also observable, that crowns and half-crowns bore the same proportion of advantage (z) Another species of false coinage, which required more skill in its creation, was said to be so lucrative as to fetch at once its full import value (a) A third sort of base money was confined to shillings, and although

---

(p) Colquhoun on the Police of the Metropolis, 7th edit. p. 211.
(q) Id. p 16.   (r) Id. p 15   (s) Id. p. 16.
(t) Id. p. 19.   (u) Colquhoun, ut supra, p. 179.
(x) Id. p 180.   (y) Id. p. 174.   (z) Id 176.
(a) Id. p. 177.

it was of inferior workmanship, so much so, as to lose its small share of pure metal in a very short time ; yet it appears to have cost the makers no more than one halfpenny for each shilling, and to have passed at the full nominal value (*b*) And, moreover, it was soon resold to the Jews as bad money, and forthwith re-coloured for fresh circulation (*c*) Fourthly, came the crooked money, which many of us can remember, before the late new coinage. Now, the intrinsic value of this was not one halfpenny in a shilling, and the deception was so good, that it soon gained an unsuspicious circulation (*d*) " Even after this the itinerant Jews will purchase them at three-pence each, though six times their intrinsic value, well knowing that they can again be re-coloured at the expense of half a farthing, so as to pass without difficulty for their nominal value of twelve pence (*e*) Lastly, there was a very inferior composition, the value being no more than one farthing in half a crown The smallest profit made upon this last kind was from 50 to 80 per cent whilst it was not by any means uncommon to get from five hundred to a thousand per cent. and sometimes more (*f*)

With respect to the copper coinage, it was said that the quan-tity of counterfeits at one time in circulation, might be said to equal three-fourths of the whole (*g*) Now, although the punish-ment for this latter offence was only an imprisonment for a year and a day, and that for falsifying the silver coin was capital, yet there seems to be but little difference between the aggregate amount of counterfeits, (that is to say, of silver and copper,) espe-cially when considered with reference to the vast disproportion of the respective penalties.—" For," says Colquhoun, " at no time can any person minutely examine either the one coin or the other, which may come into his possession, without finding a con-siderable proportion counterfeit "(*h*) The test, therefore, of the decrease of coining must be the ceasing of pecuniary gain, and not the severity of punishment, for it appears quite certain, that as long as a probability (and much more when a *certainty*) of profit exists, men will be found quite prepared to run all hazards for the acquisition of a competent though ill-gotten inde-pendence.

We next invite the attention of the reader to a table of capital convictions and executions, from the beginning of the century to the time of the issuing of the new silver coinage, referring, at the same time, to two returns by the officers of the Mint, respect-ing the gold and silver coinage

---

(*b*) Colquhoun p. 177.   (*c*) Ibid.
(*d*) Id. 178.   (*e*) Ibid.   (*f*) Id. 179.
(*g*) Id. 185.   (*h*) Ibid.

V.—A Table of Convictions and Executions in London and Middlesex,(1) for Counterfeiting Gold and Silver Coin, from the year 1801 to the time of issuing the new Silver Coinage:—

	Con.		Ex.
†1801	...0		0
†1802	1	Shillings	0
†1803	1	Shillings	0
†1804	0		0
†1805	5	3 Colouring sixpences, and 2 others, silver..	1 Colouring
†1806	0		0
†1807	0		0
†1808	1	Silver..	0
†1809	0		0
†1810	3	2 Silver, 1 cutting-engine..	0
†1811	1	Colouring silver..	0
†1812	... 3	Colouring silver..	0
†1813	0		0
†1814	... 4	Colouring silver..	0
1815	3	Colouring silver..	0
1816	... 11	6 Colouring silver, and 5 coining silver ..	0

Total .. 33 1

The silver coinage bill was passed in the summer of 1816.

---

(1) See the Parl. Papers for 1812, vol. ix. p. 299 , and for 1818, vol. xiv. p. 83.

The grand total is as follows

From 1783 to 1796, being 14 years preceding the suspension of cash payments,

		Pros.	Con.
	Gold	30	
	Silver	778	
		808	537

From 1797 to 1812,	Gold	263	
	Silver	1322	
		1586	

From February, 1797, to February, 1818,

Total Gold and Silver 2681   2132

VI.—A similar Table, showing the Convictions and Executions at the Assizes,(*k*) from 1805 to 1816.

	Con.	Ex.		Con.	Ex.
1805(*l*)	2	2	1811	0	0
1806	4	3	1812(*m*)	1	0
1807	3	0	1813	9	1
1808	0	0	1814	10	0
1809	1	1	1815	3	0
1810	0	0	1816	6	0
			Total....39		7

The first observation which will naturally arise upon the perusal of the two last tables, will be that a greater exercise of the prerogative of mercy was allowed to interfere in favour of the coiners when compared with the executions of former years But it may also be said, that in consequence of this leniency, the crime itself began to increase about the year 1812, and the number of convictions from that period to 1816, will be referred to as a proof of this. In order to repel this plausible argument, it should be noticed, first, that the offences in question were by no means several, nor arising at different places; and secondly, that the apprehension of two or three gangs of coiners which happened about this time was entirely fortuitous, and might have occurred in other years; for an attentive consideration of the history of coining will prove that the offence has thriven, for a long period, in various places, entirely in defiance of the vigilance of the police; that, at length, some clue has been discovered, and the nest of culprits has been disclosed. Thus, in prior years it will be occasionally found, that a happy circumstance had led to the detection and breaking up of a mischievous gang. Convictions have ensued, and the evil has been interrupted in that particular quarter upon principles totally independent either of severity or clemency. Because by the fact of seizing the instruments employed in fabricating the coin, you of course check the offence thus far; whereas, it is well known, that if the coiner alone be taken,

---

(*k*) Home, Western, Midland, Oxford, Norfolk, and Northern Circuits; also North Wales, Brecon, and Carmarthen Circuits. Upon the other Welsh Circuits, as well as at Chester and the Isle of Ely, there do not appear to have been many, if, indeed, any, convictions or executions for coining; but the returns from these latter places have not been regular.

(*l*) No Return for the Oxford.

(*m*) No Returns for the Western, Oxford, and Norfolk.

other parties will immediately succeed to his materials. Then, again, with reference to the year 1816, in which so large a catalogue appears, it will be found that there are not more than three, or at most four, separate convictions out of the eleven   They are five, three, and three; thus, as to the quantity of offence, bearing no greater proportion than in other years, whilst the number of persons included in each indictment makes good the points which we have suggested respecting the casual taking of *gangs* of coiners.   Again, it will appear upon inquiry, that the practices here alluded to have not prevailed in different parts of the kingdom, and in proof of this it may be asserted that the Midland Circuit returns contain perhaps as much as one-half of the country convictions for coining, and Newcastle engrosses a considerable proportion of the remainder   Lastly, we will refer to the observation of the Chancellor of the Exchequer,(n) when the measure for creating the new silver coinage was agreed to "From the present cheapness of silver," he said, "there are no other means of preventing the country from being inundated with fabricated pieces, the continuance of which must daily increase the evil "(o) On the whole, therefore, the cheapness of the article upon which the false issues are worked is one proposition, and the security of the profit which is to ensue upon the execution of the fraud is another, but the punishment of death has not been admitted into the scale; and consequently, as it operates not by way of example or influence, it surely is quite right in this instance to abandon it

We will now subjoin a table of the capital convictions and executions, from the issuing of the new coinage until the present day, as nearly as we can; and it will be instantly apparent, that the wholesome change both crippled the advantages, as well as diminished the profits of the fraudulent imitators The increase of offences in 1827 and 1828, *or rather of convictions*, may be considered upon the two principles which we have so much insisted on — that is to say, first, the union of several persons in the same indictment, which proves the joint nature of the crime; and, secondly, the critical apprehensions of long-concealed tribes of coiners.

VII.—A Table of Convictions and Executions for Coining, from 1817 to 1830, inclusive of both years, in England and Wales.(p)

	Con.	Ex		Con	Ex.
1817	2	0	1820	0	0
1818	0	0	1821	0	0
1819	0	0	1822	2	1

(n) Mr. Vansittart.   (o) Parl. Debates, vol. xxxiv. p. 965
(p) Including London and Middlesex

	Con.	Ex.			Con.	Ex.
1823	1	1		1828	9	6
1824	2	1		1829	0	0
1825	1	0		1830	0	0(q)
1826	10	1		1831	7	0
1827	20	6		1832	0	0

There was another offence relating to the coin, which the 15 Geo 2 c. 28, declared to be capital, namely, the uttering of counterfeit money after prior convictions This penalty ensued in two cases : first, where a party had been found guilty of uttering generally for the *third* time,(r) and secondly, (which was by far the most common occurrence) where having been previously convicted as a *common utterer*,(s) he was again attainted of uttering, and this would follow upon the *second*, instead of the third indictment   However, as there was only one execution(t) upon this statute, and as that proceeded upon very particular circumstances, which we proceed to mention, it does not appear necessary to enlarge upon this head.   Yet as there have been numerous convictions for the offence of a second uttering, it is impossible not to see in a moment, that a law which by reason of its severity could not be carried into execution, must needs have been mitigated (u)

With reference to the single execution which took place, the sufferer was a man named Joseph Cope.   He had been indicted for coining sixpences, together with four others, and acquitted. He was then charged with colouring base coin so as to produce the resemblance of a sixpence, and acquitted ; and lastly, he was arraigned upon a third indictment for the offence in question, and found guilty.   His former conviction was for putting off forty bad sixpences , and, as it seemed manifest that he was the

---

(q) Return of Mint Prosecutions from 1790 to 1820
Gold, 213 . Silver, 2978.
Same from 1818 to 1827 .. Total Gold and Silver, 2237.

(r) The same with respect to foreign coin, 37 Geo. 3. c. 126. Very few convictions have happened upon this clause, and, I believe, no execution.   The convictions have taken place principally, if not exclusively, in the Circuits.

(s) That is, being proved to have had other counterfeit money about him in his custody at the time of the first uttering, or being proved to have uttered other false money, " either on the same day, or within the space of ten days then next."

(t) At all events, one only in London and Middlesex.

(u) From the passing the act until 1818, there were 36 capital convictions in London and Middlesex , from 1821 to 1829, 11 ; in England and Wales, 1821 to 1829, 20.

chief of a gang of persons who made a livelihood by coining six-pences, he was considered to be a proper subject for execution. We shall have an opportunity, upon a future occasion, of con-demning the principle upon which this man suffered, (r) and will, therefore, forbear for the present   There was one other circum-stance relating to the coin which formerly produced a capital conviction, namely, where the prisoner was found guilty upon a charge which would have made it necessary for him to have prayed the benefit of clergy in case that privilege had not been before allowed him. There have been four convictions at the Old Bailey within the last century, for putting off base coin at a lower rate than its denomination imparted, benefit of clergy hav-ing been previously allowed, but no execution has followed ; but, upon one occasion, a man named Smith, otherwise Storer, was convicted for coining halfpence, having had his clergy, and was executed.

APPENDIX, No. II.

Stealing in a Dwelling-House to the amount of Five Pounds.

The offence of larceny in a building communicating *immediately* with a dwelling house, or " by means of a covered and enclosed passage leading from the one to the other, and à fortiori in the dwelling-house was itself, as far as the punishment of death ap-plies, the capital offence which the late act has repealed. (b)   In fact, the buildings which thus communicate are neither more nor less than the dwelling-house.

The crime consists in stealing to the amount of 5*l*, without any breaking. The tables, however, of the old act, which fixed the sum at 40*s*, will be found applicable to the matter now under consideration, especially as the value of money has increased greatly since those days

In very old days, the offence of stealing (*furtum*) was pu-nished by several proportioned penalties. To commit larceny upon the king was visited by a nine-fold compensation (b); upon a freeman, three times, with a *wite* for the king if the thief were

---

(r) In the Second Part to be published hereafter.
(a) See the old acts.   East, P. C. pp. 535, 629, 640, &c.
(b) Wilkins. p. 4. pl. 2.

a freeman; (c) in a dwelling-house, three times (d) If a slave purloined, he was to pay twice the value. (e) The same system of compensation prevailed in the reigns of the kings of Canterbury. (f) King Ina was also friendly to this mode of recompence, but when the thieves amounted to seven in a gang, he called them (*fures*), and demanded the weregild of them, or put them to death in default of payment. (g) As to a slave, if he were often accused of purloining, and at length caught in the act of selling his spoil, either his hand or foot might be cut off. (h) But it was always understood, that if a thief were taken in the *mainour*, he must be at the king's mercy, that is, to die, or pay the full price of his life. (i)

King Alfred sanctioned the system of compensation, and Athelstan seems to have added a kind of suretyship on the part of the criminal's relatives, (k) a notion which is well worth our attention at present, although it was much opposed during the discussions on the Game Laws in the House of Commons. (l)

By the Constitutions of London made by Athelstan, a similar rigour was enforced, with this addition, namely, that when the thief was killed, his goods were first of all to satisfy the amount of his theft, and then were to be divided into two parts,—one for his wife and family, if they were clear of his transgression,—the other also into two parts, one for the king, the second for the benefit of the state. (m) The value, however, of the property stolen must have amounted to eight denarii (about 5s. 4d.) under these laws of Athelstan, and it seems proper to observe here, that with one exception, all the laws above referred to have reference to the *furtum* only, consequently, for the penalties in question to have operated, there must have been seven in a gang. The exception was the very act of *stealing in the dwelling-house*, and the word used is *abstulerit*, instead of *furaverit*. Therefore, stealing in a dwelling-house was punished by the threefold restitution if the thief were alone, but if he were in company with six others, the weregild was demandable. The old mode of making compensation for the *furtum* continued, with sureties, as

---

(c) Id. ibid. pl. 9.
(d) Id. p. 4, pl. 29.   (e) Id. p. 7, pl. 89.
(f) Wilkins, p. 7, 10.
(g) Id. p. 17, pl. 12. and see Id. p. 16, pl. 7 and 57. Reeves, 1. 17.
(h) Id. p. 18, pl. 18. So a (*Colonus*) p. 20, pl. 37.
(i) Id. p. 12. Id. p. 56, pl. 1. Leges Ælthelstani, Id. p. 137, pl. 23. Leges Cnuti, and pl. 61.
(k) Id. pl. 56, pl. 1.
(l) One of the chief points of our new economy must be to devise some plan for compelling parents to respect the moral education of their offspring.   (m) Wilkins p. 65.

it seems; (n) and a law of Edward the Confessor declared that thieves might have sanctuary. (o) The Conqueror permitted an appeal of the *furtum*, and ordained, that if the accused person could not find compurgators, he should be compelled to undergo the ordeal.(p) It was reserved for Henry I. to abolish the weregild in cases of theft and robbery. This was effected in 1108, and the punishment of hanging was prescribed against such felons, *when taken in the mainour*.(q) Now, in order to prevent any possible mistake, let us add, that the result of these various institutions was to punish stealing in the dwelling-house (the subject now before us) capitally, if there were seven persons in a gang; redeemable, however, by the weregild, and a *wite* to the king. Henry I abolished the weregild, and then, if taken in the manner, the thief was irretrievably hanged Cases of open theft now came to be tried before the sheriff or the lord by virtue of his infangethef and utfangethef (r) If the party were not taken with the *mainour*, then the king's justices only had the power of taking cognizance. (s) Nevertheless, although at first the punishment for theft seems to have been very uncertain and discretionary,(t) (we mean, of course, where the crime was not manifest, for then it was capital) the matter did not remain long in doubt, and the distinction between grand and petty larceny (which we have lately abolished) began to obtain. So that in the reign of Edward the First, it was probably a capital felony, redeemable only by reading, to steal above the value of 12d., either in the dwelling-house or elsewhere. (u) And instead of being under the sheriff's jurisdiction, theft came now to be reckoned generally amongst the *placita coronæ* (x)

Thus, the stealing of goods *to the amount*, as some say of twelve pence, and, at all events, *above* the shilling, was punishable capitally in this reign But in the reign of Henry VII a notion was raised, that a taking must be in all cases *vi et armis*, that there must be a seizure of the thing stolen. And the inference which the judges drew from this idea was, that if a butler robbed his master of plate confided to him, or a shepherd the fold, neither could be convicted of larceny, because the words

---

(n) Id. p 110, 197, pl. 6.   (o) Id. p. 197, pl. 6.
(p) Wilkins p. 222, pl. 16.
(q) Id. p 304. Hayward's Norman Kings, p. 279
(r) Reeves, i. 250. ii. 40.   (s) Id ii. 41.
(t) Richard I. in his voyage to the Holy Land, ordained thus :—" If any one is convicted of theft, let his head be shaved, like a champion's, let melted pitch be poured upon it, and feathers shaken over it, that he may be known, and let him be set on shore at the first land to which the ship approaches."—Henry's Gt. Britain, iii. p. 368.
(u) See Reeves, ii. 274, 275. iii. 122.
(x) Reeves, i. 251.

vi et armis could never be satisfied. they said, by a man taking that, which, in fact, was in his own possession (*y*) And hence, it followed, that the embezzlement of goods by servants to the amount of forty shillings, was made felony by 21 Henry 8, provided such goods had been delivered over to the keeping of the servant. This was the origin of larceny in a dwelling-house, to the amount of forty shillings, which so long prevailed amongst us. In a subsequent year of Henry VIII. clergy was taken from persons stealing in any of the king's houses, whether by a breaking or without it (*z*) So that the reader observes it was now no longer felony for persons to steal goods committed to their care in dwelling-houses or elsewhere, under forty shillings, but that in other cases, they were capitally punishable if they took more than twelve pence. And this naturally brings us to mention the circumstance of clergy, whose immunities being more and more extended, many persons were enabled to commit larceny with comparatively a light punishment. Accordingly, the legislature of William III. fruitful in capital penalties, introduced the celebrated statute against privily stealing in a shop, warehouse, coach-house, stable, &c, and that of Queen Anne took away clergy also from larceny in a dwelling-house, or outhouse belonging to it, to the value of forty shillings. In both these cases, (as indeed it was until lately) it signified not at all whether the shop or house were broken or not, nor whether any person were within.

This is the short history of the capital punishment(*a*) for larceny in a dwelling-house without force. We now proceed to state the results of the penalty, and more especially from the days of King William and Queen Anne, when the new acts excluding clergy were passed.

Results.

It is impossible not to see that the provisions of the legislature upon this subject have had respect chiefly to the dishonesty of servants. Masters and mistresses who have accustomed themselves for many centuries to treat their domestics like cattle, to dispense with them at a moment's notice upon some occasions, and at others to discard them after a very short interval—who have never for an instant considered the difference of education between themselves and those who serve them, but always inveigh bitterly against any conduct (which they are pleased to call ingratitude) in their people which happens to displease them—became seriously indignant when they found themselves most unmercifully plundered by their hired servants. When they had spread the pains of death around their mansions, they naturally

---

(*y*) Id. iv. 285.
(*z*) Reeves, iv. 288   (*a*) East. P. C. pp. 640, 644.

concluded themselves secure, but it was only (like the poor bankers who fell into the trap of the forgery laws) to beg with tears in their eyes that they might be allowed to forego prosecution, or that mercy might be extended to their convicted hirelings It will be found that their alarm has not been without foundation. The offence of stealing in a dwelling-house has been particularly fatal to servants, and although it is one of those which has been less rigorously visited than others, the executions which have happened have been chiefly amongst domestics, shopmen, and confidential people. The judges soon caught the notion that it was a most aggravated crime for a servant to rob his master, and accordingly, prepared themselves to resist all applications for mercy on that score (*c*) The popular sanction soon shifted to the side of mercy, because, to *hang* a man in an enlightened age for stealing without force, was a most melancholy mistake, and consequently, the unfortunate prosecutor has had to contend with the three-fold miseries of an angry populace, an inexorable judge, and a force of conscience truly painful And so sure has been the rule which the magistrates of the land adopted, that a man had as well been " born a dog," as stand a convicted criminal at the bar for robbing his master's dwelling-house.

Juries also have taken up the quality of mercy. They began by annihilating the grand larcenies with their verdicts of " guilty, 10*d* " When the statutes of Elizabeth and William III. fixed 5*s* as the price of blood, the juries said, " guilty, 4*s* 10*d* " When Queen Anne's law made the amount 40*s.*, the verdicts ran, " guilty, 39*s* " The acumen of prosecutors in lowering the estimate of their property so as to bring the total amount below 40*s.*, has often presented a most curious and interesting scene.

Not to detain the reader ; the fact is, that it was soon found impossible to carry the sentence of the law into effect upon these occasions. The severity of the legislature entirely outdid itself. There were numerous candidates for death at every sessions, and at all assizes, and it was soon concluded that none excepting *servants, watchmen,* and house-breakers (whom the jury should find guilty of stealing from the dwelling-house for want of sufficient proof of the breaking) should suffer death. A reference to the tables, especially the last, will shew, nevertheless, that this limitation was made under an infelicitous mistake Many servants were convicted of the inexpiable crime, many suffered death, but the greatest grievance of all was, that masters would on no consideration prosecute their dishonest domestics,

---

(*c*) " You have done your duty, Sir," said Chief Justice Best to a clergyman, at Salisbury, whose servant had been convicted of robbing him, " I must now do mine."—Judgment of death was then passed, and the man was executed.

and, consequently, the executions were merely voluntary Perhaps not one case out of ten was prosecuted capitally.

The offence, however, being now liable to a less rigorous punishment, it is unnecessary to make any further comments We subjoin the tables.

I.—Convictions and Executions in London, from 1712(d) to 1755, for stealing in a Dwelling-house. Amount, 40s.

Con	Ex.
125	35

II.—Executions in London and Middlesex, from 1731 to 1755. (MS.)

	Ex.
25 years,	46

III —Convictions and Executions in London and Middlesex, from 1756 to 1827. Amount, 40s.

Con	Ex
1,499	141

IV.—Convictions and Executions on the Circuits.

		Con.	Ex.
Home	1712—1718	3	1
	1755—1817	202	22
Western	1770—1818	291	14
Oxford	1799—1819 (Lent)	143 convictions.	
Midland	1805—1817	62	0
Norfolk	1768—1818 (Lent)	118	12
Lancaster	1798—1819 (Lent)	47	2 (1 female)
Durham	1755—1819 (Lent)	16	0
Northern	1804—1817	52	0

England and Wales. Ten years of Peace, from 1821 to 1830.

Year.	Com.	Con.	Ex.	Acq.	No Bills, &c
1821	203	134	5	46	and 23
1822	191	133	6	40	and 18
1823	211	145	3	40	and 26
1824	275	188	1	54	and 33
1825	265	186	2	46	and 33
1826	300	222	5	59	and 19
1827	295	223	4	52	and 20

(d) When the act passed.

Year.	Committed.	Con.	Acq.	No Bill, &c.	
1828 (Peel's Acts)	122(c)	81	1	33 and	15
1829	119	81	1	31 and	7
1830	134	100	2	26 and	8

Convictions, Executions, &c. in London and Middlesex, from 18 to 1832.

Year.	Con.	Ex	Acq.	No Bill, &c	Total
1815	32	0		19	51
1816	51	1(d)		18	69
1817	53	0		11	64
1818	63	1(e)		0	0
1819	53	3(f)		0	0 } No returns
1820	49	2(g)		0	0
1821	36	3(h)		35	71
1822	49	4(i)		34	83
1823	47	1(k)		40	87
1824	75	1(l)		48	123
1825	77	2(m)		35	112
1826	73	5(n)		37	110
1827	68	3(o)		32	100

(c) This decrease was owing to the new enactments which—
    1. Facilitated the means of convicting persons for house-breaking
    2. Ordained a new punishment for breaking the curtilage not immediately communicating with the dwelling-house.

(d) 1816, A case of burglary.

(e) 1818, A watchman.

(f) 1819, All servants

(g) 1820, 2 Servants for robbing their master.

(h) 1821, 1, Robbing his master of plate and apparel to the amount of £99. 1, Like offence. 1, Stealing bank notes and guineas. This was a case of *house-breaking*

(i) 1822, 2, This was a *robbery.* 1, This in reality was a *burglary* 1, Stealing to a very large amount in his master's house.

(k) 1823, 1, I cannot find this.

(l) 1824, Stealing gold coin in the dwelling-house.

(m) 1825, 1, Confidential servant for robbing his employers. 1, An apprentice, stealing silk from his employers to the amount of £150, and upwards.

(n) 1826, 1, Stealing property to the amount of £230, from his master's cash box. 1, Robbing a house where he had lived servant. This was a *burglary.* 1, Robbing *her* master of plate, &c. to the amount of £400. The figure 5, I think, is a misprint for 3. There were not more than 3 executed for the offence in this year.

(o) 1827, 1, Robbing his master. 1, Robbing Sewell and Cross, his employers. 1, A case of house-breaking.

Years.	Committed.	Conv.	Exec.	Acq. No bill, &c.
1828 (Peel's Acts.)	26	1(p)	32	58
1823	30	1	25	55
1820	44	0	20	64(q)

APPENDIX, No. III.

I.—Table of Convictions and Executions in London for Horse-stealing.—(Parl Returns.)

Year	Con.	Ex.		Year	Con.	Ex.
1709	5	0		1734	1	0
1710	1	0		1737	1	0
1711	3	1		1738	1	0
1712	4	2		1744	1	0
1713	5	2		1747	1	0
1719	1	1		1748	2	0
1721	1	0		1749	1	0
1725	4	2		1753	1	1
1727	1	0		1755	1	0
1728	2	1			—	—
1730	1	1		Total	38	11

II.—Table of Executions in London and Middlesex, for Horse-stealing from 1731 to 1755.—(From a M.S.

Year	Con.		Year	Con.
1731	2		1748	1
1733	1		1749	2
1734	1		1750	2
1735	3		1751	0
1736	3		1753	1
1738	2(r)		1754	3
1739	2		1755	2
1741	3			

(p) 1828, 1, Robbing his master

(q) In 1831 there were convicted 41, of whom one was executed, namely, a man who was used to take care of houses.

1832, including the July Sessions, after which the new act came into operation, 16 were convicted, but no one suffered death.

(r) One of these was probably convicted in the preceding year, and if so, the tables will be consistent.

III.—Table of Convictions and Executions in London and Middlesex, from 1756 to 1832, when the act passed for repealing capital Punishment.—(Parlt. Returns.)

	Con.	Ex.		Con.	Ex.
1756	1	0	1796	2	0(t)
1757	1	1	1797	3	0
1758	2	1	1798	2	0
1759	6	2	1799	6	0
1760	1	1	1800	8	1(u)
1761	1	0	1801	6	0
1763	2	1	1802	4	0
1764	2	0	1803	10	0
1765	2	0	1804	5	2
1766	5	2	1805	2	0
1767	4	0	1806	2	0
1768	4	0	1807	3	1
1769	7	0	1808	1	0
1770	3	1	1809	9	0
1771	4	0	1010	10	1
1772	1	0	1811	5	0
1773	4	0	1812	2	0
1774	4	0	1813	5	0
1775	3	0	1814	4	0
1776	3	0	1815	4	0
1777	4	0	1816	7	0
1778	3	0	1817	5	0
1779	4	0	1818	11	0
1780	4	0	1819	6	0
1781	3	0	1820	6	1
1782	3	0	1821	5	0
1783	9	0	1822	7	0
1784	12	1	1823	7	0
1785	5	2	1824	5	0
1786	12	5	1825	12	4
1787	5	0	1826	13 !	1
1788	11	0	1827	16 !	3
1789	4	1	1828	12 !	1
1790	2	0	1829	3	0
1791	6	3	1830	4	0
1792	4	1	1831	8	0
1793	1	0	1832	5	0
1794	2	0			
1795	2	0(s)	Total	381	37

(s) In this year one man was hung for this offence.
(t) And in this year another.   (u) Qu. ? 2.

IV.—Table of Convictions and Executions on the Circuits

				Con.	Ex.
Home	..1689	to	1718	158	53
	1755	to	1817	588	73
Western	1770	to	1818	355	50
Oxford	.1799	Lent	1819	241	—
Midland..	1805	to	1817	91	2
Norfolk	1768	Lent	1818	262	36 left for ex
Lancaster	1718	Lent	1819	55	3
Durham .	1755	Lent	1819	26	0
Northern	1804	to	1817	50	0

V.—England and Wales—1821 to 1830

Years	Charged	Con.	Ex.	Acq	No Bill, &c
1821	173	129	3	31	and 13
1822	136	102	1	20	14
1823 ..	179	134	4	30	15
1824	150	104	1	32	14
1825	229	165	8	49	15
1826	171	120	7	36	14
1827	229	147	10	60	22
1828..	180	138	6	32	10
1829	184	147	6	27	10
1830	.185	139	0	37	9

APPENDIX, No. IV.

I —Table of Convictions and Executions in London for *Sheep-Stealing*, from 1741 to 1755. *(none)*—Parl Return

II —Table of Executions in London and Middlesex, from 1741 to 1755

⁎ The first convict for sheep-stealing, was reprieved in 1741.

Years. Ex
1742 1
1744 2 Fifteen ewe sheep.
1745. 1
1746..0 One reprieved, for stealing twenty lambs.
1752 .1 Twenty sheep.
1754 1
—
Total ...6

III —Table of Convictions and Executions in London and Middlesex, from 1756 to 1832, when the Act passed for repealing the Capital Punishment.

Years	Con	Ex.		Years	Con.	Ex.	
1756	2	0		1801	11	0	
1757..	1	0		1802	2	0	One 37 sheep;
1758	1	0		1803	1	1	[one 23 sh.
1762	2	0		1807	3	3	
1766.	1	0		1808 .	3	0	
1768.	2	0		1809.	1	0	
1772	1	0		1810	1	0	
1773	4	0		1811	1	0	
1774	2	0		1812	1	0	
1776.	1	0		1813..	6	0	
1779	1	0		1814	2	0	
1782	1	0		1816.	4	0	
1783	4	0		1817 .	2	0	
1785	3	2 1, 20 sheep, 1, 7 sh. & 2 lmbs		1818	9	0	
1786	1	0		1819 .	5	1	19 sheep
1787	2	1 7 sheep		1820.	2	0	
1789	2	0		1821	2	1	
1790.	1	0		1822..	2	0	
1791.	5	1 8 sheep.		1823..	1	0	
1792.	2	0		1825..	2	0	
1793	1	43 ewe sheep.		1826.	7	2	
1794,	1	0		1827..	5	1	
1795	2	0		1828.	2	0	
1796.	2	0		1829.	5	1	
1798.	6	0		1830..	3	0	
1799	4	0		1831	3	1	51 sheep
1800	6	0		1832..	2	0	
				Totals ..	149	15	

IV —Convictions and Executions upon the Circuits.

	Years	Con.	Ex.	
Home .	..1755—1817	438	37	
Western	..1770—1818	457	48	
Oxford	..1799—Lent, 1819	348	—	
Midland	..1805—1817	101	2	
Norfolk	. 1768—Lent, 1818.	280	24 left for ex.	
Lancaster	1798—Lent, 1819........	15	1	
Durham	..1755—Lent, 1819..... ..	29	2	
Northern	..1804—1817...............	31	0	

England and Wales —1821 to 1830.

Year	Charged.	Con.	Ex	Acq , No Bill, &c.
1821	169	90	5	51 and 28
1822	105	66	1	20 and 19
1823	130	79	0	23 and 28
1824	155	105	1	32 and 18
1825	166	104	3	41 and 21
1826	190	127	3	40 and 23
1827	248	153	3	60 and 35
1828	199	120	1	37 and 22
1829	237	155	5	63 and 19
1830	297	213	1	52 and 32

APPENDIX, No. V.

I Table of Convictions and Executions in London for *Cattle-Stealing.* (Pail Return), 1741-1755, *(none)*

II Table of Executions in London and Middlesex for the same, 1741-1755, *(none)*.

III Table of Convictions and Executions for the same, in London and Middlesex, 1756-1832, when the act passed for repealing the Capital Punishment.

Year	Con.	Ex	Year	Con.	Ex.	
1756	1	0	1806	2	0	
1759	1	0	1807	3	0	
1764	1	0	1812	3	0	
1766	1	0	1813	1	0	
1773	1 (a)	0	1814	2	0	
1775	3	0	1816	2	0	
1777	1	0	1817	2	0	⌠fers
1780	1	0	1818	1	D	3 hei-
1781	2	0	1819	1	0	
1784	2	0	1820	2	0	
1785	1	0	1824	1	0	
1786	3	0	1826	2	0	
1788	1	0	1827	3	0	
1789	1	0	1828	3	1	
1794	1	0	1829	2	0	
1795	1	0	1830	1	0	
1796	1	0	1831	1	0	
1797	1	0	1832	2 (b)	0	
1798	1	0		—	—	
1800	2	0	Total	63	1	
1801	2	0				

(a) There were also 2 persons convicted this year for stealing cows.
(b) One of these men was actually ordered for execution.

IV Table of the like Convictions and Executions on the Circuits

		Con.	Ex
Home ..1755—1817 . ..	45	7
Western 1770—1818.........	98	15
Oxford .. 1799—Lent, 1819 ..	44	—
Midland. . 1805—1817 .. .	14	0
Norfolk . ..1768—Lent, 1818	38	4
Lancaster . 1798—Lent, 1819 ..	15	0
Durham... 1755—Lent, 1819	6	0
Northern ..1804—1817 . .	14	0

———

V. England and Wales—1821—1830

Year	Charged.	Con	Ex.	Acq. No bill, &c.
1821	14	14	0	— —
1822	18	9	0	4 and 5
1823	29	24	0	3 and 2
1824	23	19	0	4 — 0
1825	42	24	0	10 and 8
1826	24	21	0	2 and 1
1827	45	31	0	10 and 4
1828	38	28	0	8 and 2
1829	30	25	0	4 and 1
1830	30	25	0	3 and 2

THE END.

[signature]
1/29/24

PRINTED BY STEWART AND CO , OLD BAILEY.

CPSIA information can be obtained
at www.ICGtesting.com
Printed in the USA
LVOW03s1748091115

461720LV00019B/533/P